....

Bride & Groom

....

Wedding Date

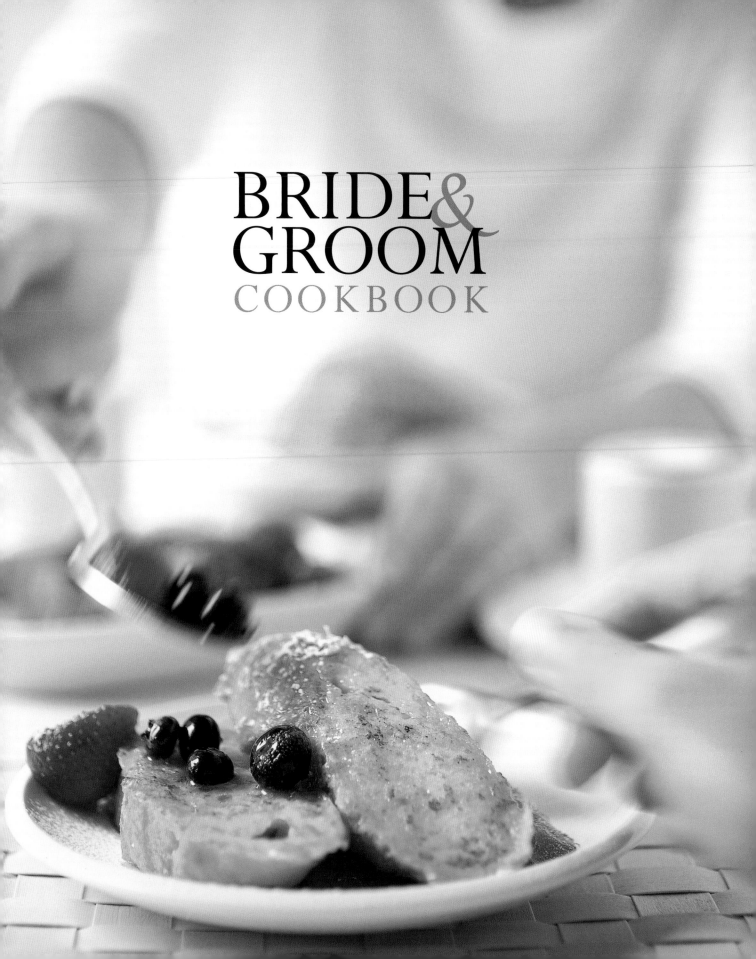

BRIDE&
GROOM
COOKBOOK

WILLIAMS-SONOMA

BRIDE& GROOM
COOKBOOK

AUTHORS

Gayle Pirie & John Clark

GENERAL EDITOR

Chuck Williams

PHOTOGRAPHER

David Matheson

FREE PRESS

NEW YORK · LONDON · TORONTO · SYDNEY

Contents

Breakfast and brunch

Starters

Soups and salads

Meat, poultry, and seafood

continued >

Desserts

About this book

This cookbook aims to help you navigate an important part of your new married life: the business of cooking, and eating, together. A fine set of cookware is often bestowed on a new couple by their family and friends, but it won't be much help if you're not sure what to do with it.

This is a cookbook you'll be able to use for years to come. If you're new to cooking, you'll learn how to arrange your kitchen, what equipment you'll need, and how to stock a pantry. You'll gain a basic understanding of the different ways of cooking and which foods they apply to. And you'll gain a wonderful collection of recipes. The dishes in this cookbook are classics that every family should be able to prepare and enjoy, but they're not stuffy or old-fashioned. Most of the recipes are quite simple, but you'll soon be able to work your way up to the more challenging ones. Some recipes are intended as weeknight meals and serve two, but most serve more with an eye to entertaining and a growing family.

I wish you happiness in the coming years and hope the recipes and knowledge shared in this book will sustain you for the journey ahead.

Chuck Williams

Creating a meal

Cooking together in your own kitchen, then sitting down together to eat dinner, enjoy your food, and talk, is at the core of many strong marriages and happy family lives. But cooking can seem mysterious, even intimidating, if it's not something you've always seen done at home.

Knowing that many of our readers have not learned the art of cooking at their grandmother's knee, we've included in this book all the basics for getting started. We've tried to answer every common question: What equipment do I need? How do I know what's in season? What foods should I keep in the cupboards? How do I peel a tomato? Which wine should I pour with this pork roast? When should I serve a cheese course?

Once you learn a few essentials, you'll find that cooking is not as hard as it sometimes looks. Dishes won't always turn out perfectly at first, but if you approach them methodically and keep practicing, you can soon become a very good cook. It all boils down to determination and a sense of humor—two qualities that will serve you well in your marriage, too!

Before you attempt cooking for guests, get comfortable cooking for yourselves. True novices can start out by preparing one cooked dish at a time. You can round out any meal with a good loaf of bread and a simple green salad, which lets you focus your efforts on a main course. When you're ready for a course in hosting, turn to page 236 for entertaining basics and page 240 for menus.

RECIPE KEY

preparation **30** minutes | cooking **50** minutes | **2** servings

The spoon icon at the top of each recipe lets you know how difficult the recipe is: one spoon indicates a simple recipe, two an intermediate one, and three a relatively complex dish.

The preparation and cooking times given with each recipe will help you estimate when you should start cooking if you want to eat at a particular hour. However, keep in mind that these and other time estimates are just that: approximate calculations. Allow yourself additional time if you are new to cooking.

Planning the dishes

When you're ready to cook up a multicourse meal, either for yourselves or for guests, the first thing you need to do is to figure out what you feel like eating. Always think seasonally. Is it hot midsummer, when lighter foods like salads and cold soups or grilled foods sound good? Is it spring, when the markets are overflowing with asparagus and artichokes? Is it chilly autumn or winter, when you want a satisfying stew or roasted meat to warm you up?

You might start with one dish or even one ingredient you want to eat, and build a menu from there. When selecting dishes to make for a meal, scan the recipes to make sure they work together in terms of time and how they are cooked (right).

Once you've decided what to serve, the next step is a shopping list. Here's where a well-stocked pantry comes into play. On pages 24–29, we list commonly used ingredients that you can keep on hand all the time if you find them useful. It's less daunting to cook dinner when you don't need to shop for a lot of groceries first.

On pages 24–29

COMBINING DISHES

Compare the ingredients lists of recipes you're considering for a meal, both to make sure the dishes mesh well together and to see whether you can combine the preparation of common ingredients.

Compare recipe methods to look for conflicts. For example, if you are planning to roast a chicken in the oven, it won't be free for baking a pie, especially if the pie cooks at a higher temperature (and you don't want your pie to taste like chicken). Choose another dessert that cooks on the stove top.

Make it easy on yourself. If one of the dishes that you've chosen—such as a pan sauce or a soufflé—requires a bit of last-minute attention, make sure the other parts of the meal lend themselves to advance preparation, so that you can take care of them earlier.

When you're ready to start cooking, pull out all the items on your ingredients lists, then check your tools lists and do the same.

Next, create a written timeline. This can be as general or as detailed as you like. Estimate when you'll need to start cooking each dish so that everything will be ready around the same time. As you grow more experienced as a cook, you'll be able to keep this schedule in your head, but even an old hand will make a time-line for a more complex dinner. Use a timer to keep track of various items as they cook.

A spouse who's not actively cooking can turn off the TV, lower the lights, put on some soft music, and set the table. Make sure a carafe of fresh water is available at dinner, flavored with a lemon wedge or slice of cucumber left over from cooking.

Serving it forth

If you're new to cooking, just getting the food onto the plate will be enough. But once you start to feel comfortable in the kitchen, try to pay attention to the niceties of presentation, making the food and the setting visually appealing.

About ten minutes before serving, place plates in a low (200°F/95°C) oven to warm or in the refrigerator to chill, depending on whether the food is hot or cold. Food is more enjoyable when it stays at the correct temperature as you eat it.

Keep portion sizes moderate, and arrange the food on the plate in an attractive way. Place a chicken thigh atop a bed of polenta instead, of plopping it alongside, or swirl a spoonful of sauce over a fillet of fish. Use a kitchen towel to wipe spatters from the rim of the plate. Garnish the food with a little herb or citrus used in the recipe, for both color and a hint of freshness, or scatter with cheese shavings or coarsely cracked pepper. Fill your wineglasses, don't forget to toast the chef, and appreciate your meal together.

Dinner for four

Here we take you through the steps of creating a simple meal for four. We began putting together our menu *(right)* by choosing an easy and quick pasta. This main dish will leave plenty of time to prepare a starter, a salad or vegetable, and a dessert. Since the pasta is Italian, we continue the Mediterranean theme by adding a starter of olives and a summery tomato salad that follows the main. The salad is served at room temperature, so you can make this dish first and let it sit while you attend to the others. Roasted figs need only a few minutes in the oven, so you can pop them in after you finish your savory courses and they'll be ready when you are.

MENU

Warm Marinated Olives • 58

Pasta Carbonara • 136

Tomato, Mozzarella,
and Basil Salad • 84

Mascarpone-Stuffed Figs • 196

TIMELINE

This sample timeline anticipates serving the starter to the guests just after they arrive and the main-dish pasta about 40 minutes later. This plan assumes 2 sets of hands in the kitchen; with 1 cook, allow a bit more time for advance preparation before your guests arrive.

40 MINUTES AHEAD
Prepare and measure out all ingredients; arrange salad on plates.

20 MINUTES AHEAD
Chill wine; blend eggs and cheese for pasta; stuff figs; sauté olives.

GUESTS ARRIVE
Serve wine and olives.

20 MINUTES AFTER
Put pasta water on to boil.

30 MINUTES AFTER
Put pasta in boiling water; put plates in oven to warm; cook bacon for pasta.

JUST BEFORE SERVING
Blend pasta, eggs, and bacon.

AFTER SALAD COURSE
Pop figs into oven.

SHOPPING LIST

FROM THE PANTRY

- OLIVES
- LEMON
- GARLIC
- SPAGHETTINI (OR OTHER LONG NOODLES)
- BACON
- OLIVE OIL
- EGGS
- NUTMEG
- PECORINO OR PARMESAN
- ALMONDS
- HONEY

FROM THE MARKET

- ORANGES
- FRESH THYME
- TOMATOES
- FRESH MOZZARELLA
- FRESH BASIL
- FRESH FIGS
- MASCARPONE

Setting the scene

The same dishes can be presented in different ways depending on the mood you want to create. For this menu, choosing simple white dishes and classic stemware will let the different colors of the foods shine. For a more casual feel, you might pick up the green of the olives, red of the tomatoes, or purple of the figs in place mats, candles, or flowers. To invoke the dishes' rustic Mediterranean origins, choose sturdy earthenware dishes and tumblers for wine.

Use citrus wedges or zest left over from the olives and figs to flavor the water included at each place setting.

Choose a pretty dish for the olives, and provide an empty bowl to hold discarded pits. Use tongs to twist each serving of carbonara into a neat coil, then top with a small pile of grated cheese and cracked black pepper. For the salad, overlap alternating slices of tomato and mozzarella cheese, and tuck varying sizes of basil leaves here and there. Arrange three figs per person on small dessert plates—odd numbers look better than even ones.

WINE PAIRINGS

Offer the olives paired with a crisp white wine, such as Sauvignon Blanc or Pinot Grigio, or a festive glass of Champagne. Champagne is often overlooked as a wine choice, but goes well with many appetizers and acts as an aperitif itself, whetting the appetite for the meal to come.

You can match the same wines with the pasta to cut the richness of the egg, bacon, and Pecorino. Alternatively, select a light-bodied red, such as Pinot Noir or Beaujolais, to reinforce these savory flavors with fuller body. Lighter reds can be served slightly chilled, especially Beaujolais.

Serve a late-harvest dessert wine, such as a Muscat, or tawny port with the figs. To appreciate the sweetness of a dessert wine, the wine should taste sweeter than the dessert.

Keep an over-the-sink colander on one side of the sink for rinsing vegetables or draining clean dishes.

Store your most commonly used appliances on the countertop, but put others away to reduce clutter.

Keep everyday dishes on shelves near the sink or the dishwasher to simplify putting them away.

Keep serving bowls and platters on shelves near the stove for ease in warming and serving.

Put specialized tools and gadgets into drawers near the sink, work space, or range, depending on use.

Keep cleaning supplies near the sink but away from foodstuffs, to avoid contact and contamination.

Use dividers to keep drawers orderly and tools easy to find. Group like items such as graters or sieves.

Keep a portion of commonly used items like salt, pepper, herbs, spices, and/or olive oil within reach of the stove.

Hang commonly used tools or pots and pans near the stove top, or knives on a magnetic strip near a work space.

Keep a crock of essential tools, like spoons and spatulas, near the stove top.

Put heavy items like pots and appliances on lower, rather than upper, shelves for ease of handling.

Use vertical dividers in a cupboard for storing narrow items like pot lids, cutting boards, and baking sheets.

Organizing the kitchen

After the two of you have spent some time working together in your kitchen—or before you move into a new one—take the time to think about how best to organize it. An efficient use of space will help make cooking a pleasure, whether your kitchen is big or small (but especially if it's small). Think about your usual cooking routines and how you tend to work in the kitchen, and examine what has gone smoothly in the past and what hasn't.

Planning the space

If you have to hustle across the room to get a pot holder when a saucepan needs to come off the stove, or search madly through a drawer for tongs while your chicken breast fillets start to scorch, your kitchen organization is not working for you.

Think of your kitchen as made up of three zones: the prep area (refrigerator, sink, and work surfaces); the cooking area (stove and work surfaces); and the cleanup area (sink, work surfaces, and refrigerator). For the best use of space, the paths between stove, refrigerator, and sink should form a triangle, and a work surface should be only a step or two away from each. You may not be able to change the layout of your kitchen, but this basic concept can help you figure out how to arrange the items you can move. You may also be able to add a movable butcher block to help create a work surface in an area that lacks one.

A basic rule is to store equipment and tools near the areas where they'll be used. Keep knives near the cutting board, pans and spatulas near the stove, food storage containers and wrappers between the sink and refrigerator. This is common sense, but it's surprising how often a tool can end up stored in an awkward place. Keeping work surfaces clear and uncluttered will make your kitchen more inviting to work in. Find spots in cupboards or a pantry for appliances you don't use every day. And adopting the professional cook's habit of cleaning up after yourself as you cook—clearing counters and washing tools—will reduce frustration and even accidents, and both of you will be grateful when it's time to wash up.

Outfitting the kitchen

You'll likely have received a selection of cooking equipment as wedding gifts, but it's rare that you'll get everything you need—or want. Even if you have a lot of gaps to fill in, don't worry. Experienced cooks know it's best to outfit a kitchen tool by tool.

You don't need a matched set of cookware. In fact, different materials are often best for different tools. The only rule is to buy the best equipment you can afford, because good-quality pieces will last longer and will make cooking easier, and your food will turn out better. This is especially true of pans: a good heavy-gauge, thick-bottomed pan will heat evenly and prevent food from burning.

The bare necessities

With the basic pots, pans, tools, and machines at right, you'll be able to create a wide range of dishes, from a batch of cookies to a pot of stew, an omelet, or a roast chicken—nearly anything that comes to mind. As you develop your own style of cooking and signature dishes, turn to pages 22–23 to see which specialized tools will help you pursue your particular cooking interests.

When choosing cookware in particular, you'll be faced with choices of materials. Each type of metal conducts heat differently, and aluminum and cast iron react to acidic foods and eggs, resulting in off flavors or color. For everyday pots and pans, two very good choices are stainless steel and anodized aluminum. Steel heats up more slowly and less evenly than aluminum, but is more sturdy and long-lasting and is nonreactive. Some steel pans have aluminum cores to help them heat quickly and evenly. Anodized aluminum has been treated to strengthen it and to prevent the aluminum from reacting with acidic foods or eggs.

Copper is the best conductor of heat and an excellent choice for cookware, but requires more maintenance and can be costly. Cast iron is used for some pans, and although this metal has a mild reaction with acidic foods, it heats up evenly and holds heat well. Enameled cast-iron cookware is good for long-simmered dishes, and the enamel coating makes the pan nonreactive.

COOKWARE

- baking dishes
  - square
  - rectangular
- frying pans
  - large, cast-iron
  - small nonstick
- roasting pan, medium, with rack
- saucepans
  - medium
  - large
- sauté pans
  - medium
  - large
- stockpot or soup pot

BAKEWARE

- 2 baking sheets, rimmed
- 2 round cake pans, 9 inch (23 cm)
- loaf pan, 8½ by 4½ inch (21.5 by 11.5 cm)
- pie dish, deep dish
- pie pan, 9 inch (23 cm)

KNIVES

- chef's knife
- slicing knife
- paring knife
- serrated bread knife
- serrated small utility knife
- sharpening steel

ELECTRICS

- blender
- coffeemaker
- food processor
- stand mixer
- toaster

TOOLS

- bowls, stainless-steel
    - medium
    - large
- box grater
- brush
- can opener
- citrus reamer
- colander
- corkscrew
- cutting boards
- ladle
- measuring cups
    - large glass liquid measure
    - nested dry measures
- measuring spoons
- mortar and pestle
- pepper mill
- potato masher
- pot holders
- salad spinner
- kitchen shears
- sieve, fine-mesh
- spatulas
    - metal
    - silicone rubber
    - wooden
- spoons
    - solid metal
    - slotted
    - wooden
- kitchen string
- thermometer, instant-read
- kitchen timer
- tongs
- vegetable peeler
- whisk
- wire racks

Caring for cookware and tools

Good-quality cookware and tools will last for many years—in some cases, a lifetime. They will serve you best when you follow the manufacturer's instructions for using and cleaning. Some pots and pans are better washed by hand than in a dishwasher, which may be an important consideration in your selection.

In the case of wooden tools and cutting boards, avoid washing in the dishwasher or soaking them in water, as this causes the wood to swell and eventually split. Wooden cutting boards should be rubbed occasionally with mineral oil to keep the wood from drying out.

Caring for knives

Knives are considered by many cooks to be the most important tools in the kitchen, and they require particular care. With a well-made, keenly sharpened kitchen blade of the right size and shape, you can easily and efficiently prepare any dish. Start with a good-quality chef's knife and paring knife that fit your budget and feel good in your hand. Add others from the list as dictated by the way you like to cook and the kinds of foods you like to prepare.

Like wooden tools, knives should not be soaked in water, which can cause the handles to swell and loosen. They should kept in a wooden knife block or hung from a magnetic strip rather than loose in a drawer, where they will be nicked by collisions with other tools as well as present a danger to anyone reaching into the drawer.

Get yourself into the habit of honing your knives *(left)* each time you use them, whether before slicing or after washing. The reason that knives should be kept honed is not only that they slice better when sharp, but because a dull knife is a dangerous one. Cutting with a dull knife requires more pressure, which can result in slippage and a threat of injury.

Even with regular honing, you will sense a knife's edge becoming dull over time; have it professionally sharpened. Check with the shop where you bought them or with a local butcher shop or food-store meat department. The personnel should be able to recommend a professional who can bring your knives back to razor sharpness at a reasonable cost.

HONING A KNIFE

Before you put a knife away after each use, it's a good idea to hone it to keep it sharp. The best home tool to use is a sharpening steel, available wherever good-quality knives are sold. Swipe each side of the blade's cutting edge across and along the length of the steel, holding the blade at about a 15-degree angle to the long metal rod. Repeat to swipe each side 3 times.

Follow your passion

It's not only handymen who live by the motto "The right tool for the job." Cooks, too, find that specialized equipment makes specialized dishes much easier to create. Once you've gotten your bearings in the kitchen and have discovered a type of cooking that appeals to you, it's time to develop your specialty. A few extra tools will help you become accomplished at whatever you choose.

For example, many cooks settle on baking for their specialty, which typically embraces breads, pies and tarts, cakes, cookies, and pastries, and is sometimes even stretched to include all desserts, whether baked or not. Baking usually requires precision—careful measuring, specific mixing techniques, attention to timing—and an array of specialized equipment. But you will be rewarded for that attention to detail and for using the proper tools when your batter of eggs, butter, and flour emerges from the oven as beautifully risen cake layers.

On pages 22–23 we list basic items you need to tackle a wide range of specialties, from baking to Asian food to breakfast. Be warned: whatever specialty you choose, it can become an obsession.

On pages 22–23

CHOOSING QUALITY

Stocking a kitchen with a selection of tools that are useful for the way you like to cook is a lifelong process. Specialty tools make particular tasks easier and cooking more pleasant.

Once you have acquired the basics, you may wish to add a few extras. Base these choices on the things you enjoy preparing, rather than what you simply think you ought to have. If you find yourself doing a certain task repeatedly, that's your cue to pick up a tool that will help you with it. When selecting a tool, be sure to hold it and consider how it feels in your hand. Handles should be comfortable and the tool should feel sturdy, not flimsy.

Gadgets, as opposed to tools, will quickly lose their initial appeal, while poorly made tools will wear out or break. If you invest in good-quality tools, on the other hand, they will last for years. Well-made ones will never let you down.

FOR GENERAL COOKING

- small pot
- small sauté pan
- asparagus pot
- deep fryer
- grill pan
- paella pan
- clam knife
- double boiler
- fondue pot
- lobster and crab cracker
- mallet
- mandoline
- oyster knife and oyster glove
- potato ricer
- wide spatula (for fish)
- oil and candy thermometer
- citrus zester

FOR GRILLING

- grill (charcoal or gas)
- chimney starter
- grill basket
- long-handled tongs, spatula, brush
- sauce mop
- instant-read thermometer

FOR BREAKFAST

- griddle
- crepe pan
- coffee grinder
- espresso machine
- waffle iron
- double boiler
- egg poacher
- wide spatula

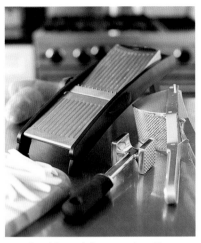

Specialty tools for general cooking

Specialty tools for soups and stews

Specialty tools for breakfast

FOR PIZZA AND PASTA

- pasta maker
- pizza peel
- pizza stone
- pizza cutter
- stand mixer with dough hook
- multipot
- lasagna pan
- pasta fork

FOR SOUPS, STEWS, SAUCES, AND STOCKS

- multipot
- Dutch oven
- cheesecloth (muslin)
- food mill
- stick blender
- perforated metal skimmer
- sauce whisk

FOR ASIAN FOOD

- wok
- cleaver
- boning knife
- Santoku knife
- steamer insert or bamboo steamer
- Asian skimmer
- rice cooker

FOR HOLIDAY MEALS

- roasting pan, large
- carving board
- degreasing cup
- meat fork
- meat slicer

FOR GENERAL BAKING

- springform pan
- electric handheld mixer
- ice cream maker
- ceramic or glass nesting bowls
- citrus zester
- small prep bowls
- brush, reserved for sweet items
- dough scraper
- flour sifter
- graduated canisters
- ice cream scoop
- nonstick baking liner
- oven thermometer
- parchment (baking) paper
- ramekins, ½ cup (4 fl oz/125 ml)
- rolling pin
- kitchen scale
- skewers, metal or wooden
- wooden spoon, for sweets only
- balloon whisk

FOR CAKES

- Bundt pan
- icing spatula, straight or offset
- oven thermometer
- pastry bag and tips
- cake comb
- decorating turntable

Specialty tools for general baking

Specialty tools for pies and tarts

Specialty tools for yeast and quick breads

FOR COOKIES

- cookie sheets, rimless
- cookie cutters
- pastry bag and tips
- pastry board, wood or marble
- rolling pin, wood or marble
- oven thermometer

FOR PIES AND TARTS

- tart pan, 9 inch (23 cm)
- tartlet pans
- cherry pitter
- pastry board, wood or marble
- rolling pin, wood or marble

FOR CUSTARDS AND SOUFFLÉS

- double boiler
- soufflé dishes, large (7½-inch/19-cm diameter) and small (4-inch/10-cm diameter)
- ramekins
- pastry bag and tips
- oil and candy thermometer
- oven thermometer
- kitchen torch

FOR YEAST AND QUICK BREADS

- muffin pans, regular or jumbo
- popover pan
- ceramic nesting bowls
- wooden board for kneading
- stand mixer with dough hook

FOR THE SPICE RACK

SPICES

CAYENNE PEPPER, GROUND

CHILI FLAKES, RED

CHILI POWDER (SPICE BLEND)

CINNAMON, WHOLE & GROUND

CLOVES, WHOLE & GROUND

CREAM OF TARTAR

CUMIN, SEEDS & GROUND

FENNEL SEEDS

MACE, GROUND

NUTMEG, WHOLE

PAPRIKA, SWEET & HOT

VANILLA EXTRACT (ESSENCE)

DRIED WOODY HERBS

BAY LEAVES

MARJORAM

OREGANO

ROSEMARY

SAGE

THYME

SALT AND PEPPER

SALT, KOSHER AND/OR SEA

PEPPERCORNS, WHOLE BLACK

USING SPICES

• For best flavor, purchase spices whole and grind them yourself in a mortar and pestle, a spice grinder, or a coffee grinder reserved for spices only.

• Toast spices briefly in a dry frying pan over medium heat to bring out their aromas and flavors before using.

The well-stocked pantry

Having to stop at the market on the way home from work to buy all you'll need for a meal can make cooking dinner a discouraging prospect. Keeping a number of the items you commonly use on hand—in the fridge and freezer as well as the cupboards—simplifies the planning and preparing of good home-cooked meals.

Get yourself into the habit of sitting down at the same time every week to plan the meals you want to cook—even if it's just two or three—and do a weekly shopping trip for the fresh items you'll need. If you can come home after a long day knowing that all the ingredients for supper are on hand, cooking dinner becomes a pleasure, rather than a chore. What follows are lists of the common pantry items called for in the recipes in this book. As you cook meals, take note of the items you find yourself needing often, and use the checklists in this section to help jog your memory as you make a shopping list. Tailor your pantry to suit your own taste, keeping on hand the ingredients you need for your favorite dishes. That way you'll always be able to whip up a good meal without a lot of fuss.

Herbs and spices

Spices and herbs are aromatic flavorings derived from plants. In general, spices are the hard seeds, bark, roots, and dried buds of various plants, while herbs are leaves and stems. Spices have a more concentrated flavor than herbs, and both have their role in the kitchen.

The herbs and spices on the page opposite represent the basis of a spice rack. If you live near a store that sells bulk items, you can purchase spices in small quantities. This is ideal, because they start to lose flavor after six months and ought to be replaced every year.

Herbs can be divided into two main types: woody and tender. "Woody" describes the stems, and these are the herbs that dry well and can be kept on hand for up to six months before losing flavor. Tender herbs are practically flavorless when dried and are best used fresh. This category includes basil, chives, cilantro, mint, parsley, and tarragon. Herbs are hardy and easy to grow, even on a sunny windowsill—and that way you always have a fresh handful on hand.

FRESH AND DRIED HERBS

- Dried herbs have a more concentrated flavor than fresh and should be used in smaller quantities when substituted.

- Put the stems of purchased fresh herbs in a glass of water, like a flower bouquet. Drape a plastic bag over the top and refrigerate for up to 1 week.

- Keep dried herbs in a dark cupboard or drawer; if you want to keep them in a light area, such as on a countertop, use opaque containers to prevent them from being bleached by the sun.

SALT AND PEPPER

These most common spices deserve a special mention. Salt, indeed, is essential to all kinds of cooking. It brings out and balances the flavors of foods, making it useful in every type of dish, including desserts. Pepper, too, is ubiquitous and goes into many dishes both savory and sweet, pleasing the palate with its subtle heat. Since these flavorings are used in practically every dish, put care into the types you use.

Kosher and sea salt are your best choices for everyday cooking. Both have a clean, pure salt flavor. Kosher salt has large, flat crystals that are easy to grab (for cooking, keep the salt in a bowl rather than a shaker), adhere well to food, and give a mild salt flavor. You'll need to use almost twice as much kosher salt as regular salt for the same degree of saltiness, giving you good control when seasoning a dish. Sea salt is also an excellent natural choice. Choose fine grains for even seasoning. Reserve very high-quality sea salt, such as the French *fleur de sel*, for sprinkling on food at the table.

Peppercorns should always be ground fresh just before use. The flavor begins to dissipate soon after grinding.

In the cupboard

The items in the list opposite constitute a well-stocked pantry or cupboard, and they appear in many of the recipes in this book. Group similar items together in cupboards so you can find things quickly. For example, you might have one area for liquids like oils, vinegars, sauces, and honey; another area for dry goods for baking like flour, sugar, and baking powder; yet another area for canned goods; and finally an area for rice, pasta, and polenta.

All these items will keep longest when stored in a cool, dark cupboard rather than out in the kitchen exposed to light and heat. If you need to keep items like oil or flour on an exposed shelf, use opaque metal or ceramic containers. Beware of open packages and spills in the cupboard, which can attract insects and other vermin. Keep flour and other dry goods in canisters or sealed containers, and wipe spills from jars and bottles before placing them back in the pantry.

OILS FOR THE PANTRY

Different cooking tasks require different types of oil. For most savory uses, olive oil is a good and healthful choice, high in monounsaturated fat. But there's more than one kind of olive oil. A good extra-virgin olive oil, which is created without the use of heat, is best reserved for uncooked uses. Its wonderful flavor is destroyed by heat. An ordinary extra-virgin or a "pure" olive oil is better used for cooking.

Another good all-purpose oil is canola. This oil, made from rapeseed, is also high in healthful monounsaturated fat, like olive oil. Unlike extra-virgin, it is neutral in flavor, ideal for baking.

For high-heat cooking, such as deep-frying, peanut and grape seed oils are good choices.

FOR THE CUPBOARD

CANNED GOODS

FISH, CANNED

— ANCHOVY FILLETS

— TUNA

STOCK

— CHICKEN

— VEGETABLE

TOMATOES

— CANNED, DICED & WHOLE

BOTTLES & JARS

ARTICHOKE HEARTS, WATER
 PACKED OR MARINATED

CAPERS

HONEY

MOLASSES, DARK

SPIRITS

— BRANDY

— VERMOUTH (WHITE)

TABASCO SAUCE

VINEGAR

— BALSAMIC

— RED WINE

WINE

— DRY RED

— DRY WHITE

WORCESTERSHIRE SAUCE

OILS

OLIVE OIL

EXTRA-VIRGIN OLIVE OIL

CANOLA OIL

PEANUT OR GRAPE SEED OIL

DRY GOODS FOR BAKING

BAKING POWDER

BAKING SODA (BICARBONATE
 OF SODA)

CHOCOLATE, BITTERSWEET

FLOUR, ALL-PURPOSE (PLAIN)

SUGAR

— BROWN SUGAR

— GRANULATED SUGAR

— POWDERED (ICING) SUGAR

OTHER DRY GOODS

BEANS, DRIED OR CANNED

— BLACK

— CANNELLINI

— LENTILS

BREAD CRUMBS, FINE DRIED

CORNMEAL

— FINE STONE-GROUND

— POLENTA, STONE-GROUND

FRUIT, DRIED

GARLIC

ONIONS

— YELLOW ONIONS

— SHALLOTS

PASTA, DRIED

POTATOES

— BAKING OR RUSSET (STARCHY)

— BOILING, WHITE OR RED (WAXY)

RICE

— LONG-GRAIN WHITE

— BROWN

Nota bene

- Oils are high in fat and therefore perishable. Some unrefined oils, notably nut oils and sesame oil, are best stored in the fridge. The oils will become cloudy, but this will not affect their flavor.

- Flours and meals are perishable as well. This is especially true of whole-grain flours and meals and nut meals. More perishable flours and even plain flour that is kept for more than a year should be stored in the refrigerator.

- Keep white vermouth on hand for cooking. When you need a little white wine for a dish but don't want to open a bottle solely for that purpose, vermouth can be used. Because it's fortified, it keeps for months.

- There are many brands of balsamic vinegar in the market, but most of them are not true balsamic. Look for the Consorzio label for true aged balsamic from Modena, Italy. Choose a younger one for cooking and for use in salad dressings, and save a long-aged one to use as a condiment. When choosing a red wine vinegar, look for an aged one.

- Light and dark brown sugars are often interchangeable. Dark contains more molasses and has more flavor.

- Canned items should be free of dents or bulges, which encourage bacterial growth and spoilage. Do not store food in an open can in the refrigerator; transfer it to a storage container.

In the refrigerator

The modern pantry includes items that are stored in the fridge or freezer, not just the cupboard. We find that keeping the items shown at left on hand in the refrigerator makes it easier to put together a square meal on short notice. And here's another reason to keep the fridge stocked: a full refrigerator works more efficiently than an empty one. Cold foods help keep their neighboring foods cold.

Note that the chilliest areas of the refrigerator are usually the rear and the lowest shelf. The warmest is the door. Keep dairy, eggs, and meats in the coldest spots, cheeses and oils in the warmest. A refrigerator thermometer will let you know whether you're keeping foods cold enough—35°–38°F (2°–3°C) is ideal.

Although they may seem like cupboard items, nuts, whole grains, and whole-grain flours all contain oils that will eventually go rancid, so keep them in the refrigerator or freezer for longer storage.

In the freezer

One of the most useful items to keep on hand in the freezer is home-made stock (pages 216–17). You can make your own on a free after-noon, divide it into useful portions of 1 cup (8 fl oz / 250 ml) or 1 quart (1 l), and freeze it for up to six months. Some delis sell freshly made stock. Or, look for good-quality frozen stock in concen-trate. If you buy canned broth, look for a reduced-sodium version so that you can more easily control the seasoning of the dish to which the broth is added.

Butter, meat, and poultry freeze well for longer storage. Keep these foods in the freezer—they'll keep for six to eight months—and you'll always be able to make a satisfying pantry meal.

If bread goes stale, chop it into crumbs in the food processor and freeze it for later use. If your fresh herbs are in danger of wilting, make an herb butter (see page 67) and freeze to use for flavoring meat or vegetables.

Make sure to wrap food well for freezing. If exposed to air, the food will develop freezer burn and dry out. Use freezer paper or plastic, or self-sealing plastic containers. Label and date the items you freeze; they may not be clearly identifiable in a few weeks.

THE SCIENCE OF REFRIGERATION

Storing foods in cold conditions slows down the process of spoilage, by slowing down the activity of the microbes or the food's own enzymes that cause it. Foods do continue to deteriorate in the refrigerator and even the freezer, but at a much slower rate than when held at room temperature.

The reason food should be carefully wrapped before being put in cold storage is to prevent the dry air of the refrigerator or freezer from depleting its moisture and drying out the food.

FREEZING AND THAWING

● Wrap foods for freezing in freezer-weight plastic or in several layers of regular plastic, foil, or freezer paper. If the surface of the food is exposed to the cold air of the freezer, it will develop a condition called freezer burn, which leaves the food dry and unpalatable. This is especially true for meat and poultry. Liquids can be frozen in a freezerproof container.

● When a food is frozen, the water in its cells is converted to ice crystals, whose sharp edges pierce the cell walls and soften the food's texture. This is one reason that foods should not be thawed and re-frozen; the texture worsens with each freezing. Foods that are commercially flash-frozen suffer the least amount of damage, while foods frozen at home suffer the most because the process is slower and results in larger ice crystals.

● To minimize further damage to the texture and in the interest of food safety, frozen foods should be thawed slowly in the refrigerator, not at room temperature or in a bowl of warm water. This may take several hours. You can also use the microwave for a quick defrost, but the quality of the food will suffer.

Following a recipe

The first step of following a recipe is to read it, start to finish, before you do anything else. This prevents unpleasant surprises—like discovering one hour before dinnertime that the meat you planned to cook requires two hours of marinating before it can be grilled!

Read the ingredients list and method, then make a shopping list. If you follow our advice on pages 25–29 and stock your pantry with plenty of commonly used staples, your shopping list won't be too long. We've also created lists of required tools for each of the recipes in this book, so you will know at a glance whether you have the right equipment on hand. (If you don't, think creatively and you may be able to come up with a substitute.)

Once you have all your ingredients and tools, it's time to set up what chefs call *mise en place* (meez-on-plahs). This French phrase, which translates as "putting in place," means preparing and measuring out your ingredients according to the ingredients list and preparing your equipment according to the recipe method. Once all the ingredients are measured out and chopped as described and arranged in piles or in bowls, your oven is preheated, and your pans are greased, you're ready to start cooking.

Preparing ingredients

A recipe's ingredients list includes information about how each ingredient should be prepared before cooking: peeled, trimmed, diced, chopped. (We explain some of these techniques in detail on pages 232–35.) If you read the ingredients list carefully, you'll notice that the order of these words varies. The placement of the word "chopped" is as essential as the word itself. For example:

> *1 cup walnuts, finely chopped*

tells you to measure out 1 cup walnuts, then chop them finely after measuring. But:

> *1 cup finely chopped walnuts*

tells you to measure out 1 cup finely chopped walnuts; they are chopped before measuring.

ASSUMPTIONS

In order to keep recipes reasonably short, we've made the following assumptions for our recipes:

- Tbsp means tablespoon and tsp, teaspoon.
- Butter is unsalted.
- Eggs are large. This is most crucial in baking.
- Flour is all-purpose (plain) and unsifted.
- Sugar is granulated.
- Salt is kosher salt. To substitute fine sea salt or table salt, use half as much.
- Onions are yellow.
- Garlic, onions, and fresh ginger are peeled.
- Pepper is freshly ground.
- Fresh herbs, greens, and lettuces are washed and spun or patted dry.
- Fresh parsley is flat-leaf (Italian).
- Oven rack is placed in center of oven.

Since more of an ingredient fits into a cup after it's been chopped, these two phrases call for a different amount of walnuts. And that small difference in the amount of a single ingredient can make a big difference in how your recipe turns out.

Unless otherwise noted, ingredients should be at room temperature because they combine better when they are not cold from the refrigerator. If an item should be cold, as in the case of butter for pie dough, this is specified in the recipe. Otherwise, let food that has been refrigerated sit out for twenty minutes to take off the chill.

A word on measuring

Now that we're on to the finer points of preparing and measuring ingredients, we need to point out that there are two different types of measuring cups: one for liquids and one for dry ingredients. A liquid measure is clear glass or plastic with graduated measures indicated on the side. You'll need to hold the cup at eye level to take

an accurate reading. Dry measures are nested metal or plastic cups. If you tried to measure a dry ingredient, like sugar, using a liquid measuring cup, you wouldn't get a level, accurate amount. Instead, measure sugar by scooping it into the nested dry cup of the required size and use the dull side of a knife to sweep off the excess. Do the same when measuring dry ingredients in measuring spoons. And note that a "scant" measure is shy of the full amount. "Heaping" means a little extra. A "pinch" is as much as you can pick up between thumb and forefinger.

Preparing equipment and preheating

The recipe method tells you whether the oven should be preheated and what needs to be done to pots and pans before cooking. Allow about twenty minutes for an oven to preheat or, better yet, use an oven thermometer to check whether it's hot enough. The food will brown better if the oven's good and hot, and browning equals flavor. The same goes for pans on a stove top: let them heat up for a minute or two before you add oil or butter, and then let the cooking fat heat up before you add the food. Broilers don't need to be preheated.

Especially in baking, pans may need to be greased. This will help the cake or bread release from the pan after cooking. The recipe will suggest a fat that is used in the baked item, but butter and oil are basically interchangeable. Don't use a strongly flavored oil such as olive; canola oil is a neutral-flavored choice, and can be found in spray cans.

Testing for doneness

The time frames given in a recipe are not to be taken as gospel; they are guidelines only. With all the variables of different ingredients at different temperatures before cooking begins, different pans, and different stoves and ovens, it's impossible to say to the minute how fast any item will cook. For determining doneness, always rely on your senses rather than the clock: look for a sensory cue in the recipe, such as "cook until golden brown" or "toast until fragrant." Get into the habit of looking at, listening to, smelling, touching, and tasting food as it cooks. This is how good cooks know when something's ready to come off the stove. For meat and poultry, you may want to use a thermometer to make sure the food is cooked through. For doneness temperatures, see page 225. For egg safety, see page 226.

MEASURING FLOUR

Cooks have a special method for measuring flour. Since it's so fine, it's easy to pack differing amounts of flour into the same measuring cup—but using too much or too little can adversely affect the way a recipe turns out, especially cookies or cakes.

Most cookbooks assume a "spoon and sweep" method of measuring flour: spoon the flour into a nesting dry measuring cup, heaping it above the rim of the cup, then sweep off the excess flour with the back of a knife. This will give you a perfectly level measure.

Another common method is "scoop and sweep," where you scoop up the flour with the cup, but this results in more flour in the cup, so it's best to use this technique only when specified in a recipe or cookbook.

Professional bakers avoid the fuss by simply weighing flour, figuring 5 oz (155 g) flour for each cup. If you have a kitchen scale, you can do the same thing at home.

Seasoning

A recipe will tell you when to season food as you cook it, but you should also rely on your own judgment. Taste and season with salt, pepper, herbs, and spices at various points throughout the cooking for the deepest and most complex flavor. (Of course, exercise caution when you are working with raw egg or meat or common sense when working with raw flour—until these items are cooked through, you may want to season without tasting.) And always give a dish a final taste and season it to your liking just before you serve it. If you watch professional cooks seasoning a dish, you may be amazed at their liberality with salt and pepper, not to mention lemon juice, vinegar, fresh herbs, and spices.

About wine

In our home, wine is regarded as food, as indispensable to a fine meal as a good loaf of bread or a leafy green salad. Wine balances the food, aids in digestion, and gives the occasion a convivial feel.

Wine is the happy result of yeast fermenting in grape juice, followed by aging the juice in a wooden cask or bottle that brings on subtle or profound changes. The differences among wines begin with the grape variety or varieties from which each is made *(below)*. Each grape bestows its unique characteristics of flavor, body, and color on the finished wine. The geographical region in which the grapes are grown and made into wine also contributes to a wine's character. The ineffable effects created by a particular soil and climate are known as *terroir* (tare-WAHR). When a wine is made entirely or predominantly from one grape variety, it is called a varietal wine. While European

SPARKLING WINES	WHITE WINES	ROSÉ WINES	RED WINES	DESSERT WINES
French Champagne **California sparkling wine** **Italian Prosecco** crisp and sparkling **Spanish Cava**	**Sauvignon Blanc** light bodied, high acid **Pinot Grigio/Gris** light bodied, fruity, low alcohol **Riesling** medium bodied, fruity to off dry, low alcohol **Gewürztraminer** medium bodied, fruity to off dry, low alcohol **Chardonnay** medium to full bodied, crisp-tart to oaky **Chenin Blanc** crisp and acidic to full bodied and lush **Viognier** full bodied, aromatic, and lush **Sémillon** full bodied, aromatic, and lush	**Bordeaux** dry, crisp **Bandol** (mourvèdre) dry, crisp **Languedoc** dry, crisp to fruity, full bodied **Rosado** Spanish, full bodied **Syrah/Shiraz** full bodied, fruity, spicy	**Gamay** light bodied, fruity **Grenache** light bodied to medium bodied **Pinot Noir** medium bodied, can be fruity, low alcohol **Sangiovese** light bodied to medium bodied, high acid **Merlot** medium bodied to full bodied (if oaked) **Tempranillo** medium bodied to full bodied **Syrah/Shiraz** full bodied **Zinfandel** full bodied, fruity, high acid **Nebbiolo** full bodied **Cabernet Sauvignon** full bodied	**Eiswein/ice wine** sweet and crisp **Late-harvest wines** sweet **Muscat** sweet **Tokay** sweet **Sauternes** sweet, lush **Vin santo** sweet, fortified **Port** fortified, fruity or sweet, range of styles **Sherry** fortified, dry to sweet styles **Madeira** fortified, sweet

OPENING AND POURING WINE

Use the knife on a waiter's corkscrew to neatly slice the foil as you turn the bottle. Screw the corkscrew firmly into the center of the cork, nearly all the way in. Using the lip of the bottle for leverage, pull out the cork with a steady motion. There is no sense in letting a wine "breathe" in the bottle—wine is only aerated by the act of pouring, either into a glass or a decanter. Pour wine into a glass, rotating the bottle as you stop pouring to prevent drips.

wines are labeled according to the geographical region in which they are produced, placing the focus on terroir, most wines bottled in the New World—the Americas, Australia and New Zealand, and South Africa—are made and labeled as varietals. This shift in labeling was a revolutionary development, making understanding and choosing among these wines much simpler for nonconnoisseurs. Luckily, the European regions, as a rule, make their wines from a predominant type of grape, and each wine will also display that grape's varietal qualities, so an understanding of varietals can be applied to European wines once you know which grapes are used in which areas.

The simplest way to start making sense of wine is to focus on the color and the body. "Body" refers to how the wine feels in the mouth—light or heavy. In simplest terms, white wines—which are made either from white grapes or from red ones with the skins removed at an early stage in the process, are lighter bodied than reds. Among both white and red wines, a range of styles is available. It's up to you to decide what types you like to drink, and when. Another primary consideration is sweetness: "dry" means a wine low in sugar, "off dry" is a little sweet, and "sweet" explains itself.

Serving wine

Serving wine has some seemingly arcane rituals attached, but many of them are grounded in good sense and allow the wine to taste its best. The different shapes of wineglasses are designed to show off the characteristics of the type of wine being served. All wineglasses have a rounded bowl, which captures aromas. The wine's aroma can make up a large part of the pleasure of drinking it. Tall, narrow Champagne flutes are designed to keep the bubbles bubbling up for as long as possible. You'll notice that glasses for Champagne and white wine are fairly straight sided, appropriate for subtler aromas. A balloon-shaped wineglass is perfect for capturing the more complex aromas of a light- or medium-bodied red, allowing you to swirl and sniff. These glasses are also well suited for serving a full-bodied white. A Bordeaux glass, designed for heavy, full-bodied red wines, is large, allowing for more air to be incorporated to soften flavors, and straight sided, to prevent a blast of heady aroma being directed at your nose. The more prominent the personality of the wine, the bigger the glass. Dessert wine and port glasses are smaller than wineglasses, since these wines are served in smaller portions.

The stem of a traditional wineglass acts as a handle, allowing you to hold the glass without touching the bowl. This prevents you from heating up the wine with your hands, which would make the flavors dissipate more quickly. (Cupping the bowl with your palm is a good trick if you are ever served a glass of white wine that is too chilly, and is also part of the ritual of drinking brandy—you want to warm this spirit to bring out its flavors.) Holding a glass by the stem also protects the bowl from greasy fingerprints, which lessens the enjoyment of gazing at the beautiful color of a wine.

Sometimes a French bistro or Italian trattoria will serve wine in little tumblers. Obviously, this rustic glass is best suited to a rustic wine—the local red table wine, which in many French and Italian regions is quite good. You can decide how to serve wine at home based on the character of the wine and the mood you want to create. Using alternative wineglasses may create the right ambience for a casual or alfresco supper.

The temperatures for serving wine are also based on maximum enjoyment. Full-bodied red wines should be served at cool room temperature, while light whites benefit from chilling for twenty minutes in ice water or the freezer (don't forget you put the bottle in there, or it will break) or an hour in the fridge. If they are too cold or too warm, their flavors will be dulled. Full-bodied whites, rosés, and lighter-bodied reds fall somewhere in between: a lush Viognier, though white, should not be too cold, which would mask its tropical fruit flavors, while a light rosé, Beaujolais, or even Pinot Noir can be served lightly chilled, especially in summer. Dessert wines and port are generally served at cool room temperature.

Cooking with wine

You might think that wine for cooking calls for a cheaper bottle. While it's true that you would not want to cook with a fine old vintage—since applying heat alters the flavor and structure that the winemaker labored to produce—neither should the wine be undrinkable. A bad wine is not going to be improved by cooking. Never buy anything labeled "cooking wine." If you're braising a chicken in wine or otherwise using a lot of wine in a dish, you would do well to choose the same varietal to drink at the table, though not necessarily the same bottle or producer.

MATCHING WINE AND FOOD

Above are possible pairings for the dinner menu on page 14, shown in their proper wineglasses. A simple starter of olives matches well with a crisp white wine such as Sauvignon Blanc. A full-flavored pasta, like this carbonara made with bacon, balances with a lighter red wine such as Pinot Noir. And the figs, a dessert that is not overly sweet, can match with a sweet dessert wine such as a Muscat without making the wine taste dry.

Pairing wine with food

We believe that matching wine with food is a personal choice. While there are tried-and-true combinations that seem made for one another *(right)*, it's ultimately a matter of personal taste, the mood of the moment, or simply what you have on hand. Forget the stiff old rules about pairing reds with meat or whites with fish. Try different combinations of varietals with the same dish, and be aware of aromas and flavors that please you. Don't worry about which wine is the "correct" one. The goal is to eat foods you love with wines you love.

We've all been intimidated at one time or another by the task of choosing wine, whether at a restaurant or in a shop. To learn more about which wines you like, you need to find a good store where you feel comfortable asking questions. This could be a small wine merchant in your area, or even a supermarket with a large selection of wines. When you taste a wine or discuss it with a wine merchant, keep in mind four basic qualities:

BODY: *Does the wine feel light or heavy on the tongue?*

INTENSITY: *Is it bold and assertive, or delicate and mild?*

GENERAL FLAVOR: *What kinds of tastes and aromas does it bring to mind (citrus, berry, apple, oak)?*

FLAVOR CHARACTERISTICS: *Is it dry or fruity; what are its levels of acidity and astringency (tannin)?*

Now think about the foods you want to serve. A wine can work with a dish either by mirroring it or contrasting with it. Delicately flavored foods like sole or halibut are complemented by a delicate, fruity white like Pinot Grigio. A rich, oily salmon may contrast well with a slightly acidic, medium-bodied Pinot Noir—and this fish won't be overwhelmed by this red wine. A spicy chicken stir-fry may overpower a buttery white, but be complemented by the spicy flavor of red Syrah—or a sweet, light white like Riesling. A rich, meaty braise will need a powerful red like Cabernet Sauvignon. And what is the weather like? This may also inform which wine best suits a meal.

As a general rule, wines are better appreciated when they progress from light to heavy over the course of the meal, with whites served before reds, and dry wines before sweet ones. Sweet dessert wines should taste sweeter than the food they are served with.

PAIRING SUGGESTIONS

Salty snack foods
Choose sparkling wines: Champagne, California sparkling wine, Prosecco

Spicy dishes
Choose fruity, low-alcohol, or spicy wines: Riesling, Pinot Grigio, Pinot Noir, Zinfandel

Rich or fatty dishes
Choose full-bodied wines: Chardonnay, Merlot, Cabernet Sauvignon, Zinfandel, Syrah

Acidic dishes (tomato, citrus, goat cheese)
Choose high-acid wines: Sauvignon Blanc, Zinfandel, Chianti

Salty or smoked dishes
Choose fruity, low-alcohol wines: Riesling, Gewürztraminer, Pinot Grigio/Gris, Pinot Noir

Cheeses
For goat's milk cheeses, choose high-acid white wines: California Sauvignon Blanc, Sancerre

For double- or triple-cream cheeses, choose fruity red or sweet wines: young Pinot Noir, tawny port

For blue cheeses, choose sweet white wines (Sauternes, late-harvest wines) or full-bodied reds

Sweet fruit or dessert
Choose sweet wines, with the wine at least as sweet as the dish

Classic pairings
Caviar with Champagne/sparkling wine
Oysters or lobster with Chablis (Chardonnay)
Goat cheese with Sancerre (Sauvignon Blanc)
Sole with white Burgundy (Chardonnay)
Roast lamb and Bordeaux (Cabernet/Merlot)
Charcuterie with Beaujolais Cru (Gamay)
Beef stew or game dishes with Barolo (Nebbiolo)
Roquefort cheese with Sauternes
Stilton cheese with vintage port

About cheese

Many people like to serve cheese with wine when guests first arrive. But some types are so rich and heavy that they easily spoil appetites. As a stylish change of pace, serve a selection of cheeses as a course before dessert or in place of dessert.

Selecting cheese

A good cheese shop, which gives advice and offers tastes, makes it easy to choose a selection of cheeses. For an ample array, plan on two to four types, depending on the number of people you're serving. You can also serve just one cheese, such as a luxurious French Camembert or a buttery blue Gorgonzola, to finish a meal. In any case, you don't want to overwhelm with too much cheese. Rather, you want to intrigue the palate with a few different flavor and texture sensations.

In choosing an assortment of cheeses, aim to offer variety and counterpoint. One approach is to select cheeses made from different

milks: cow's, sheep's, and goat's. Each milk offers a different starting point of flavor, which the cheese maker develops. Try to include different degrees of pungency. Another consideration is texture. The longer the cheese is aged, the more moisture evaporates from it and the firmer its texture, ranging from fresh, soft, young cheeses to semifirm ones, to long-aged hard cheeses. Including a blue cheese among the choices is a good way to provide range. A last consideration might be appearance. Cheeses are available in so many shapes and colors, with different rinds, leaf wrappers, and ash coatings, that it's easy to create a lovely and varied arrangement that appeals to the eye as well as the palate.

Storing cheese

Cheese does not like the cold. In fact, with the exception of fresh cheeses like ricotta, cheeses actually fare better stored in a cool, dimly lit spot for a day or two rather than in the refrigerator. If you do need to put cheese in the refrigerator for longer storage, try keeping it in the vegetable bin, which is more humid and less drying. Wrap it in waxed paper and then in a paper or plastic bag.

Accompaniments to cheese

Offer a few simple accompaniments with cheese. Thin slices of a baguette or dense peasant bread provide a welcome plain backdrop. Olives and nuts, especially walnuts, hazelnuts (filberts), and almonds, toasted for a few minutes to bring out their flavors, are especially good with goat's milk cheeses. Fruit delivers contrast: classic combinations are crisp apple with Cheddar, and pear with Brie. Dried fruits such as apricots or raisins enhance strong-flavored cheeses such as Comté, Muenster, or Manchego. Pair fresh jams with buttery blue cheeses, or wildflower honeys with semifirm and hard cheeses such as Gruyère and Parmesan.

A versatile wine choice that would complement a range of cheeses is a medium-bodied red. See right and page 37 for some specific suggestions, or let the character of the cheese guide you. For example, with mild fresh cheeses serve a lighter wine, like dry rosé, young Chablis, or Sauvignon Blanc. If the cheeses are stronger, a Chianti, Barolo, or Zinfandel will stand up well. When in doubt, brandy, a lightly chilled sherry, or a sparkling wine is always a welcome touch.

A CLASSIC CHEESE TRAY

EXPLORATEUR
OR BRILLAT-SAVARIN
(triple-cream)

CABÉCOU OR HUMBOLDT FOG
(semisoft, goat's milk)

P'TIT BASQUE
(semifirm, sheep's milk)

AGED GRUYÈRE
(hard, cow's milk)

*Wine pairing: Viognier or Vouvray
(full-bodied, aromatic white)*
*Accompany with sliced baguette, olives, grapes,
honey or honeycomb*

CHEESES FOR DESSERT

PORT-SALUT OR SAINT-ANDRÉ
(double-cream, cow's milk)

LANCASHIRE
(aged, semifirm, cow's milk)

STILTON OR ROQUEFORT
(firm, blue, cow's or sheep's milk)

*Wine pairing: 10-year tawny port or
Poire Williams (pear brandy)*
*Accompany with sliced pears or crisp persimmons,
dried figs, toasted raisin-walnut bread*

A SPANISH PAIRING

MANCHEGO
(firm, sheep's milk)

GARROTXA OR RONCAL
(semifirm, goat's milk)

*Wine pairing: Rioja Crianza
(smooth, medium-bodied Spanish red aged in wood)*
*Accompany with toasted almond, quince paste, or
apricot preserves*

Breakfast and Brunch

In this chapter, you'll find homey comfort foods just right for a
cozy breakfast for two. A favorite weekend morning tradition at our
house is custardy French toast, made with a baguette left over from
the night before, or a hearty breakfast hash that never fails to stir
up fond memories of a camping trip we took early in our marriage.
We like to host brunches and here we have several ideas for an easy
yet festive table, including huevos rancheros, an updated version of
eggs Benedict, and ethereal popovers that never fail to delight.

Vanilla-Pear Muffins

preparation **15** minutes | cooking **25** minutes | **6** large muffins or **12** regular muffins

Choose firm, ripe pears with a buttery texture and sweet perfume, such as French Butter, Comice, Warren, or Bartlett (Williams'), for these muffins, perfect for a lazy winter Sunday.

tools | muffin pan | chef's knife | silicone spatula | skewer | whisk | wire rack

Butter for greasing

FOR THE TOPPING

3 Tbsp sugar

2 Tbsp finely chopped walnuts

¼ tsp ground cinnamon

FOR THE MUFFINS

2 cups (10 oz/315 g) flour

½ cup (4 oz/125 g) sugar

2 tsp ground cinnamon

1 tsp freshly grated nutmeg

2 tsp baking powder

½ tsp baking soda (bicarbonate of soda)

½ tsp kosher salt

2 large eggs

½ cup (4 fl oz/125 ml) canola oil

¾ cup (6 fl oz/180 ml) buttermilk

2 tsp vanilla extract (essence)

4 or 5 firm but ripe pears, peeled, cored, and coarsely chopped

1 cup (4 oz/125 g) walnuts, coarsely chopped

Butter, slightly softened, for serving

Preheat the oven to 350°F (180°C). Grease a large 6-cup muffin pan or regular 12-cup muffin pan with butter.

To make the topping, combine the sugar, walnuts, and cinnamon in a small bowl. Set aside.

To make the muffins, stir together the flour, sugar, cinnamon, nutmeg, baking powder, baking soda, and salt in a bowl. In another bowl, whisk together the eggs, oil, buttermilk, and vanilla until blended. Add the dry ingredients to the wet ingredients, stirring just until evenly moistened. The batter will be slightly lumpy. Using a large silicone spatula, gently fold in the pears and walnuts just until evenly distributed, no more than a few strokes. Take care not to break up the fruit or overmix.

Spoon the batter into the prepared muffin cups, filling them level with the rim. Sprinkle the muffins with the topping, dividing it evenly. Bake until golden, dry, and springy to the touch, 20–25 minutes. A wooden skewer inserted into the center of a muffin should come out clean. Transfer the pan to a wire rack and let cool for 5 minutes. Turn out the muffins. Serve warm or at room temperature, with butter.

Banana Bread

preparation **10** minutes | cooking **1** hour | **1** loaf

Banana bread makes a great, wholesome breakfast or afternoon snack with coffee or tea. Try it sliced and toasted, with a bit of butter.

tools | loaf pan | chef's knife | box grater | fine-mesh sieve | skewer | wire rack | wooden spoon

Preheat the oven to 350°F (180°C). Grease an 8½-by-4½-inch (21.5-by-11.5-cm) loaf pan with butter.

Sift the flour, baking powder, and salt together into a medium bowl and set aside. In a large bowl, use a wooden spoon to beat the butter with the sugar and lemon zest until soft and creamy. Add one-third of the flour mixture to the butter mixture and stir until fully incorporated. Repeat, adding the remaining flour mixture in 2 more batches. Mix in the eggs and the mashed banana until well blended. Gently fold in the pecans and dates.

Pour the batter into the prepared loaf pan and smooth the top. Bake until a wooden skewer inserted in the center comes out clean, about 1 hour. Remove from the oven and let cool in the pan on a wire rack. Turn out onto a plate and serve at room temperature.

Butter for greasing

1¾ cups (9 oz/280 g) flour

2¼ tsp baking powder

¾ tsp kosher salt

⅓ cup (3 oz/90 g) butter, at room temperature

⅔ cup (5 oz/155 g) sugar

1 tsp grated lemon zest

2 large eggs, lightly beaten

1¼ cups (10 oz/315 g) mashed very ripe banana (about 2 large bananas)

½ cup (2 oz/60 g) chopped pecans

½ cup (3 oz/90 g) chopped dates

Popovers

preparation **10** minutes | cooking **35** minutes | **12** popovers

Be warned: the aroma of baking popovers will fill the entire house, and it may cause a delicious sense of anticipation—or even impatience!

tools | nonstick muffin pan | whisk

Whisk together the eggs and milk in a large bowl. Whisk in the flour, salt, and butter. Stir the batter until well blended, but don't overbeat, or the eggs will lose their rising power. The batter should have the consistency of heavy (double) cream.

Divide the batter among the cups of a 12-cup nonstick muffin pan, filling them two-thirds full. Do not overfill, or the popovers will not rise properly. Place the pan in a cold oven and heat the oven to 425°F (220°C). After 20 minutes, turn the oven down to 350°F (180°C) and continue to bake until the popovers are billowing out of each cup and golden brown, 12–15 minutes more. Serve at once.

3 large eggs

1½ cups (12 fl oz/375 ml) milk

1¼ cups (6½ oz/200 g) flour

2 tsp kosher salt

3 Tbsp butter, melted

Blueberry Pancakes

preparation **15** minutes | cooking **20** minutes | **4** servings (about **12** pancakes)

The secret ingredient in these pancakes is whipped egg whites, which gives them a feather-light texture. For tips on separating eggs and whipping egg whites, turn to pages 233 and 234. To give your spouse a treat, cut the recipe in half and serve these pancakes as breakfast in bed. For a nice touch, heat a pitcher of maple syrup by placing it in a little water in a saucepan over low heat or by putting it in the microwave for a few seconds.

tools | griddle or frying pan | baking sheet | electric mixer | ladle | metal spatula | silicone spatula | wooden spoon | whisk

1½ cups (7½ oz/235 g) flour

2 Tbsp sugar

1½ tsp baking powder

1 tsp baking soda
(bicarbonate of soda)

¾ tsp kosher salt

2 large eggs, separated

2 cups (16 fl oz/500 ml) buttermilk

4 Tbsp (2 oz/60 g) butter, melted
plus extra melted butter
for brushing

1½ cups (6 oz/185 g) blueberries

Maple syrup for serving

Preheat the oven to 200°F (95°C).

Stir together the flour, sugar, baking powder, baking soda, and salt in a large bowl with a wooden spoon. In another bowl, mix the egg yolks, buttermilk, and the 4 Tbsp butter until blended. Add the egg yolk mixture to the flour mixture and stir just until evenly blended.

In another large bowl, with an electric mixer on high speed, beat the egg whites until soft peaks form when the beaters are lifted. Gently fold the whites into the batter with a silicone spatula just until no white streaks remain.

Heat a griddle or a 12-inch (30-cm) frying pan, preferably nonstick, over medium heat until hot and brush lightly with butter. For each pancake, ladle ⅓ cup (3 fl oz/ 80 ml) batter onto the griddle and use the back of the ladle to gently spread into a 4-inch (10-cm) circle. Sprinkle evenly with about 2 Tbsp blueberries. Cook until large bubbles form and pop and the edges of the pancakes turn lightly brown, about 2 minutes. Turn the pancakes over with a large metal spatula and cook the other side until lightly browned, 1½–2 minutes longer. Transfer to a baking sheet and place in the oven to keep warm. Repeat with the remaining batter.

When all the pancakes are cooked, serve warm with maple syrup.

Buttermilk Waffles with Orange Butter

preparation **15** minutes | cooking **20–30** minutes | **4–8** servings

Waffles turn any weekend morning into a festive occasion. Serve with any topping you like; other possibilities are yogurt and honey or fresh berries and whipped cream.

tools | baking sheet | waffle iron | citrus reamer | wooden spoon

Preheat a Belgian waffle iron. Preheat the oven to 200°F (95°C). Stir together the flour, baking soda, and salt in a bowl with a wooden spoon. In another bowl, stir together the buttermilk, butter, and eggs until well blended. Stir the buttermilk mixture into the flour mixture until it forms a smooth, thick batter.

Spread about ½ cup (4 fl oz/125 ml) batter evenly in the waffle iron and cook according to the manufacturer's instructions. Transfer the waffle to a baking sheet and keep warm in the oven. Repeat with the remaining batter. Serve the waffles with the orange butter and maple syrup.

> **orange butter** Combine 4 Tbsp (2 oz/60 g) room-temperature butter, 1 Tbsp fresh orange juice, 1 tsp vanilla extract (essence), a pinch of kosher salt, and a pinch of sugar in a bowl and beat with a wooden spoon until well blended and fluffy.

1³/₄ cups (9 oz/280 g) flour, plus 2 Tbsp

1½ tsp baking soda (bicarbonate of soda)

1 tsp kosher salt

2 cups (16 fl oz/500 ml) buttermilk

4 Tbsp (2 oz/60 g) butter, melted and cooled

2 large eggs, lightly beaten

Orange butter for serving *(left)*

Maple syrup for serving

Breakfast Hash

preparation **10** minutes | cooking **40** minutes | **4** servings

This homey dish can be made with just about any leftover meat you have on hand, such as grilled rib eye, roast chicken or pork, or panfried duck breast. Serve with poached eggs (page 214) for a hearty winter breakfast.

tools | medium sauté pan | chef's knife | wooden spoon

Heat the olive oil in a medium sauté pan over low heat. Add the onion and sauté until softened, about 6 minutes. Add the potatoes and season with the salt and some pepper. Increase the heat to medium and add the meat and stock. Stir well and press the mixture onto the bottom of the pan. Lower the heat to medium-low. Cover and cook until the hash forms a crust on the bottom, about 15 minutes. Stir the hash to mix some of the crust into the rest of the hash. Repeat the process and cook until crusty, another 10–15 minutes, being careful not to overcook the hash and scorch the bottom. Spoon onto 4 warmed serving plates, turning each serving upside down to show off the crusty brown bottom. Garnish with the parsley and serve at once.

3 Tbsp olive oil

³/₄ cup (4 oz/125 g) diced onion

2 cups (10 oz/315 g) diced Yukon gold or russet potatoes

Kosher salt and pepper

2 cups (12 oz/375 g) finely diced cooked meat, such as rib eye

¹/₃ cup (3 fl oz/80 ml) beef or chicken stock (page 216 or 217)

3 Tbsp chopped fresh parsley

French Toast

preparation **10** minutes | resting **15** minutes | cooking **30** minutes | **4** servings

For this recipe, use day-old bread, which absorbs the sweet egg custard mix better. When fresh bread absorbs egg, it becomes soggy and temperamental. Baguettes and peasant-style French bread give the best results: light and crisp on the surface, custardy and tender on the inside. Top the French toast with powdered (icing) sugar, mascarpone cheese, fresh fruit, your favorite fruit jam, or honey.

tools | baking sheets | cast-iron frying pan or griddle | serrated bread knife | box grater or citrus zester | citrus reamer

1 day-old baguette

4 large eggs

1 egg yolk

2 cups (16 fl oz/500 ml) milk

1 tsp vanilla extract (essence)

1 tsp grated or minced orange zest

2 Tbsp fresh orange juice

4½ tsp sugar

¾ tsp kosher salt

2 Tbsp butter, or as needed

Slice the baguette on a slight bias into 20 slices about ¾ inch (2 cm) thick.

In a bowl, beat together the eggs, yolk, milk, vanilla, orange juice and zest, sugar, and salt, blending well. Pour the mixture into a large, shallow dish. Submerge the slices of bread and prick their surfaces with a fork so that they better absorb the egg mixture. If the bread is fairly dry, turn it over a few times and press the bread into the egg mixture, massaging it into the bread. Let the bread sit in the egg mixture for at least 15 minutes, turning once; this ensures a custardlike interior when the bread is cooked.

Preheat the oven to 200°F (95°C). Melt some of the butter in a cast-iron frying pan or on a seasoned griddle over medium heat. Place the bread slices, in batches, into the foaming butter and reduce the heat to low. Cook each slice just until the surface is golden brown and the inside has the texture of pudding, 3–4 minutes on each side. Add more butter to the frying pan if necessary. As the slices are cooked, keep warm in the oven spread in a single layer on baking sheets; do not stack. Serve on warmed plates.

Zucchini-Basil Frittata

preparation **10** minutes | cooking **15** minutes | **2** servings

A fluffy frittata, which begins on the stove top and finishes in the oven, makes a savory meal any time of day. You can vary this recipe to make use of whatever ingredients you have on hand: leftover cooked greens, roasted vegetables, or cheese and herbs. Serve with crusty French bread, sliced prosciutto or salami, and potato salad (page 179).

tools | small, nonstick frying pan | chef's knife or mandoline

Preheat the oven to 350°F (180°C).

Beat the eggs in a bowl until blended and season lightly with salt. Set aside. Trim off the ends of the zucchini and cut the zucchini into long, narrow matchsticks (see below).

Heat the olive oil in an 8-inch (20-cm) nonstick, ovenproof frying pan over medium heat. Sauté the zucchini for 1–2 minutes and season lightly with salt and pepper. Stir in the ricotta and basil, mixing well, and then pour in the eggs.

Reduce the heat to low and stir for 1 minute. Place the pan in the oven and bake until the frittata has gently risen and is set, 8–12 minutes.

Slide the frittata out of the pan onto a warmed plate and serve at once, or let cool to room temperature.

> **cutting matchsticks** Cutting vegetables into narrow strips of equal size allows them to cook quickly and evenly, and their neat appearance adds a pleasing look to a dish. Small matchsticks—about ⅛ inch (3 mm) thick—are called julienne. To cut matchsticks for this recipe, using a sharp chef's knife or a mandoline, first trim off the zucchini's rounded edges, cutting the vegetable into a log that's flat on each side. Cut the zucchini crosswise into 2-inch (5-cm) lengths, then cut each piece lengthwise into slices ⅛–¼ inch (3–6 mm) thick. Stack the slices and cut lengthwise into narrow strips.

5 eggs

Kosher salt and pepper

2 medium zucchini (courgettes)

1 Tbsp olive oil

⅓ cup (2½ oz/75 g) ricotta cheese

Leaves from 2 sprigs fresh basil, torn into small pieces

Classic French Omelet

preparation **5** minutes | cooking **7** minutes | **1** serving

Omelets, with a green salad and chilled white wine, are also an elegant, but easy, midweek supper for two. Use a nonstick pan and brisk heat to create an authentic French rolled omelet, tender and plump on the outside and creamy and voluptuous within. Since you can cook only one omelet at a time, keep the first loosely tented with foil while you prepare the second.

tools | small, nonstick frying pan or omelet pan | chef's knife | silicone spatula

3 eggs

1 Tbsp Champagne or sparkling wine

Kosher salt

2 Tbsp mascarpone cheese

2 tsp finely chopped fresh chives

2 tsp finely chopped fresh chervil

1 tsp finely chopped fresh parsley

1 Tbsp butter

In a small bowl, beat the eggs lightly with a fork to blend the yolks and whites completely. Stir in the Champagne, a pinch of salt, the mascarpone, and all the herbs. Do not overbeat.

Melt the butter in a 7- or 8-inch (18- or 20-cm) nonstick frying pan or omelet pan over medium-high heat. When the butter stops foaming and just before it begins to brown, add the egg mixture to the pan. The eggs will begin to set on the bottom within 30 seconds. Begin to pull in the egg mixture from the sides of the pan toward the center with a small silicone spatula to allow the raw egg to run underneath the thin sheet of cooked egg. Repeat 2 or 3 times until most of the bottom is set, while the surface remains moist and creamy. Tilt the pan forward, sliding the omelet up the side of the pan, and use the spatula to fold in the edge of the omelet, then roll it up. Flip the omelet once or twice with the spatula to secure the roll. Slide the omelet onto a plate and serve at once.

chervil This lacy herb with a delicate parsley-anise flavor is best known as a component of the French herb blend *fines herbes*, a combination of chervil, parsley, tarragon, and chives commonly used in sauces and omelets. Chervil wilts quickly, so wrap it in a damp paper towel, place in a plastic bag, and store in the refrigerator for no longer than 2 days.

Huevos Rancheros

preparation **10** minutes | cooking **20–30** minutes | **4** servings

You can use store-bought salsa in this dish to make it quicker to prepare, but if possible, take a few extra minutes to make the simple and tasty salsa fresca *(fresh salsa). The eggs can be fried in batches; just hold the finished plates in a warm spot until all the eggs are ready.*

tools | frying pan or griddle | medium saucepan | chef's knife | citrus reamer

To make the salsa, combine all of the salsa ingredients in a bowl and stir to blend. Add 1 Tbsp water if the mixture seems dry. Taste the salsa and adjust the seasoning with salt and lime juice. Let stand for 10 minutes to allow the flavors to marry.

In a medium saucepan, combine the beans and ¼ cup (2 fl oz/60 ml) water. Heat over medium-high heat, stirring often, until hot, about 7 minutes. Set aside and cover to keep warm. Heat a large, heavy frying pan or griddle over high heat and add the tortillas one at a time, heating each for a minute or two on each side. Wrap in a clean kitchen towel to keep warm.

To fry the eggs, coat the frying pan or griddle with a thin film of olive oil. In batches as necessary, break the eggs into the pan and fry over medium-high heat until the whites are set and the yolks are nearly set.

Place 1 or 2 tortillas on each of 4 warmed plates. Spread each tortilla with 2 or 3 Tbsp beans and top with 1 or 2 eggs. Top the eggs with salsa and slices of avocado. Serve at once.

> **cutting avocados** Preparing an avocado is easier if you know a few tricks. Cut the fruit in half, working around the pit. Twist the halves in opposite directions to separate. To remove the pit, strike it carefully but firmly with the heel of the blade of a large, sharp knife, lodging the knife firmly in the pit, then ease the pit out. Slice the flesh while it's still in the peel, then scoop out the slices with a large spoon.

FOR THE SALSA

2 Tbsp finely chopped yellow onion

2 ripe small to medium tomatoes, cored and chopped

2 Tbsp chopped fresh cilantro (fresh coriander)

½ tsp kosher salt

2 tsp fresh lime juice

1 Tbsp minced jalapeño chili

1 Tbsp red wine vinegar

One small can regular or spicy refried beans

4–8 corn tortillas

Olive oil for frying

4–8 eggs

1 ripe avocado, sliced

Eggs Benedict

preparation **15** minutes | cooking **15–20** minutes | **4** servings

Serve eggs Benedict for a Mother's Day brunch or an Easter celebration, or treat your houseguests, or yourself, on a Sunday morning. In the spring, substitute sliced steamed asparagus for the spinach.

tools | double boiler | small saucepans | large sauté pans | paring knife | citrus reamer | slotted spoon | whisk

FOR THE HOLLANDAISE SAUCE

1½ Tbsp fresh lemon juice

4 Tbsp (2 oz/60 g) butter

3 large egg yolks

Kosher salt

¼ tsp ground cayenne pepper

4 English muffins, split

2 tsp olive oil

1½ lb (750 g) baby spinach, patted dry

½ tsp kosher salt

8 large eggs

8 slices Virginia ham or prosciutto, at room temperature

To make the hollandaise sauce, warm the lemon juice in a small nonreactive saucepan over low heat, or in the microwave. Bring ½ cup (4 fl oz/125 ml) water to a boil in a small saucepan over high heat. Melt the butter in another small saucepan over low heat, or in the microwave.

Set up a double boiler (page 245) over low heat. Place the egg yolks in the bowl or top pan of the double boiler and place over (but not touching) the barely simmering water in the bottom pan. Whisk the egg yolks constantly until they begin to thicken, then add 1 Tbsp of the boiling water and continue to whisk until the yolks have thickened, about 30 seconds. Add 3 more Tbsp boiling water, 1 Tbsp at a time, whisking thoroughly after each addition. Whisk in the warm lemon juice and remove the pan from the heat. Pour in the melted butter very slowly, whisking constantly, then add ¼ tsp salt and the cayenne. The sauce will thicken. Turn off the heat but leave the bowl over the water and cover to keep warm.

Toast the English muffins.

Heat the olive oil in large sauté pan over medium-low heat. Gently sauté the spinach leaves just until tender, about 4 minutes. Season with the ½ tsp salt, set aside, and cover to keep warm.

Meanwhile, poach the eggs in batches. Put 2–3 inches (5–7.5 cm) of water in a large sauté pan or shallow pot. Season the water with salt and bring to a simmer over medium heat. One at a time, and working quickly, crack each egg into a small ramekin and carefully slip it into the water. Leave space in around the eggs. Adjust the heat so that the water barely simmers. Poach the eggs gently for 3–5 minutes, depending on the desired doneness. Remove each egg from the water with a slotted spoon, and, while the egg is still in the spoon, blot the bottom dry with a kitchen towel and trim off the ragged edges with a paring knife.

Place 2 warm English muffin halves, cut side up, on each of 4 plates. Lay a ham slice on each muffin half. Arrange the warm spinach on the ham, top each bed of spinach with a poached egg, and spoon ¼ cup (2 fl oz/60 ml) hollandaise sauce over each egg. Serve at once.

Starters

The purpose of an appetizer is to stimulate the appetite for the meal to come. A dish can be extremely simple and yet play this role perfectly: think of olives gently warmed to awaken their flavors, or crunchy radishes paired with creamy butter. An uncomplicated starter allows you to focus on wonderful flavors and textures and artfully awakens anticipation for the main course, rather than sating you.

Spicy Almonds

preparation **5** minutes | cooking **15** minutes | **6–8** appetizer servings

Toasting almonds fills your kitchen with their sweet fragrance, and you are rewarded with a versatile snack that goes equally well with a chilled rosé, a classic Manhattan, or an ice-cold beer. These almonds can be added to salads, frittatas, or even pasta.

tools | baking sheet | spatula or wooden spoon

2 cups (10 oz/315 g) whole almonds with the skin

1 tsp kosher salt

2 tsp olive oil

1 or 2 pinches of finely ground red chili flakes

¼ tsp garlic powder (optional)

Preheat the oven to 325°F (165°C). In a medium bowl, combine the almonds with 2 Tbsp water and the salt, tossing the almonds to coat evenly. Spread the almonds on a baking sheet and bake for 8 minutes. Remove the baking sheet from the oven and drizzle the olive oil over the nuts. Use a spatula or wooden spoon to mix the nuts until the oil is thoroughly incorporated. Sprinkle the ground chili flakes and garlic powder, if using, onto the almonds and mix to coat well. Return the almonds to the oven and bake for 5–6 minutes more, stirring the almonds after 3 minutes to ensure even cooking. Remove from the oven and let cool. The almonds will keep in an airtight container for up to 1 week.

Warm Marinated Olives

preparation **10** minutes | cooking **5** minutes | **6–8** appetizer servings

For a touch of simple Mediterranean pleasure, fix your mate a snack of these warm olives before serving supper. We suggest a combination of olive varieties here, but feel free to choose a selection of flavors, shapes, and colors that appeal to you. Be sure to choose olives with their pits for the best flavor and quality.

tools | medium sauté pan | chef's knife | citrus zester

½ cup (2½ oz/75 g) Picholine olives

½ cup (2½ oz/75 g) Moroccan olives

½ cup (2½ oz/75 g) Niçoise olives

1 orange

1 lemon

Leaves from 2 sprigs fresh thyme

1 clove garlic, minced

1½ Tbsp extra-virgin olive oil

Rinse the olives under cold water to remove any brine. Pat dry with paper towels.

Remove half of the orange's zest in long strips with a zester. Remove half of the lemon's zest.

In a bowl, toss the olives with the orange and lemon zests, thyme, garlic, and olive oil. Just before serving, heat the olives in a medium sauté pan over low heat just long enough to bring out their flavors and gently warm them. Serve in an earthenware crock or dish with a small ramekin for discarded pits.

Gougères

preparation **20** minutes | cooking **25** minutes | **4** appetizer servings

Gougères are golden cheese-laced puffs that bake up crisp yet tender. They are delicious served warm or cold, with white or red wine, and they make delicious late-night snacks.

tools | medium saucepan | baking sheets | box grater | parchment paper | wooden spoon

Preheat the oven to 375°F (190°C) and line baking sheets with parchment (baking) paper. Combine the butter and ½ cup (4 fl oz / 125 ml) water in a medium saucepan and bring to a boil. Add the flour all at once, quickly stirring with a wooden spoon until the batter is glossy and smooth and pulls away from the sides of the saucepan. The dough will form a ball around the spoon.

Remove from the heat and add the eggs, one at a time, beating well after each addition until thoroughly incorporated. Stir in the cheese, cayenne, and salt.

Use 2 spoons or a pastry bag without a tip to form 1-inch (2.5-cm) balls on the prepared baking sheet. Bake until the balls double in size and turn golden brown and a thin-bladed knife inserted in the center comes out clean, about 25 minutes. Let cool slightly or completely before serving.

3 Tbsp butter

¾ cup (4 oz / 125 g) plus 2 Tbsp flour

3 large eggs

1⅓ cups (5½ oz / 170 g) grated Gruyère cheese

¼ tsp ground cayenne pepper

½ tsp kosher salt, or more to taste

Marinated Goat Cheese

preparation **5** minutes | resting **1** day | **4** appetizer servings

Soft, fresh goat cheese is satisfying on its own, but marinating the cheese in oil, herbs, and spices makes it completely irresistible. Serve it with crackers, fold it into an omelet, or use it to top a green salad, bruschette, or pasta.

tools | chef's knife

Place the goat cheese in a shallow dish. Drizzle with the olive oil and sprinkle with the thyme, chili flakes (if using), fennel seeds, and bay leaves. Cover and refrigerate for at least 1 day and up to 3 days. Remove from the refrigerator at least 1 hour before serving to bring the cheese to room temperature.

> **toasting seeds** To toast seeds and bring out their flavor, spread them in a dry frying pan and heat over medium heat until fragrant. Watch seeds carefully to prevent them from burning.

4 rounds fresh goat cheese, each ½ inch (12 mm) thick sliced from a log 2½ inches (6 cm) in diameter

¾ cup (6 fl oz / 180 ml) extra-virgin olive oil

3 or 4 sprigs fresh thyme

¼ tsp red chili flakes (optional)

2 tsp fennel seeds, lightly toasted (left)

2 fresh or dried bay leaves

Eggplant Caviar

preparation **10** minutes | cooking **50** minutes | resting **30** minutes | **4** appetizer servings

The name of this eggplant spread may be tongue-in-cheek—a poor man's caviar?—but it's so delicious that it holds its own alongside most elegant luxury foods. Pair with Italian-style cauliflower (page 158) and ginger carrots (page 155) to make a simple meal for two.

tools | baking sheet | chef's knife | paring knife | citrus reamer

1 large globe eggplant (aubergine)

1 Tbsp olive oil

Sea salt and pepper

2 Tbsp extra-virgin olive oil

1 Tbsp fresh lemon juice

1 Tbsp balsamic vinegar

1 clove garlic, mashed

Several sprigs fresh mint

Crostini for serving (page 215)

Preheat the oven to 375°F (190°C). Trim off the stem of the eggplant and cut in half lengthwise. Rub the cut surfaces with the olive oil and sprinkle with salt and pepper. Place the halves cut side down on a baking sheet and roast until the flesh is soft and cooked through, 40–50 minutes.

Let the eggplant to cool until is it easy to handle and then peel the skin off with a paring knife. Chop the flesh until it has the texture of salsa. Combine the chopped eggplant with the extra-virgin olive oil, lemon juice, vinegar, and garlic. Taste and adjust the seasoning with salt. Allow the mixture to rest for at least 30 minutes. When ready to serve, pick the leaves from the mint sprigs, chop coarsely, and stir them into the eggplant. Accompany with the crostini.

Radishes with Butter

preparation **10** minutes | **4** appetizer servings

Crunchy, raw radishes paired with rich unsalted butter is a French tradition. We like to use French breakfast radishes, with their pretty white and pink color, oblong shape, and mildly peppery flavor. Choose an organic or European-style butter if available. It has less water and better flavor than regular butters. Serve with a rosé.

tools | paring knife | serrated bread knife

1 bunch French breakfast radishes or other mildly spicy radishes

Fine sea salt

4 Tbsp butter, cut into 4 pats

1 baguette, cut into slices ½ inch (12 mm) thick

Trim the radish tops, leaving a few of the leaves if they are pretty and green. Trim away and discard the root ends. Submerge the radishes in a small bowl of cold water for 10 minutes to crisp. Drain and pat dry.

On each of 4 small plates, arrange a few radishes, a small pile of sea salt, a pat of butter, and a few baguette slices.

Artichoke Dip

preparation **10** minutes | cooking **30** minutes | **6–8** appetizer servings

This savory dip is rich, even a little decadent, but guests are guaranteed to devour it quickly. Luckily the recipe doubles well! Serve the dip with crostini (page 215) and classic martinis and you'll have an instant party.

tools | small baking dish or soufflé dish | baking sheet | chef's knife | box grater | citrus reamer | colander or sieve | wooden spoon

Preheat the oven to 350°F (180°C). Drain the liquid from the artichokes and discard. Chop the artichokes into ½-inch (12-mm) pieces and put in a mixing bowl. Add the mayonnaise, lemon juice, 3 Tbsp of the Parmesan, and the parsley and mix well with a wooden spoon. Spoon into a small baking dish or soufflé dish and sprinkle with the remaining Parmesan. Place the dish on a baking sheet and bake until golden on top, 25–30 minutes. The dip will be very hot; let cool slightly before serving with the crostini.

1 jar (12 oz/375 g) water-packed or marinated artichoke hearts (about 2 cups)

⅓ cup (3 fl oz/80 ml) mayonnaise

1 tsp fresh lemon juice

3½ Tbsp freshly grated Parmesan cheese (divided)

1 Tbsp chopped fresh parsley

Crostini for serving (page 215)

Guacamole

preparation **10** minutes | **6–8** appetizer servings

If you don't have a big mortar and pestle, treat yourself to a Mexican molcajete, *made of volcanic rock. It is so handsome that you can serve the dip in it, too. We are purists when it comes to guacamole, relying on the irresistible flavor and texture of perfectly ripe avocado: buttery, nutty, and fruity.*

tools | chef's knife | citrus reamer | mortar and pestle (optional)

Use a mortar and pestle or a bowl and fork to mash the onion, chili, chopped cilantro, and a pinch of salt with a grinding motion to form a coarse paste. Cut the avocados in half, remove their pits, and scoop out the flesh with a spoon. Add to the mixture and mash until well incorporated. Add salt to taste and lime juice to balance the flavors. (The flavors of the lime and salt should be prominent, but the guacamole should not be too salty or acidic.) Let the mixture stand for a few minutes before serving to allow the flavors to marry. Garnish the guacamole with the cilantro sprigs and serve.

¼ cup (1 oz/30 g) finely chopped white onion

1 jalapeño chili, seeded and finely chopped

¼ cup (⅓ oz/10 g) coarsely chopped fresh cilantro (fresh coriander), plus 4 sprigs

Kosher salt

2 ripe Hass avocados

1 Tbsp fresh lime juice, or to taste

Bruschette Two Ways

preparation **20** minutes | resting **1** hour | cooking **10** minutes | **12** servings

Bruschette—open-faced sandwiches of toasted or grilled bread with savory toppings—are a fun way to start any social gathering. Halve the recipe to make a light summertime lunch for two with a glass of Chianti or Viognier. The number of bruschetta toppings you can create are infinite, and we hope you will be inspired to create your own with any ingredients that sound appealing to you. The two toppings here are classics.

tools | large sauté pan | chef's knife | serrated bread knife | colander or sieve | grill, toaster oven, or broiler

12 slices sourdough or peasant bread, ½ inch (12 mm) thick

FOR THE TAPENADE AND GREENS TOPPING

1 cup (5 oz/155 g) fruity green olives, pitted

5 cloves garlic (divided)

2 anchovy fillets, rinsed and patted dry

2 Tbsp capers, rinsed and chopped

2 tsp grappa (optional)

Extra-virgin olive oil

1 bunch kale, escarole (Batavian endive), or Swiss chard

½ tsp kosher salt

Pinch of red chili flakes (optional)

FOR THE WHITE BEAN TOPPING

1½ cups (10½ oz/330 g) canned white beans (see Note)

2 fresh sage leaves, chopped

Sea salt and freshly ground pepper

Extra-virgin olive oil

1 large clove garlic

1 medium ripe tomato

Using a grill with glowing embers, a toaster oven, or the broiler (grill), toast the bread slices on both sides until golden brown, taking care not to burn them.

To make the tapenade and greens topping, roughly chop the olives, keeping the texture slightly coarse. Finely mince 4 cloves of the garlic and the anchovy fillets. Combine the olives, minced garlic, anchovies, capers, and grappa (if using) in a bowl and drizzle with ¼ cup (2 fl oz/60 ml) extra-virgin olive oil. Taste and add more olive oil if needed for flavor or texture. The tapenade should glisten and have a texture similar to that of salsa, loose but not overly oily. Let stand at room temperature for at least 1 hour to allow the flavors to marry.

When nearly ready to serve, trim the stems from the greens and pat dry. Chop into bite-sized pieces. Mince the remaining 1 clove garlic. Heat 1 Tbsp olive oil in a large sauté pan over medium heat and add the greens. Sprinkle with 1 Tbsp water to create steam. Reduce the heat to low, season the greens with the salt, garlic, and chili flakes (if using), and cook until the greens are tender, 8–10 minutes, depending on the type of greens. Taste and adjust the seasoning with salt. Spread the tapenade over 6 toasted bread slices and arrange the warm greens on top.

To make the white bean topping, rinse and drain the beans. Combine the beans, sage, a pinch of salt, a grinding of pepper, and 2 Tbsp extra-virgin olive oil in a bowl and mash with a fork until the beans are pasty and the ingredients thoroughly combined. Rub 6 slices of the toasted bread lightly and evenly with the garlic clove to flavor well. Slice off the top of the tomato and rub the bread slices with the cut side of the tomato to moisten and give them flavor. Divide the bean mixture among the bread slices and spread evenly. Drizzle each bruschetta with olive oil and serve at once.

Note: If you have leftover white beans and sage (page 189), you can use this in place of canned white beans.

Shrimp with Parsley-Garlic Butter

preparation **30** minutes | cooking **5** minutes | **6–8** appetizer servings

This appetizer inevitably disappears as soon as it hits the table. The shrimp are butterflied, or cut almost in half and opened flat, then topped with a flavored butter and quickly broiled while still in their shells. When prepared like this, the shrimp are easy to peel, and very flavorful and attractive.

tools | baking sheet or roasting pan | chef's knife | paring knife | box grater or citrus zester | wooden spoon

Make the parsley-garlic butter.

Preheat the broiler (grill). Remove the legs from the shrimp. With a sharp paring knife, make an incision ¼ inch (6 mm) deep all the way along the curved back of each shrimp up to the tail. Don't cut all the way through the shrimp; cut just enough to open it up, or butterfly it. Lift any dark vein with the tip of the knife and pull it out, and then press down on the opened shrimp to flatten it without separating the halves. Rinse the shrimp under cold water and pat dry.

Arrange the butterflied shrimp in a single layer on a baking sheet or in a roasting pan (you may need to do this in batches). Place 1–2 tsp of the parsley-garlic butter (depending on the size of the shrimp) in the center of each shrimp. Slide the pan under the broiler and broil (grill) until the shrimp turn pink and are just cooked through, 4–5 minutes. Transfer the shrimp to a serving platter or individual plates, pour any drippings from the pan over the shrimp, and serve with plenty of napkins and a plate for the shells.

> **parsley-garlic butter** The ingredients in this flavored butter can be changed to suit your taste: Try chives instead of parsley, or orange zest instead of lemon zest. In a bowl, combine 1 cup (8 oz/250 g) butter, slightly softened; leaves from 1 bunch fresh parsley, minced; 5 or 6 medium to large cloves garlic, minced; 1 Tbsp grated or minced lemon zest; 2 tsp fine sea salt; and 1 tsp pepper. Mash together well with a wooden spoon. The butter can be refrigerated for up to 3 days before using, and any leftover butter will keep for up to 1 month in the freezer.

Parsley-garlic butter (below)

2 lb (1 kg) unpeeled jumbo shrimp (prawns) (about 28)

Grilled Mozzarella Sandwiches

preparation **10** minutes | cooking **8** minutes | **6** appetizer servings

The keys to a sensational appetizer are simplicity, an appealing texture, and a savory taste that sharpens the appetite. These little sandwiches fit the bill perfectly, and they go very well with tumblers of red or white wine.

tools | cast-iron frying pan or nonstick flat grill pan | chef's knife | serrated bread knife | brush (optional)

1 loaf peasant bread, preferably day-old

1½ lb (750 g) fresh mozzarella

Kosher salt

2 Tbsp olive oil

1 Tbsp chopped fresh parsley

Cut the bread into 12 slices ¼ inch (6 mm) thick. Arrange half of the slices on your work surface. Cut the mozzarella into slices ¼ inch thick and place on top of the arranged bread slices. Season the mozzarella with salt and cover with the remaining bread slices. Make sure the top bread slices fit the bottoms so that the cheese is not exposed or falling out of the sandwich.

Brush the surface of a cast-iron frying pan or nonstick, flat-surfaced grill pan with a thin film of olive oil and heat over medium heat. Brush the tops of the sandwiches with oil as well. When the pan is hot, add the sandwiches oiled side down, in batches as necessary, and cook until the bottoms are golden and the cheese starts to melt, 3–5 minutes. Brush the other side of the bread with oil and turn the sandwiches over, adding a little more oil to the pan if needed. Cook for a few minutes longer. The sandwiches should be toasted golden on both sides and the cheese should be melted.

Remove the sandwiches from the pan and cut into neat, bite-sized pieces (triangles or rectangles, depending on the shape of the bread). Sprinkle with the chopped parsley and serve warm on a serving platter lined with a cloth napkin.

Crab Cakes

preparation **30** minutes | cooking **15** minutes | **4** appetizer servings or **2** main-course servings

Once you master the knack of making crab cakes, you'll see how easily you can vary them. Try adding minced ginger, chopped bell peppers (capsicums), or chopped sautéed spinach. If you want truly knockout crab cakes, make spicy mayonnaise to top them with, and use some of the unflavored homemade mayonnaise in the crab cakes as well. This recipe yields an excellent appetizer for four, or serves two as a main course with a green salad (page 82) and a bowl of corn soup (page 81).

tools | small and large sauté pans | chef's knife | citrus reamer | spatula or tongs

Heat the olive oil in a small sauté pan over medium-low heat. Add the onion and celery and sauté until tender, about 10 minutes; do not let brown. Season lightly with salt, remove from the heat, and let cool completely. Meanwhile, in a medium bowl, combine the crabmeat, fresh bread crumbs, mashed potatoes, mustard, mayonnaise, chives, tarragon, cayenne, and lemon juice. Season with salt and pepper. Mix together gently with a fork to keep the mixture fluffy, with big flakes of crabmeat intact. Carefully stir in the cooled onion mixture and taste. Add a little more lemon juice, cayenne, or salt to suit your taste.

To form the cakes, spread the toasted bread crumbs on a plate. Use a ¼-cup (2–fl oz/60-ml) measure to scoop out the crab mixture and drop into the crumbs. Coat each side lightly with the crumbs, patting them on so they adhere, and form a compact cake about ¾ inch (2 cm) thick. You should be able to form 8 crab cakes. At this point, you can refrigerate the cakes until just before ready to cook and serve.

When ready to serve, preheat the oven to 200°F (95°C). Heat half of the oil in a large sauté pan over medium heat. Place 4 of the cakes in the pan and cook on one side until a golden crust forms, about 3 minutes. Use tongs or a spatula to turn the cakes over and continue cooking until a golden crust forms on the second side, about 3 minutes more. Remove the cakes from the pan and keep warm in the oven while adding the remaining half of the oil to the sauté pan and cooking the remaining 4 cakes.

To serve, place the crab cakes on individual plates with a dollop of spicy mayonnaise, if using, and a sprinkling of arugula leaves.

1 Tbsp olive oil

⅓ cup (2 oz/60 g) minced yellow onion

⅓ cup (2 oz/60 g) minced celery

Kosher salt and pepper

1 lb (500 g) fresh or thawed frozen lump crabmeat, picked over for shell pieces and cartilage

¾ cup (1½ oz/45 g) fine fresh bread crumbs (page 215)

½ cup (4 oz/125 g) mashed potatoes, cooled (page 178)

3 Tbsp Dijon mustard

¼ cup (2 fl oz/60 ml) mayonnaise

2 Tbsp chopped fresh chives

2 Tbsp chopped fresh tarragon

¼ tsp ground cayenne pepper

Juice of ½ lemon, or to taste

1 cup (4 oz/125 g) fine toasted bread crumbs (page 215)

¼ cup (2 fl oz/60 ml) grape seed or olive oil (divided)

Spicy mayonnaise for serving (page 213; optional)

Arugula (rocket) leaves for serving

Soups and Salads

These versatile recipes can start a multicourse dinner or double as light meals, lunches for two, or late-night snacks. Fun-to-assemble salads such as tomato, mozzarella, and basil require some timely shopping, but they make up for it by coming together in minutes. Some of the soups, such as gazpacho or butternut squash, can be made ahead of time and served as a weeknight supper. Clam chowder can be the centerpiece of any gathering, and frisée with lardons and poached egg is a perfect brunch main course.

Gazpacho

preparation **15** minutes | chilling **2** hours | **4** servings

Don't attempt to make gazpacho with canned tomatoes. Wait until summertime, visit your local farmers' market, and ask the vendors to help you select the ripest specimens.

tools | chef's knife | food mill, food processor, or blender

1 English (hothouse) cucumber

1 small red bell pepper (capsicum)

8 ripe tomatoes

¼ cup (1 oz/30 g) chopped sweet red onion

1 tsp minced garlic

Extra-virgin olive oil

Red wine vinegar

6 Tbsp (¾ oz/20 g) fresh bread crumbs (page 215)

Kosher salt

Peel the cucumber and slice in half lengthwise, then scoop out any seeds with a small spoon. Finely dice enough cucumber to measure out 2 Tbsp, set aside, and chop the rest. Remove the core and seeds from the bell pepper. Chop the pepper and tomatoes.

Combine the chopped cucumber, bell pepper, tomatoes, onion, garlic, ¼ cup (2 fl oz/60 ml) olive oil, and 2 Tbsp vinegar and purée until smooth using a food mill, food processor, or blender. Stir in the bread crumbs. Taste for salt and vinegar and adjust according to your taste. Cover and refrigerate for at least 2 hours or up to 2 days. Serve cold in chilled bowls, drizzled with extra-virgin olive oil and garnished with the reserved diced cucumber.

Leek and Potato Soup

preparation **15** minutes | cooking **15** minutes | **4** servings

The arrival of stormy days and chilly nights is your cue to simmer up a pot of this soup. It can be made some days in advance, so it's ready and waiting when you need a quick meal.

tools | small pot | chef's knife | colander | ladle | vegetable peeler

5 medium leeks

2 large boiling potatoes such as Yukon gold or Yellow Finn

8 cups (64 fl oz/2 l) vegetable stock

1 tsp kosher salt, or to taste

3 sprigs fresh thyme

1 clove garlic, lightly crushed

¼ cup (2 fl oz/60 ml) crème fraîche or sour cream

1 Tbsp chopped fresh chives

Clean the leeks by trimming off their roots and green tops. Peel away the tough outer green leaves, exposing the tender stalk. Quarter each stalk lengthwise, and cut into ¼-inch (6-mm) dice. Rinse the leeks under cold water in a colander to remove any sand or dirt. Let the leeks drain. Peel the potatoes and dice finely.

Bring the stock to a boil in a small pot over medium-high heat and add the salt, potatoes, thyme, and garlic. Return to a boil and cook, covered, for 5 minutes. Add the leeks, lower the heat to medium, and simmer, uncovered, until the leeks and potatoes are tender, about 10 minutes. Taste and adjust the seasoning.

Remove the thyme sprigs. Ladle the soup into warmed bowls, garnish with a dollop of crème fraîche and a sprinkle of chives, and serve at once.

New England Clam Chowder

preparation **20** minutes | cooking **30** minutes | **6–8** servings

There is something comforting in creating and serving supper out of a single pot— not to mention what a gift it is to the appointed dishwasher. Serve this classic chowder with warm crusty French bread and lemony Caesar salad (page 88). To serve at a dinner party, make the chowder base ahead of time and add the clams right before serving.

tools | medium and large sauté pans | soup pot | chef's knife | cheesecloth | fine-mesh sieve | ladle | vegetable peeler | wooden spoon

To make the roux, melt the butter in a medium sauté pan over low heat. Add the flour and cook the mixture, stirring constantly with a wooden spoon, until pastelike, about 4 minutes. Do not allow the flour to brown. Remove from the heat and set aside.

To open the clams and make the clam stock, combine 2½ cups (20 fl oz/625 ml) water and the clams in a large sauté pan, discarding any clams that do not close to the touch. Place over medium heat, cover, and cook until the clams open, 2–5 minutes. Remove from the heat and let the clams and their liquid (now clam stock) cool slightly. Discard any clams that failed to open. Use your fingers or a small spoon to pick the meats out of the clam shells, letting any juices fall back into the pan; put the clam meats on a cutting board and discard the shells. Pour the stock through a fine-mesh sieve lined with damp cheesecloth (muslin) to remove any grit. Chop the clams coarsely for a finer texture in the final chowder. Set the clams and the stock aside.

To make the chowder, melt the butter in a soup pot over low heat. Gently sauté the bacon, onions, celery, and carrot, stirring constantly, until tender, about 10 minutes. Do not brown. Add the clam stock, cream, milk, potatoes, thyme, and bay leaf. Bring to a gentle simmer and cook for 5 minutes. Stir 1 Tbsp of the chowder mixture into the roux until smooth. Add the roux to the pot of chowder, stirring thoroughly to incorporate. Simmer, stirring constantly, to thicken the chowder, 4–5 minutes.

When just about ready to serve, add the chopped clams to the chowder and simmer for 2 minutes longer. Add the salt, taste, and adjust the seasoning. Ladle into warmed bowls, sprinkle with the parsley, and serve.

FOR THE ROUX

1 Tbsp butter

2½ Tbsp flour

FOR THE CLAMS AND CLAM STOCK

2½ lb (1.25 kg) fresh clams such as littleneck or Manila, scrubbed well

FOR THE CHOWDER

2 Tbsp butter or olive oil

2 thick slices bacon, minced

2 small yellow onions, finely diced

1 large rib celery, finely diced

1 large carrot, peeled and finely diced

1 cup (8 fl oz/250 ml) heavy (double) cream

1½ cups (12 fl oz/375 ml) milk

1 large or 2 small yellow-fleshed boiling potatoes such as Yukon gold or Yellow Finn, peeled and finely diced

Leaves from 3 sprigs fresh thyme

1 bay leaf

½ tsp kosher salt

1 Tbsp chopped fresh parsley

Black Bean Soup

soaking **4** hours | preparation **20** minutes | cooking **2** hours | **6–8** servings

Plan ahead and start soaking the beans the night before you prepare this recipe, which makes enough soup for more than one delicious meal. If you live in an area where there are Latin markets, look for epazote, an herb commonly used in Mexican cooking, to give the soup an authentic flavor. Ask the butcher to saw a ham hock or bone in half for you. While the beans soak and the soup simmers, you'll have plenty of time to make a delicious tomatillo salsa topping, if you'd like to dress up the soup for company.

tools | soup pot | chef's knife | food processor or blender | citrus zester | ladle | large metal spoon

1 lb (500 g) dried black beans

1 yellow onion, diced

1 large carrot, peeled and diced

1 rib celery, diced

4 cloves garlic, lightly crushed

1 sprig fresh epazote or cilantro (fresh coriander)

½ small ham hock or ham bone

2½ qt (2.5 l) chicken or vegetable stock (page 216), or as needed

1 Tbsp ground ancho chili powder

1 Tbsp ground cumin

1 Tbsp kosher salt

½ cup (4 fl oz/125 ml) crème fraîche or sour cream

Thin strips of lime zest for garnish

Tomatillo salsa for garnish (right; optional)

Rinse and pick over the beans, discarding any debris and any misshapen or discolored beans. Put in a bowl, add water to cover by 3 inches (7.5 cm), and soak for 4 hours or up to overnight.

Drain the beans and put them in a soup pot with the onion, carrot, celery, garlic, epazote, ham hock, and stock. Bring to a boil and skim off any foam with a large metal spoon. Reduce the heat to low and simmer slowly, uncovered, until the beans are creamy and tender, about 2 hours. Add more stock to the beans if needed to keep them barely covered. Stir often so that the beans cook evenly.

When the beans are tender, remove the ham hock and epazote and discard. Let cool slightly for easier handling. Ladle the bean mixture into a food processor or blender in small batches, adding cooking liquid as necessary, and process to an even and smooth purée. Return to the pot and stir in the chili powder and cumin. The soup should be smooth and pourable, without being too runny or too thick. Add water to thin the soup, if necessary; if it is too runny, simmer over medium heat until slightly thickened. Add the salt (if using prepared broth you may not need as much), taste, and adjust the seasoning.

When ready to serve, reheat the soup over medium heat and ladle into warmed bowls. Garnish with the crème fraîche, lime zest, and the tomatillo salsa, if using.

> **tomatillo salsa** Tomatillos look like miniature green tomatoes in a papery husk, but they are actually unrelated to tomatoes. Remove the husks from 10 tomatillos, rinse, and finely chop. Finely chop 1 small red onion. Stem, seed, and finely chop 1 serrano chili. In a nonreactive bowl, combine the tomatillos, onion, chili, ¼ cup (⅓ oz/10 g) chopped fresh cilantro (fresh coriander) leaves, 1 Tbsp olive oil, 1 tsp champagne vinegar or white wine vinegar, and 1 tsp kosher salt. Mix well and let stand for 30 minutes to allow the flavors to marry.

Butternut Squash Soup

preparation **20** minutes | cooking **1½** hours | **4–6** servings

Butternut squash soup is velvety in texture, restorative, and delicious. You can also substitute other squash varieties, such as acorn or delicata. Garnish the soup with cumin, toasted for a minute in a dry pan, or top it with mascarpone cheese or whipped cream flavored with a pinch of cayenne or nutmeg.

tools | soup pot | baking sheet or roasting pan | chef's knife | food processor or blender | ladle | whisk

Preheat the oven to 375°F (190°C). Split the butternut squash in half lengthwise and scrape out the seeds and fibrous pulp with a large spoon. Coat the cut surfaces with 1 Tbsp of the olive oil and season generously with salt and pepper. Place the halves cut side down on a baking sheet or in a roasting pan and slip 2 sage leaves and 2 garlic cloves under each cavity. Roast the squash in the oven until the flesh is tender to the touch, 40–50 minutes.

Let the squash cool completely. Peel off the skin and discard. Chop the flesh coarsely and set aside. Squeeze the roasted garlic from its skins and reserve.

Heat the remaining 2 Tbsp olive oil in a soup pot over low heat. Add the onions and cook, stirring occasionally, until tender and translucent, about 15 minutes. Add the butternut squash, roasted garlic, vegetable stock, mace, cloves, and salt and pepper to taste. Whisk until the soup is blended. Cover partially and simmer, stirring often, for about 20 minutes.

Remove from the heat and let cool slightly for easier handling. Ladle into a food processor or blender in small batches and process until very smooth. Return the soup to the pot and add warm water to thin to the desired consistency, if necessary.

When ready to serve, reheat the soup over low heat and stir in the cream. Taste and adjust the seasoning with salt. Ladle into warmed bowls and serve with a little cream on top of each serving, if desired. Serve at once.

2 lb (1 kg) butternut squash

3 Tbsp olive oil (divided)

Kosher salt and pepper

4 fresh sage leaves

4 small unpeeled cloves garlic

2 large yellow onions, diced

4 cups (32 fl oz/1 l) vegetable stock (page 216) or water

½ tsp ground mace

¼ tsp ground cloves

½ cup (4 fl oz/125 ml) heavy (double) cream, plus cream for garnish (optional)

> **butternut squash purée** Follow the directions above to roast a butternut squash. Let cool until cool enough to handle, then scoop the squash flesh from the skin and purée in a food mill or potato ricer. Reheat the purée in a saucepan and add 4 Tbsp (2 oz/60 g) butter. Season with salt and pepper to taste. Serve with brined pork chops (page 105).

Minestrone Thickened with Bread

preparation **30** minutes | cooking **1½–2** hours | **6** servings

Many traditional Italian dishes, like this one, are vehicles for using up stale bread, which comes in handy because a fresh-baked loaf doesn't keep long. Here, toasted day-old bread absorbs flavorful liquid and thickens this substantial soup, which makes a hearty meal in autumn or winter.

tools | medium saucepan | soup pot | baking sheet | chef's knife | serrated bread knife | ladle | box grater or vegetable peeler

1 loaf day-old peasant bread

5 Tbsp (2½ fl oz/75 ml) extra-virgin olive oil (divided), plus oil for drizzling

Kosher salt and pepper

1 lb (500 g) fresh shelling beans such as cranberry, cannellini, or flageolets, or 1 can (15 oz/ 470 g) cannellini

2 small yellow onions, diced

3 thin slices pancetta or bacon

1 bay leaf

1 tsp chopped fresh sage

3 ribs celery, diced

2 carrots, peeled and diced

1 small bulb fennel, diced

4 cloves garlic, thinly sliced

1 head kale or other sturdy greens, coarsely chopped

6 drained canned whole tomatoes

1 cup (3 oz/90 g) sliced savoy cabbage

6 cups (48 fl oz/1.5 l) chicken stock (page 216) or water, or as needed

Parmesan cheese for garnish

Preheat the oven to 350°F (180°C). Cut the crust off the bread and tear the bread into bite-sized pieces. Toss the bread pieces until evenly coated with 3 Tbsp of the olive oil and salt to taste, spread on a baking sheet, and bake until lightly golden, 10–12 minutes.

If using fresh beans, shell them and put them in a medium saucepan with water to cover by 2 inches (5 cm), a little olive oil, and salt to taste. Simmer over low heat until the beans are soft but not falling apart, about 30 minutes. Set them aside in their cooking liquid. If using canned beans, rinse and drain.

Heat the remaining 2 Tbsp olive oil in a soup pot over medium-low heat. Add the onions, pancetta, bay leaf, and sage and sauté until the pancetta and onions soften slightly, about 10 minutes. Stir in the celery, carrots, fennel, and garlic. Add the kale, tomatoes, and cabbage and sauté until the vegetables soften slightly, 3–4 minutes. Season with salt. Add the stock, raise the heat to high, bring to a boil, reduce the heat to low, and simmer until all the vegetables are tender, about 40 minutes. Add the beans and half of their cooking liquid, or 1 cup (8 fl oz/ 250 ml) water if using canned beans, and simmer for 10 minutes more to blend the flavors. Add the toasted bread, stir, cover, and continue to simmer until the bread absorbs the liquid and melts into the soup, about 15 minutes more. If the soup is too thick, thin with water, stock, or additional bean-cooking liquid.

To serve, ladle the soup into warmed bowls and garnish each bowl with grated or shaved Parmesan, a drizzle of olive oil, and a grinding or two of pepper.

Sweet Corn Soup

preparation **10** minutes | cooking **40** minutes | **6** first-course servings

Corn is inherently sweet and a little starchy, so it gives both flavor and body to this simple soup. Try to get recently picked corn for the sweetest flavor.

tools | soup pot | baking sheet | chef's knife | serrated bread knife | blender | ladle | sieve

Preheat the oven to 375°F (190°C). Melt 2 Tbsp of the butter. Cut the bread into ½-inch (12-mm) cubes and toss with the melted butter and a pinch of salt. Spread on a baking sheet and bake until golden, about 10 minutes.

Heat the olive oil and remaining butter in a soup pot and add the onions. Sauté over low heat until the onions are very soft, about 30 minutes. Add 4 cups (32 fl oz/1 qt) water to the onions, raise the heat to high, bring to a boil, lower the heat to medium, and add the corn. Simmer for 5 minutes. Season with salt. Remove from the heat. Let cool slightly for easier handling. Purée until smooth with a food mill or blender, in batches as needed. Pass the soup through a sieve to achieve a uniform smooth texture. Press the solids with the back of a spoon to extract as much liquid as possible. Reheat gently, stirring, taste, and adjust the seasoning. Ladle into warmed bowls and garnish with the croutons and a dollop of crème fraîche.

4 slices day-old peasant bread

5 Tbsp melted butter

Kosher salt

3 Tbsp olive oil

2 yellow onions, coarsely chopped

Kernels cut from 8 ears white or yellow corn

¼ cup (2 fl oz/60 ml) crème fraîche or sour cream

French Onion Soup

preparation **20** minutes | cooking **1** hour | **6–8** servings

On a cold winter's night, nothing is more satisfying than soup made from onions slowly cooked until caramelized and fortified with bread and melted cheese.

tools | soup pot | chef's knife | serrated bread knife | box grater | ladle | kitchen string

In a soup pot over medium-low heat, melt the butter. Add the onions and cook, stirring occasionally, until softened but not browned, about 15 minutes. The onions will "throw" their moisture into the pot and then reabsorb it. Season the onion mixture liberally with salt and pepper. Continue to cook until the onions start to caramelize slightly, about 10 minutes more.

Add the sherry, beef and chicken stocks, and thyme. Reduce the heat to low and simmer, partially covered, until the flavor is developed and the onions are tender, another 20–30 minutes. Taste and adjust the seasoning with salt and pepper.

To serve, preheat the broiler (grill). Ladle the soup into individual flameproof soup bowls. Place 2 slices of bread on top of each bowl and sprinkle evenly with the cheese. Slide under the broiler and broil (grill) until the cheese is bubbly and lightly browned, 3–4 minutes. Serve at once.

3 Tbsp butter

4 large yellow onions, thinly sliced

Kosher salt and pepper

2½ Tbsp cream sherry

4 cups (32 fl oz/1 l) beef stock

4 cups (32 fl oz/1 l) chicken stock

6 sprigs thyme, tied in a bundle

12–16 slices baguette, ¼ inch (6 mm) thick, toasted

¾ cup (3 oz/90 g) grated Gruyère cheese

Tossed Green Salad

preparation **10** minutes | **4** servings

For a delicious variety of salad greens throughout the year, visit your local farmers' market. Assemble your own blend of greens, balancing different flavors and textures to suit the season. To allow the flavor of the greens to shine through, dress them simply with fruity olive oil, a hint of vinegar, salt, and pepper. Spin or pat the the greens completely dry to avoid diluting the vinaigrette.

tools | salad spinner

FOR AUTUMN AND WINTER SALADS

1 small bunch watercress, stems discarded

1 large handful arugula (rocket) leaves

2 heads Belgian endive (chicory/witloof), 1 medium or 2 small heads curly endive, or 1 small head radicchio

1 bunch fresh chervil (optional), stems discarded

FOR SPRING AND SUMMER SALADS

¾ lb (375 g) mixed lettuces and other greens and herbs such as red or green leaf lettuce, oak leaf lettuce, dandelion greens, arugula (rocket), mâche, garden cress, chervil, and/or butter (Boston) lettuce

Basic vinaigrette (page 212)

Separate any heads of lettuce, endive, and radicchio into individual leaves. Swish all the greens in a large bowl of cold water. Lift the greens out, allowing the dirt to settle to the bottom of the bowl, spin dry in a salad spinner, and place the greens between layers of paper towels to dry completely. Combine all the greens in a large bowl, cover, and refrigerate until needed, or roll up the greens in their towels, place in plastic bags, and refrigerate until needed. Tear the greens into bite-sized pieces as necessary.

Just before serving, put the greens in a serving bowl and pour some of the vinaigrette over the greens. Toss gently, using your hands, which are the best tools for gently coating the leaves without damaging them. Taste the greens; they may need a pinch of salt or more vinaigrette, but do not overdress. Serve at once.

Panzanella

preparation **15** minutes | cooking **10** minutes | resting **30** minutes | **8** servings

Here, rustic Tuscan-style bread meets juicy tomatoes and aromatic vegetables for simple summertime pleasure. Make this a few hours in advance for a slightly softer texture.

tools | baking sheet | chef's knife | serrated bread knife

Preheat the oven to 450°F (230°C). Cut the crust off the bread and tear the bread into bite-sized pieces. Arrange in a single layer on a baking sheet and toast until the bread is crisp and golden, about 10 minutes. Core the tomatoes and cut into wedges. Put the toasted bread in a large bowl and toss with the tomatoes. Let sit for 30 minutes–3 hours. Meanwhile, combine the celery and onions in a bowl and season with 2 tsp salt, which will tenderize the vegetables.

Drain the excess moisture from the celery mixture and add to the tomato and bread mixture. Add the basil, tearing the leaves into pieces. Add 6 Tbsp (3 fl oz/90 ml) olive oil, 3 Tbsp vinegar, the capers, and several grindings of pepper and toss well. Taste and adjust the seasoning, adding more oil, vinegar, pepper, or salt to taste.

1 lb (500 g) peasant bread, preferably stale

1½ lb (750 g) ripe tomatoes

1 lb (500 g) celery, finely diced

1 lb (500 g) sweet red or yellow onions, thinly sliced

Kosher salt and pepper

½ cup (½ oz/15 g) basil leaves

Extra-virgin olive oil

Red wine vinegar

3 Tbsp capers, rinsed and chopped

Winter Chicory and Apple Salad

preparation **15** minutes | cooking **7** minutes | **4** servings

Your bowl of chicories will brighten a winter meal with a beautiful mixture of colors. The creamy white dressing that lightly coats it also makes a great dip for raw vegetables.

tools | baking sheet | chef's knife | paring knife | salad spinner | whisk

Preheat the oven to 350°F (180°C). Spread the pecans on a baking sheet and toast in the oven until warm and fragrant, about 7 minutes. Coarsely chop and set aside.

Combine the cream and 1 Tbsp vinegar in a serving bowl and whisk lightly. Crumble in the cheese. Add 1 tsp salt and pepper to taste and whisk until the dressing is smooth. Taste and adjust the seasoning with additional vinegar, salt, or pepper if necessary. The dressing should taste fairly bold to complement the bitter chicories. Tear the greens into bite-sized pieces, discarding any wilted outer leaves, and add to the bowl. Sprinkle with salt, then toss with the dressing.

Peel the apple if desired, core, and slice. Add the slices to the salad, tossing gently. Arrange the dressed salad on chilled plates, distributing equal amounts of apple on each plate. Sprinkle each salad with the pecans and serve at once.

¼ cup (1 oz/30 g) pecans

6 Tbsp (3 fl oz/90 ml) heavy (double) cream

Cider vinegar

3 oz (90 g) Roquefort cheese

Kosher salt and pepper

1 lb (500 g) mixed chicories such as hearts of escarole (Batavian endive), frisée, and radicchio

1 Gala, Fuji, or Sierra Beauty apple

Smoked Trout and Grapefruit Salad

preparation **15** minutes | **6** servings

Though they may seem an unlikely combination, the ingredients in this salad marry harmoniously. Serve for brunch with toasted bagels, radishes (page 62), and fluffy scrambled eggs.

tools | chef's knife | whisk

2 ruby grapefruits

1 Tbsp champagne vinegar

1 Tbsp minced shallot

3 Tbsp crème fraîche or sour cream

2 Tbsp extra-virgin olive oil

Kosher salt and pepper

4 large heads Belgian endive (chicory/witloof)

2 Hass avocados, diced (page 53)

1 lb (500 g) boneless smoked trout, skinned

Cut the peel off the grapefruits with a chef's knife and cut out the segments over a bowl to catch the juices (page 233). Transfer the segments to a plate. Squeeze the membranes over the bowl to extract any extra grapefruit juice. Stir in the vinegar and shallot, then whisk in the crème fraîche and olive oil. Season the dressing with salt and pepper to taste and pour into a cruet or small pitcher.

Trim the ends from the endive and separate into individual leaves. Arrange the leaves on a large platter. Nestle in the grapefruit sections, alternating with the diced avocado and pieces of smoked trout, flaked by hand into bite-sized pieces. Assemble this salad freely like a mosaic, but aim to offer a taste of all the ingredients with each bite. Serve at once, passing the vinaigrette at the table.

Tomato, Mozzarella, and Basil Salad

preparation **10** minutes | **4–6** servings

This simple salad relies on two perfect allies: ripe, juicy summer tomatoes and sweet fresh mozzarella. Use your best extra-virgin olive oil here, since its flavor will shine. If your local tomatoes are good, you may find yourselves eating this every day all summer.

tools | chef's knife | serrated utility knife

8 very ripe red or gold tomatoes

1 lb (500 g) fresh mozzarella cheese

½ cup (½ oz/15 g) fresh basil leaves

¼ cup (2 fl oz/60 ml) best-quality extra-virgin olive oil

Fine sea salt and ground pepper

Slice the tomatoes ¼ inch (6 mm) thick with a serrated knife. Slice the mozzarella into thin slices.

On a serving platter, arrange overlapping slices of tomato and mozzarella in an alternating pattern. Garnish the platter generously with basil leaves, tucking some underneath the tomatoes. Drizzle the olive oil over everything and sprinkle generously with salt and pepper. Serve at once.

Frisée with Bacon and Poached Egg

preparation **10** minutes | cooking **15** minutes | **4** servings

This classic French bistro salad is too good, simple, and satisfying not to become a staple at home. Frisée is a member of the endive family, a bitter-flavored green, and lardons *are the French version of bacon bits. Here we offer a slight variation on the classic, adding a touch of reduced balsamic vinegar to enhance the poached egg on top.*

tools | small nonreactive saucepan | small and large sauté pans | chef's knife | paring knife | salad spinner | slotted spoon | whisk

Pat the frisée leaves dry and tear into bite-sized pieces if desired. Put them in a medium bowl.

In a small bowl, combine the shallot with the sherry vinegar, ½ tsp salt, and a few grindings of pepper. Let stand to pickle for 10 minutes. Drizzle in the olive oil while whisking to make a vinaigrette. Taste and adjust the seasoning with salt and pepper.

Meanwhile, put the bacon in a sauté pan over medium heat and fry until crisp, about 5 minutes. Transfer the bacon pieces to the bowl with the frisée. (If you like, add a little of the bacon fat to the frisée to enhance the flavor of the salad.) Add the vinaigrette to the bowl and toss the salad to combine all the ingredients. Taste and add a pinch of salt, if necessary. Divide the salad among serving plates.

Put the balsamic vinegar in a small, nonreactive saucepan over medium heat. Simmer until reduced by half, 3–4 minutes. Set aside.

Meanwhile, poach the eggs. Put 2–3 inches (5–7.5 cm) of water in a large sauté pan or shallow pot. Season the water with salt and bring to a simmer over medium heat. One at a time, and working quickly, crack each egg into a small ramekin and carefully slip it into the water. Leave space in around the eggs. Adjust the heat so that the water barely simmers. Poach the eggs gently for 3–5 minutes, depending on the desired doneness. Remove each egg from the water with a slotted spoon, and while the egg is still in the spoon, blot the bottom dry with a kitchen towel and trim off the ragged edges with a paring knife.

Gently place an egg on each salad. Drizzle an equal amount of the balsamic reduction on each salad and serve at once.

2 heads of frisée, leaves separated

1 small shallot, minced

2 Tbsp sherry vinegar or red wine vinegar

Kosher salt and pepper

½ cup (4 fl oz/125 ml) extra-virgin olive oil

4 thick slices bacon, cut into ½-inch (12-mm) pieces

¼ cup (2 fl oz/60 ml) balsamic vinegar

4 eggs

Caesar Salad with Garlic Croutons

preparation **20** minutes | cooking **12** minutes | **4** servings

A Caesar salad is hearty enough to constitute a lunch by itself, especially when served with warm fresh bread. Though you'll often see chicken and other items thrown into this classic salad, we like the traditional version. Since this recipe uses so few ingredients, don't skimp on the quality: this is the time to use your very best olive oil and a hunk of well-aged Parmesan cheese. Look for hearts of romaine in well-stocked produce markets. You can also make your own by removing the outer leaves from heads of romaine—but you may need to buy an extra head to be sure of getting enough tender inner leaves.

tools | baking sheet | chef's knife | box grater | citrus reamer | salad spinner | vegetable peeler | whisk

FOR THE DRESSING

1 egg

2 Tbsp fresh lemon juice

½ tsp Worcestershire sauce

1 tsp red wine vinegar

1½ Tbsp chopped anchovy fillets

1 small clove garlic, minced

½ cup (4 fl oz/125 ml) extra-virgin olive oil

½ cup (2 oz/60 g) freshly grated Parmesan cheese

Kosher salt and ground pepper

2 hearts romaine (cos) lettuce, about ½ lb (250 g) each, leaves separated and cut into bite-sized pieces

Garlic croutons (right)

A hunk of good Parmesan cheese for shaving

To make the dressing, crack the egg into a small bowl. Add the lemon juice, Worcestershire sauce, vinegar, anchovies, and garlic and whisk to combine well. Gradually whisk in the olive oil. Stir in the grated cheese. Season to taste with salt and pepper.

In a large bowl, combine the lettuce, croutons, and dressing and toss well. Divide the salad among 4 chilled plates. Using a vegetable peeler, shave thin curls of Parmesan over each salad. Serve at once.

Note: This recipe includes uncooked egg. For more information, see page 226.

garlic croutons These croutons are torn instead of cubed for a more homey, rustic look. Preheat the oven to 350°F (180°C). In a small bowl, whisk together 2 Tbsp extra-virgin olive oil and 1 large clove garlic, crushed and finely chopped. Tear ¼ loaf of day-old rustic levain (sourdough wheat) or white French bread into about 20 bite-sized pieces and toss in a large bowl with the garlic-oil mixture and a pinch of kosher salt. Spread the pieces on a baking sheet in a single layer. Toast, stirring occasionally, until the pieces are golden brown, 9–12 minutes. Let cool completely before using.

Salade Niçoise

preparation **30** minutes | cooking **15** minutes | **2** servings

"Niçoise" refers to the cooking style of the city of Nice; dishes with this name typically include tomato, garlic, anchovies, and the famous purple-black, briny olives from the south of France. Make sure that each ingredient is high quality and appealing, and you will have a simple and sparkling brunch, lunch, or light summer supper.

tools | large saucepan | chef's knife | paring knife | salad spinner | slotted spoon | whisk

Bring a large saucepan of salted water to a boil. Add the potatoes and cook just until tender, about 10 minutes. Scoop the potatoes out with a slotted spoon and set aside to drain and cool. Add the green beans to the boiling water and cook until al dente, tender but firm, 3–5 minutes, depending on their size. Scoop out and let drain and cool.

Use a paring knife to peel the potatoes and cut them into wedges. Combine the potatoes in a mixing bowl with the green beans, tomatoes, and olives. Season with salt and toss with a few tablespoons of the vinaigrette. Break the tuna into bite-sized pieces into a separate small bowl. Lightly season with salt and pepper and toss with a few teaspoons of the vinaigrette. In another bowl, toss the salad greens with some of the remaining vinaigrette to taste.

Divide the salad greens between serving plates. Tuck the vegetables in and around the greens, then distribute the tuna. Slice the anchovy fillets into thin strips and arrange on top of the salad. Moisten the salads with more vinaigrette, if necessary. Garnish with the eggs, tucking the wedges into each salad. Serve at once.

> **pitting olives** To pit a number of olives quickly, put them in a plastic bag and crush with a pan. This will expose the pits and make them easier to cut out.

6 small new potatoes

1 handful green beans such as haricots verts or Blue Lake, trimmed

2 small ripe tomatoes, diced and lightly salted

15 Niçoise olives, rinsed and pitted

Fine sea salt and pepper

Basic vinaigrette (page 212)

1 can (6 oz/185 g) good-quality tuna, packed in olive oil or spring water, drained

1 handful mixed salad greens, 2½–3 oz (75–90 g)

Anchovy fillets, rinsed in cold water and patted dry

2 hard-cooked eggs (page 214), peeled and cut into wedges

Roasted Beet and Feta Salad

preparation **10** minutes │ cooking **1** hour │ **4** servings

Vegetable salads are a colorful way to begin a meal. Here, roasted beets contribute substance, richness, and texture to tender salad greens. Substitute mâche (sometimes called lamb's lettuce) if available for the butter lettuce, or try crisp, mildly bitter Belgian endive (chicory/witloof). We like Bulgarian feta for its tangy, creamy character, but other types of feta work nicely as well.

tools │ baking dish │ chef's knife │ paring knife │ salad spinner │ whisk

FOR THE BEETS

1 lb (500 g) small to medium red or gold beets

2 tsp red wine vinegar

2 tsp olive oil

Kosher salt

1 Tbsp sherry vinegar

1 Tbsp red wine vinegar

¼ cup (2 fl oz/60 ml) extra-virgin olive oil

Kosher salt and freshly ground pepper

1 small head butter (Boston) lettuce, ½ lb (250 g) mâche, or 1 Belgian endive (chicory/witloof), patted dry

⅓ cup (1½ oz/50 g) crumbled feta cheese

To prepare the beets, preheat the oven to 400°F (200°C). Trim the beet stems, leaving about ½ inch (12 mm) intact. Leave the root ends untrimmed. Wash the beets thoroughly and put them in a baking dish with enough water to cover the bottom of the dish. Cover the dish with foil and bake the beets until they can be easily pierced with a sharp knife, 45 minutes–1 hour. Do not overcook, or the beets will be mushy. Let cool.

Using a small paring knife, trim off the tops and bottoms of the beets, then peel away the skins with the knife. Cut the beets in half, then in quarters or wedges. Sprinkle the beets with the red wine vinegar, olive oil, and a pinch of salt. At this point the beets can be covered and refrigerated for several days.

In a nonreactive bowl, whisk together the sherry and red wine vinegars and the extra-virgin olive oil, then season with salt and pepper. Taste and adjust the seasoning to your liking. Separate the lettuce leaves and tear into bite-sized pieces. Toss in a bowl with the vinaigrette to coat thoroughly. Divide the greens among salad plates and nestle the roasted beets into the greens. Sprinkle the feta evenly over each salad and serve at once, offering freshly ground pepper at the table.

Meat, Poultry, and Seafood

Whether you're serving a midweek supper or a celebratory meal, the recipes in this chapter will help you answer the eternal question of what to make for dinner. We find that having a great dish in mind as the centerpiece for a meal makes it easy to round out the menu—and this chapter is packed with memorable menus. We share some recipes here that are family traditions for us—from an heirloom oven-fried chicken to a roasted crab dish we feast on together every year at holiday time.

Rib-Eye Steak with Pan Jus

preparation **5** minutes | cooking **25** minutes | **2** servings

This is a nice way to prepare a rib eye for two: ask the butcher for a steak cut thicker than usual, sear it, roast it, and then thinly slice it on the bias. The pan juices are used to create a rich, simple pan sauce to accompany the meat. Serve with mashed potatoes (page 178) and a green salad (page 82).

tools | ovenproof sauté pan | chef's knife | tongs | wooden spatula

1 rib-eye steak, 18–20 oz (560–625 g) and about 1½ inches (4 cm) thick (see Note)

Kosher salt and pepper

1 sprig fresh rosemary

1 Tbsp olive oil

¼ cup (2 fl oz/60 ml) dry red wine

½ cup (4 fl oz/125 ml) beef or chicken stock (page 216 or 217)

2 small sprigs fresh thyme

Preheat the oven to 400°F (200°C). Season the steak liberally with salt and pepper. Pick the rosemary leaves from the stem and press them into the steak. Heat the olive oil in an ovenproof sauté pan over medium-high heat. Let the oil get quite hot, but before it starts to smoke, sear and brown the steak on one side for about 1 minute. Turn the steak over to sear the other side for 1 minute. Use tongs to hold the steak upright and sear the sides of the rib eye, another minute per side.

Place the pan with the steak in the oven and roast for 10–12 minutes for medium-rare, or until it reaches the desired doneness (see page 225). Press the center of the steak to gauge doneness; it will still have some give for medium-rare, more firmness for medium. Remove the pan from the oven and transfer the meat to a carving board. Let rest for 10 minutes.

Meanwhile, add the wine, stock, and thyme to the drippings in the pan and place over medium-high heat. (Be careful not to burn yourself on the hot pan.) Deglaze the pan, stirring with a wooden spatula and loosening any caramelized bits stuck to the bottom, and simmer until reduced by half. Taste and adjust the seasoning with salt and pepper. Remove the thyme sprigs.

Using a chef's knife, carve the steak with a sharp knife across the grain into thin slices. Arrange the slices on warmed plates and spoon the pan juices over the top.

Note: This is a large portion of steak for 2 people, but using a big, thick piece makes for better end results—wide, perfectly cooked slices still rare in the center. Save remaining steak to use in breakfast hash (page 47). Refrigerate for up to 3 days, or wrap well and freeze for up to 1 month.

Grilled T-Bone with Garlic Butter

preparation **15** minutes | cooking **12** minutes | resting **5** minutes | **4** servings

On a summer night when when you are hosting an intimate gathering for close friends, grilling sets a relaxed mood. Thick T-bone steaks cook up succulent and juicy, and they taste especially savory when they absorb charcoal or wood smoke flavors from the grill. Serve with Tuscan farro (page 190), or accompany with handfuls of fresh undressed arugula (rocket) leaves placed underneath each steak. The juices from the steak will provide all the dressing the arugula needs. To serve two, simply cut the recipe in half.

tools | grill | tongs

Make the garlic butter.

Season the steaks by rubbing them with the olive oil, thyme, salt, and pepper to taste. Prepare a charcoal or gas grill for direct-heat grilling (page 228). When the coals are ready, they will have burned down to glowing embers covered with gray ash. Place the steaks on the grill and cook for 5–6 minutes on each side for medium-rare, or until they reach the desired doneness (see page 225). Press the center of a steak to gauge its doneness; it will still have some give for medium-rare, more firmness for medium. Remove the steaks from the grill and place them on a platter.

Place a pat or two of the flavored butter on each steak along with a sprinkling of parsley. Let rest for 3–5 minutes, then serve.

> **garlic butter** Topping a steak with flavored butter is a quick way to add delicious flavor. Let ½ cup (4 oz/125 g) salted butter come to room temperature. Use a fork to blend in 1 Tbsp minced fresh thyme, 4 cloves minced garlic, 1 or 2 dashes of Worcestershire sauce, and 1 or 2 dashes of Tabasco sauce. Roll into a log using waxed paper and set aside.

Garlic butter (below)

4 T-bone steaks, 10 oz (315 g) each

2 Tbsp extra-virgin olive oil

Leaves from 3 sprigs fresh thyme

1½ tsp kosher salt or ¾ tsp fine sea salt

Freshly ground pepper

2 Tbsp chopped fresh parsley

Roast Beef with Yorkshire Pudding

seasoning **12** hours | preparation **10** minutes | cooking **2** hours | **8** servings

This is the perfect recipe for the first holiday feast you host as a married couple. It's impressive, but it's also extremely easy to prepare. Plan on roasting the beef for 15 minutes per pound. The Yorkshire pudding, which is like a giant popover, contains juices from the roast, so it's prepared while the roast rests. You may want to make two batches of Yorkshire pudding—because you can never have enough!

tools | 9-inch (23-cm) cast-iron frying pan or pie dish | large roasting pan | brush | fine-mesh sieve | instant-read thermometer | meat slicer | meat fork | whisk | wooden spoon

FOR THE ROAST BEEF

5 lb (2½ kg) beef rib or sirloin tip roast

2½ tsp kosher salt

Freshly ground pepper

FOR THE YORKSHIRE PUDDING

2 large eggs

1¼ cups (10 fl oz/310 ml) milk

¾ cup plus 2 tablespoons (4½ oz/140 g) flour

Pinch of kosher salt

One day before serving, season the roast with the salt and pepper to taste. Cover and refrigerate overnight. Let the roast sit at room temperature to temper for 1–2 hours before roasting. This will help the meat cook more evenly.

To roast the beef, preheat the oven to 425°F (220°C). Place the beef in a large roasting pan and place in the oven. Roast for 15 minutes, then lower the heat to 375°F (190°C). Continue roasting, basting the meat frequently with the pan juices, until an instant-read thermometer inserted into the center of the roast away from the bone registers 135°F (57°C) for medium-rare, about 1¼ hours. (The temperature of the meat will continue to rise outside of the oven. If using a boneless roast, start checking the temperature a little earlier.) Transfer the roast to a carving board and let rest, loosely covered with foil, for 30 minutes. This allows time for the juices to distribute evenly throughout the meat and makes carving easier. Reserve the roasting pan with the drippings and keep the oven on. While the roast rests, make the Yorkshire pudding.

To make the Yorkshire pudding, place a 9-inch (23-cm) cast-iron frying pan or Pyrex pie dish in the oven to preheat. Meanwhile, in a bowl, whisk the eggs and milk together until blended. Add the flour a little at a time, whisking constantly until smooth. The batter should have the consistency of heavy (double) cream. Add the salt. Remove the frying pan from the oven and transfer 2 Tbsp of beef fat from the roasting pan into the frying pan. (Tilt the roasting pan and spoon off the clear fat from the brown drippings.) Pour the batter into the pan and place in the oven. Bake until the pudding is puffy and crisp, about 25 minutes. Cut the pudding into wedges and serve at once with slices of the roast beef.

> **beef jus** While the Yorkshire pudding bakes, you can also create a beef jus to use as a sauce, if desired. Skim off any excess clear fat from the brown drippings in the roasting pan and add 2 cups (16 fl oz/500 ml) chicken stock (page 216) to the pan. Place the pan on 1 or 2 burners over medium heat and deglaze, stirring and loosening any caramelized bits stuck to the bottom with a wooden spatula. Cook for about 4 minutes, stirring constantly. Strain the juices through a fine-mesh sieve. Keep warm until serving.

Beef Daube

preparation **20** minutes | cooking **3** hours **40** minutes | **4–6** servings

In this version of daube (say "dobe"), a traditional French stew, we use white wine for a lighter touch, and add tomatoes and Dijon mustard for a Provençal accent. To finish the dish, we whisk in a little crème fraîche to add body and sweetness. Serve with warm buttered fettuccine or pappardelle *noodles. This dish tastes even better the next day.*

tools | large sauté pan or Dutch oven | chef's knife | wooden spatula | slotted spoon | kitchen string | tongs | whisk

Season the beef liberally with salt and pepper. In a large sauté pan or Dutch oven with a tight-fitting lid, heat the olive oil over medium heat. In several small batches to avoid crowding, brown the pieces of beef on all sides. Watch carefully and adjust the heat if necessary to avoid scorching the meat. With tongs, set each batch aside on a platter as it is finished, and continue in the same manner until all the pieces are evenly browned. Don't rush this step: browning the meat on all sides imparts flavor to the stew.

Preheat the oven to 300°F (150°C). Pour off and discard any excess fat left in the pan, leaving only a thin film. While the pan is off the heat (to avoid flare-ups), add the brandy and wine to it. Return to medium heat and deglaze, stirring and scraping with a wooden spatula to loosen any caramelized bits from the bottom, 3–4 minutes. Let the liquid simmer, uncovered, until most of the alcohol is cooked off, about 8 minutes after the liquid reaches a simmer. Whisk in the mustard until thoroughly blended. Add the meat and any juices on the platter, the tomatoes and their liquid, the onions, and the garlic. Tie the thyme, tarragon, and savory tightly together with kitchen string and add to the pan. Cover and braise in the oven until the meat is fork-tender, 2½–3 hours. Remove and discard the bundle of herbs. (The dish can be prepared to this point up to 2 days in advance.)

Using a slotted spoon, transfer the meat, tomatoes, and onions to a platter. Bring the liquid to boil over high heat and cook until reduced by about one-third, 8–10 minutes. Stir in the crème fraîche until blended. Taste, adjust the seasoning, and return the meat, tomatoes, and onions to the pan to heat through. Spoon into warmed bowls to serve.

2 lb (1 kg) boneless braising beef such as beef shoulder, chuck, or brisket, cut into 2-inch (5-cm) pieces

Kosher salt and pepper

3 Tbsp olive oil

¼ cup (2 fl oz/60 ml) brandy

1 bottle (24 fl oz/750 ml) dry white wine

2 Tbsp Dijon mustard

1 can (1 lb/500 g) plum (Roma) tomatoes

3 small yellow onions, thinly sliced

6 cloves garlic, lightly crushed

3 sprigs fresh thyme

3 sprigs fresh tarragon

2 sprigs winter or summer savory

5 Tbsp (2½ fl oz/75 ml) crème fraîche or ¼ cup (2 oz/60 g) sour cream

cuts for braising The best meats for braises and stews contain plenty of fat and connective tissue, which contribute flavor and keep the meat succulent during its long cooking time. Sirloin and round are sometimes labeled as "stew beef" but are too lean for simmering at length and can become dry and chewy. For this dish, ask the butcher for a large piece of chuck or brisket. Have the butcher cut it into 2-inch (5-cm) pieces for you, or do it yourself at home.

Osso Buco

preparation **30** minutes | cooking **2** hours **40** minutes | **4** servings

Osso buco, which literally means "bone with a hole," refers to the thick round slices of veal shank, or shin, that are braised with aromatic vegetables. If you don't see them at the butcher's, ask the butcher to order them for you. The highlight of this wintertime feast is scooping out the flavorful marrow lodged in the center of each shank—considered a delicacy by the Italians. Serve with orzo or risotto (page 149).

tools | ovenproof sauté pan with tight-fitting lid | large baking sheet | chef's knife | citrus zester | wooden spatula | kitchen string | tongs

³/₄ cup (4 oz/125 g) flour

Kosher salt

½ tsp freshly ground pepper

4 center-cut slices veal shank, each about 1½ inches (4 cm) thick and meat tied around the middle with kitchen string

5 Tbsp (2½ fl oz/75 ml) olive oil (divided)

1 small yellow onion, finely diced

1 large carrot, peeled and finely diced

2 small to medium ribs celery, finely diced

3–4 cloves garlic, minced

2 bay leaves

³/₄ cup (6 fl oz/180 ml) white wine

1 cup (8 fl oz/250 ml) beef stock (page 217), or more as needed

1 can (28 oz/875 g) diced plum (Roma) tomatoes, drained

2 tsp chopped orange zest

2 sprigs fresh thyme

1 small sprig fresh rosemary

Orange *gremolata* for serving (right)

Preheat the oven to 350°F (180°C). Combine the flour with ½ teaspoon salt and the pepper and spread on a plate. Dredge the veal shanks in the flour mixture, turning them to coat evenly. Shake off the excess flour. Select a heavy, ovenproof sauté pan with a tight-fitting lid large enough to hold the veal shanks in a single layer and heat 3 Tbsp of the olive oil over high heat. When the oil is hot, place the veal in the pan and brown evenly, about 3 minutes on each side. Using tongs, transfer the veal to a plate and set aside. Without cleaning the pan, add the remaining 2 Tbsp olive oil. When the oil is hot, add the onion, carrot, celery, garlic, bay leaves, and a pinch of salt. Cook, stirring occasionally, until the onion is golden, about 8 minutes; watch carefully to avoid burning the vegetables. Add the wine and deglaze the pan, stirring and scraping with a wooden spatula to loosen any caramelized bits on the bottom. Add the stock and cook until reduced by half, about 5 minutes. Add the tomatoes, orange zest, thyme, and rosemary. Cook, stirring occasionally, for 5 minutes. Season with 1 tsp salt.

Return the veal shanks to the pan. The tomato mixture should come about two-thirds of the way up the shanks. If it doesn't, add a little more beef stock or water. Cover the pan with the lid and place in the oven on a large baking sheet. Braise the shanks for 2 hours, turning them every 30 minutes to ensure that they cook evenly. Add extra stock or water if the liquid in the pan is getting too low or too thick. When the shanks are done, they should be extremely tender and the meat should fall away from the bone. Remove from the oven and place the shanks on a large platter until ready to serve. Remove and discard the bay leaves from the pan, place over medium heat and simmer until the liquid is reduced to a saucelike consistency, about 10 minutes. The sauce should have a velvety texture, but not be too thick. Taste and adjust the seasoning with salt and pepper. To serve, spoon the sauce over the warm veal shanks and sprinkle with orange *gremolata*.

orange gremolata To make this variation on the traditional lemon-and-parsley accompaniment to osso buco, combine 2 Tbsp chopped fresh parsley, 1 tsp minced garlic, and 2 tsp chopped orange zest in a bowl and mix well.

Rack of Lamb with Mustard and Herbs

preparation **10** minutes | cooking **30** minutes | resting **10** minutes | **6–8** servings

A rack of lamb is a loin roast made up of about eight rib chops. When the rack is seared in a pan and then roasted whole in the oven, the meat stays juicy and succulent. Slice the rack into chops to serve. This dish is a good choice for a celebratory meal. To save trouble, ask the butcher to remove all but a thin layer of fat from each rack.

tools | large sauté pan | large baking dish | chef's knife | instant-read thermometer | tongs | brush (optional)

Preheat the oven to 400°F (200°C). Season the lamb racks with salt and pepper. Heat the olive oil in a large sauté pan over medium-high heat. Sear the lamb, one rack at a time, browning on each side (about 2½ minutes per side). Using a pair of tongs, hold each rack upright and sear the ends, about 20 seconds each. The racks should look golden. Transfer the racks to a 13-by-9-inch (33-by-23-cm) baking dish.

Stir together the bread crumbs, garlic, thyme, rosemary, and melted butter in a bowl. Season with a pinch of salt and mix well. Brush or smear the seared lamb thoroughly with a thin layer of mustard. Sprinkle the bread-crumb mixture over the surface of the lamb, gently pressing the mixture onto the lamb so that it adheres.

Roast the lamb until an instant-read thermometer inserted into the center of the meat but not touching bone registers 120°F (49°C) for rare, about 20 minutes, or 130°F (54°C) for medium-rare, 25–30 minutes. (The temperature of the meat will continue to rise outside of the oven.) Transfer the lamb to a cutting board or serving platter. Allow to rest for 10 minutes to allow the juices to redistribute before slicing into chops and serving.

2 racks of lamb , about 1½ lb (750 g) and 8 chops each, trimmed of all but a thin layer of fat

Kosher salt and freshly ground pepper

1 Tbsp olive oil

¾ cup (1½ oz/45 g) fine fresh bread crumbs (page 215)

1 clove garlic, minced

1 tsp chopped fresh thyme

½ tsp chopped fresh rosemary

2 Tbsp butter, melted

3 Tbsp Dijon mustard

Provençal Roast Leg of Lamb

preparation **10** minutes | cooking **1** hour **35** minutes | resting **20** minutes | **6–8** servings

Rosemary, thyme, and bay leaves grow wild in the south of France. In this recipe, we use these herbs, along with a generous amount of garlic, to infuse the fragrances of Provence into a leg of lamb as it roasts. If time permits, season the lamb one day before cooking it. Serve with soft or grilled polenta (page 186) or rosemary roasted potatoes (page 177).

tools | roasting pan | small roasting rack | chef's knife | fine-mesh sieve | wooden spatula | instant-read thermometer

1 leg of lamb, 6–8 lb (3–4 kg), boned, trimmed, and tied by the butcher

Kosher salt and pepper

4 Tbsp (2 fl oz/60 ml) extra-virgin olive oil (divided)

1 small bunch fresh rosemary

1 small bunch fresh thyme

6 heads garlic

2 bay leaves

Remove the lamb from the refrigerator up to 2 hours before cooking it to ensure even roasting. Preheat the oven to 425°F (220°C). Season the lamb generously with 2 tsp salt and pepper to taste and rub with 3 Tbsp of the olive oil. Pick a few of the leaves from the rosemary and thyme sprigs and rub them into the lamb. Trim off one-third of each head of garlic with a sharp chef's knife.

Place the garlic heads in a roasting pan with the remaining rosemary and thyme leaves, and the bay leaves. Nestle a small rack on top of the herbs and garlic and place the lamb on the rack. Drizzle the garlic heads with the remaining 1 Tbsp olive oil.

Roast the lamb for 20 minutes, then lower the oven temperature to 350°F (180°C). Continue roasting, turning occasionally, until an instant-read thermometer inserted into the thickest part of the lamb registers 120°F (49°C) for rare or 130°F (54°C) for medium-rare. (The temperature of the meat will continue to rise outside of the oven.) The total cooking time should be about 15 minutes per pound; start checking the lamb after 1¼ hours. Transfer the lamb to a platter and let rest for 20 minutes.

Carve the meat thinly and serve with the roasted garlic, which will be mellow and softened. Encourage diners to squeeze out the softened garlic and spread it on the meat.

> **lamb jus** To create a simple sauce to serve with the lamb, remove the garlic and herbs and spoon off the excess clear fat from the brown drippings. Place the pan on 1 or 2 burners over medium-low heat and add 1 cup (8 fl oz/250 ml) chicken stock (page 216), 2 Tbsp water, and 2 Tbsp dry white wine. Deglaze the pan, stirring and loosening any caramelized bits stuck to the bottom with a wooden spatula. Cook for about 5 minutes. Strain the juice through a fine-mesh sieve. Keep warm until serving.

Brined Pork Chops

preparation **10** minutes | cooking **12** minutes | **2** servings

Pork has been bred to be so lean nowadays that it tends to dry out easily during cooking. Soaking pork in brine is our secret weapon for juicy chops—and thicker, bone-in chops won't dry out as quickly during cooking as thinner, boneless ones. Put the chops in the brine in the morning, and you'll have a quick dinner ready to go at the end of the day. Serve with braised fennel (page 167) or butternut squash purée (page 77).

tools | cast-iron frying pan | stockpot or large bowl

To make the brine, combine the sugar and salt with 4 cups (32 fl oz/1 l) cold water in a stockpot or a large bowl and stir to dissolve. Add the thyme, bay leaf, peppercorns, cloves, and chili flakes.

Place the pork chops in the brine. Cover and refrigerate, turning occasionally, for at least 8 hours but no longer than 2 days.

When ready to cook, lift the chops out of the brine and pat dry thoroughly with paper towels. Heat the olive oil in a cast-iron frying pan. Add the chops and cook over medium heat until brown on one side, about 8 minutes. Turn the chops over and cook the other side until just cooked through, about 4 minutes. Press the center of a chop to gauge doneness; it should still have some give for medium-rare chops that are juicy in the middle. Let rest for a minute or two, then serve.

Note: If thick chops aren't available, reduce the cooking time by a few minutes.

FOR THE BRINE

¼ cup (2 oz/60 g) sugar

1 Tbsp plus 2 tsp kosher salt

½ tsp fresh thyme leaves

1 bay leaf

6 peppercorns

4 whole cloves

⅛ tsp red chili flakes

2 bone-in center-cut pork chops, 1½ inches (4 cm) thick (see Note)

2 Tbsp olive oil

Roast Pork Loin with Apricots

seasoning **6** hours | preparation **10** minutes | cooking **35** minutes | resting **15** minutes | **4** servings

Stuffing a pork roast is easy, and you can use almost any dried fruit you like. Dried figs, cherries, cranberries, or prunes—or a combination of two or three of these—are all classic accompaniments for roast pork and yield a juicy stuffing. Serve with braised fennel (page 167) and soft polenta (page 186) for a classic autumn meal.

tools | roasting pan | roasting rack | boning knife | mortar and pestle | wooden spatula | instant-read thermometer

1 boneless center-cut pork loin, about 2 lb (1 kg)

½ cup (3 oz/90 g) dried apricots

2½ tsp kosher salt

Freshly ground pepper

Leaves from 2 sprigs fresh rosemary

1 tsp cumin seeds, lightly toasted (page 61) and crushed

2 tsp fennel seeds, lightly toasted (page 61) and crushed

Light cream sauce (below; optional)

One day or at least 6 hours before cooking, stuff and season the pork loin. Use a thin boning knife to make an incision from each end that runs the length of the loin through its center. The incision should be no wider than 1 inch (2.5 cm). Stuff the dried apricots into the center, one at a time, until the incision is completely filled with apricots. Season the pork liberally with the salt and pepper to taste. Rub with the rosemary, cumin seeds, and fennel seeds.

Preheat the oven to 450°F (230°C). Place the pork on a rack in a roasting pan and put it in the oven. Roast for 10 minutes, then lower the oven temperature to 375°F (190°C). Cook until an instant-read thermometer inserted into the center of the roast registers 135°F (57°C) for medium-rare, about 25 minutes more. Remove from the oven and let rest for 15 minutes. This allows time for the juices to redistribute evenly throughout the roast.

Slice the pork, about ¼ inch (6 mm) thick, in order to show off the center stuffing. Arrange on a large platter or on individual plates and serve. Pass the light cream sauce at the table, if desired.

light cream sauce To make a light pan sauce to pass at the table, after removing the pork from the roasting pan, place the pan on 1 or 2 burners over medium-low heat. Add ½ cup (4 fl oz/125 ml) dry white wine and deglaze the pan, stirring and loosening any caramelized bits stuck to the bottom with a wooden spatula. Simmer to reduce the liquid by half, 1–2 minutes. Add 1 cup (8 fl oz/250 ml) chicken stock (page 216) and continue to simmer, stirring once or twice, until reduced by half, about 3 minutes. Add ¼ cup (2 fl oz/ 60 ml) heavy (double) cream, stir once more, and serve warm in a cruet or small pitcher.

"Barbecued" Ribs with Asian Flavors

preparation **10** minutes | marinating **5** hours | cooking **1** hour **35** minutes | **4–6** servings

Although this recipe requires marinating the ribs in advance—preferably the day before cooking—the results are well worth the wait. The ribs are slowly cooked in the oven until the meat is falling off the bones, making them reminiscent of ribs cooked in a covered barbecue over slow-burning coals.

tools | baking dish | large saucepan | sauté pan | chef's knife | blender or food processor | large brush or sauce mop

To make the marinade, trim the root ends from the garlic cloves. Combine all the marinade ingredients in a blender or food processor. Purée until smooth, about 30 seconds. Rub the marinade liberally on the ribs at least 5 hours before cooking, or, preferably, the day before.

Meanwhile, make the barbecue sauce: Heat the olive oil in a sauté pan over medium heat. Add the onion and cook until softened, 10–15 minutes. Transfer to a blender or food processor and purée until smooth. Put the onion purée in a large saucepan and add all of the remaining barbecue sauce ingredients and ⅓ cup (3 fl oz/80 ml) water. Cook over low heat, stirring frequently, for 15 minutes to blend the flavors. Watch the sauce carefully, as it can scorch.

Preheat the oven to 375°F (190°C). Place the marinated whole ribs in a shallow baking dish and cover with foil. Bake until the meat starts to soften but is not falling off the bone, 45–60 minutes, depending on the size of the ribs.

Remove the ribs from the oven and uncover. Coat the ribs liberally on all sides with the barbecue sauce, cover, and return to the oven for 15 minutes. Remove from the oven and slice into individual ribs. Toss the ribs in the sauce in the pan, re-cover, and return to the oven once more, for 10 minutes. Remove and let cool slightly. Serve on a platter, garnished with cilantro sprigs.

Note: You will have leftover barbecue sauce. Store it in the refrigerator for up to 10 days, or freeze for up to 2 months.

FOR THE MARINADE

8–10 cloves garlic

⅓ cup (⅓ oz/10 g) tightly packed cilantro (fresh coriander) leaves

2 Tbsp olive oil

1 Tbsp dark brown sugar

2 Tbsp soy sauce

1 Tbsp Chinese five-spice powder

2 Tbsp kosher salt

4 lb (2 kg) baby-back ribs, in slabs

FOR THE BARBECUE SAUCE

¼ cup (2 fl oz/60 ml) olive oil

1 cup (4 oz/125 g) diced onion

1½ cups (12 oz/375 g) tomato paste

¾ cup (6 fl oz/180 ml) cider vinegar

1 Tbsp dry mustard

1 Tbsp ground ginger

½ cup (4 fl oz/125 ml) soy sauce

⅓ cup (4 oz/125 g) honey

⅓ cup (3½ oz/105 g) dark molasses

1 Tbsp Chinese five-spice powder

Fresh cilantro (fresh coriander) sprigs for garnish

Goat Cheese–Stuffed Chicken Breasts

preparation **15** minutes | cooking **10** minutes | **4** servings

This savory chicken dish is quite fun to assemble once you get the hang of it. Accompany these tender stuffed chicken breasts with braised red cabbage (page 158) in the winter or a simple tomato salad (page 84) in the summer.

tools | large sauté pan | boning knife | mallet or small frying pan | tongs |

4 skinless, boneless chicken breast halves

Kosher salt and pepper

2 oz (60 g) fresh goat cheese

4 thin slices prosciutto

8 fresh sage leaves

2 cups (10 oz/315 g) flour

2 eggs, lightly beaten with 2 Tbsp water

2 cups (8 oz/250 g) fine dried bread crumbs

¼ cup (2 fl oz/60 ml) olive or grape seed oil, or as needed

Season the chicken breasts with salt and pepper on both sides. Use a boning knife to cut a horizontal incision into each breast, without cutting the breasts in half, creating a pocket for stuffing.

Place each chicken breast between 2 pieces of parchment (baking) or waxed paper. Pound lightly with a mallet or small frying pan, until each breast is about ¾ inch (2 cm) thick. When all the breasts have been pounded, rub each piece lightly all over with a little of the oil.

Stuff each pocket with about 1½ Tbsp of the goat cheese, spreading evenly, then follow with 1 slice of prosciutto and 2 sage leaves.

Arrange a plate with the flour, a bowl with the eggs, and a plate with the bread crumbs on a work surface. Dredge each stuffed breast in the flour, shaking off the excess. Dip it into the beaten egg mixture, then dredge in the bread crumbs.

Heat 2 Tbsp of the oil in large sauté pan over medium heat. When the oil is hot but not smoking, add 2 of the breaded chicken breasts to the pan. Do not overlap the pieces, or the breasts will cook unevenly. Cook for 1 minute, then lower the heat to low and continue to cook for 2 minutes more. Using tongs, carefully turn the breasts and cook until golden on the second side and just becoming firm to the touch, about 2 minutes.

Transfer the chicken breasts to a plate and tent with foil to keep warm while you cook the others in the same way, adding more oil to the pan as needed. Serve at once.

Grandmother's Oven-Fried Chicken

preparation **30** minutes | cooking **1** hour **20** minutes | **8** servings

This recipe, passed down in our family, calls for studding chicken with garlic, breading it, and baking it slowly with butter until it is crisp and golden, almost like fried chicken. If you're watching your waistline (or your spouse's!), you can remove the skin from the chicken. We find the dish more succulent with the skin intact, but the recipe works fine without it. Leftovers make excellent cold picnic chicken.

tools | large glass baking dish | chef's knife | paring knife | whisk or fork

Preheat the oven to 350°F (180°C). Separate the garlic heads into cloves, peel the cloves, and then cut the cloves lengthwise into at least 32 small slivers about ⅛ inch (3 mm) thick. Place the chicken pieces on a large platter and season each piece liberally with salt and pepper. Pierce each chicken piece with the tip of a paring knife to make 4 small incisions, each just large enough to hold a garlic sliver. Insert 4 slivers into each chicken piece, reserving any leftover garlic.

Stir together the parsley, oregano, and bread crumbs in a shallow bowl large enough to dip the chicken pieces in one at a time. Put the flour in a separate shallow bowl of similar size. In a third bowl of the same size, beat the eggs with 2 Tbsp water until well blended.

Melt the butter in a large glass baking dish by placing it in the preheated oven for several minutes. Meanwhile, dredge each piece of chicken in the flour, shaking off any excess, coat it in the egg mixture, and then dredge it in the herbed bread crumbs.

When the butter has melted, remove the dish from the oven and nestle the coated chicken pieces, skin side down, in the warm butter, arranging the pieces to fit tightly. Tuck any leftover garlic between the chicken pieces.

Bake for 45 minutes, then carefully turn over each piece of chicken. Continue baking until the chicken is well browned and crisped on the edges, about 35 minutes longer. Remove the chicken from the oven and let cool slightly before serving with any caramelized garlic slivers sprinkled on top.

---

2 heads garlic

8 whole chicken legs (drumsticks and thighs), with the skin or without

Kosher salt and pepper

1 Tbsp chopped fresh parsley

1 Tbsp chopped fresh oregano

1½ cups (6 oz/185 g) fine toasted bread crumbs (page 215)

1 cup (5 oz/ 155 g) flour

3 eggs

½ cup (4 oz/125 g) butter

Roast Chicken with Lemon and Herbs

seasoning **5** hours | preparation **10** minutes | cooking **45–55** minutes | resting **10** minutes | **4** servings

The trick to making a great roast chicken is to purchase a chicken that isn't too large. A 3-lb (1.5-kg) bird is just about the right size for four, or for two with leftovers, and it roasts evenly: the center cooks through before the outer parts are overdone and dry, as is sometimes the problem with large birds. Serve with crisp rosemary roasted potatoes (page 177) and a tossed green salad (page 82). Use leftovers to make fried rice (page 128) or chicken potpie (page 118).

tools | cast-iron frying pan or small roasting pan

1 roasting chicken, about 3 lb (1.5 kg)

1 Tbsp kosher salt

½ tsp pepper

3 cloves garlic, lightly crushed

4 small sprigs fresh rosemary

½ scrubbed lemon

If possible, season the chicken 3–5 hours or a day before you roast it for more tender, succulent results. Remove any organs from the cavity. Rub the salt and pepper over the entire surface of the chicken, including inside the cavity and on the back, wings, and inner and outer thighs. Using your index finger, separate the skin from the breast meat without tearing it. Cut 1 garlic clove in half and place the halves and 1 rosemary sprig under the skin. Place the other 2 cloves and remaining 3 rosemary sprigs inside the cavity. Cover and refrigerate until about 1 hour before you are ready to cook the chicken, then take the chicken out of the fridge. Allowing the bird to temper, or come closer to room temperature, will help the meat cook more evenly.

Preheat the oven to 450°F (230°C). Just before roasting, squeeze the juice from the lemon half over the chicken and place the squeezed lemon half inside the cavity to perfume the meat. (If you have any extra lemon and rosemary, you can add them to the pan.) Put the chicken in a cast-iron frying pan or small roasting pan.

Place the chicken in the oven for 10 minutes. Lower the oven temperature to 350°F (180°C) and continue to roast, turning the pan around once halfway through to ensure even cooking, until the skin is crispy and golden brown and an instant-read thermometer inserted in the thigh away from the bone registers 175°F (80°C); start checking the temperature after about 35 minutes. Remove from the oven and let the chicken rest for 10 minutes before carving. The temperature of the bird will continue to rise outside of the oven, and the resting time allows the juices to redistribute evenly throughout the bird for more succulent meat.

Chicken Braised in Red Wine

preparation **20** minutes | cooking **50** minutes | **4–6** servings

This hearty and restorative dish is perfect for a cozy cold-weather get-together. For the best results, choose a good bottle of fruity red wine such as California Pinot Noir, Zinfandel, or any Burgundian-style red. Avoid wines with heavy oak or other wood flavors. Serve with celery root purée (page 169) and caramelized Brussels sprouts (page 164).

tools | large sauté pan or cast-iron frying pan | 2 large saucepans | chef's knife | ladle | slotted spoon | whisk

Pour the wine into a large saucepan and bring to a boil over medium heat. Cook until reduced by half and set aside.

Season the chicken pieces with salt and pepper. Spread the ½ cup flour in a shallow dish and lightly dredge the chicken in the flour, shaking off any excess. In a large sauté pan or cast-iron frying pan, melt 2 Tbsp of the butter over medium heat. In batches as necessary to avoid crowding, brown each piece of chicken on all sides. Transfer the chicken to a platter and set aside. Add the remaining 2 Tbsp butter to the pan, melt, and add the onion, bacon, and garlic. Sauté until the onion is soft, about 10 minutes. Stir often and lower the heat, if necessary, to avoid browning the onion. Add the mushrooms, thyme, bay leaves, ½ tsp salt, and a little pepper. Raise the heat to medium and sauté until the mushrooms release their moisture, about 5 minutes. Add the brandy and continue cooking for another minute.

Transfer the onion and mushroom mixture to another large saucepan or Dutch oven. Sprinkle the 2 Tbsp flour over the onion and mushroom mixture, then add the stock, browned chicken pieces, and reduced brandy. Bring the mixture to a boil, lower the heat to low, and simmer gently, uncovered, until the chicken is opaque throughout and fork-tender and the flavors have married, 15–20 minutes. Make sure the mixture does not boil, or the chicken will toughen.

To serve, remove and discard the thyme sprig and bay leaves, then use a slotted spoon to transfer the chicken pieces to a serving platter. Return the pan with the sauce to medium-high heat and whisk until the sauce combines and thickens. Taste and adjust the seasoning with more salt and pepper, if necessary. Ladle the sauce over the chicken pieces and garnish with the parsley. Serve at once.

1 bottle (24 fl oz/750 ml) fruity red wine

8 chicken drumsticks and thighs, with the skin

Kosher salt and pepper

½ cup (2½ oz/75 g) flour, plus 2 scant Tbsp

4 Tbsp (2 oz/60 g) butter (divided)

1 large yellow onion, thinly sliced

4 thick slices bacon, cut into 1-inch (2.5-cm) pieces

3 cloves garlic, crushed

1 lb (500 g) button mushrooms, stemmed, brushed clean, and quartered

1 sprig fresh thyme

2 bay leaves

¼ cup (2 fl oz/60 ml) brandy

2 cups (16 fl oz/500 ml) chicken stock (page 216)

1 Tbsp chopped fresh parsley

Spiced Roast Turkey with Gravy

seasoning **4** hours | preparation **15** minutes | cooking **2½–3** hours | resting **30** minutes | **12** servings

Once you serve this turkey to your relatives, you'll never need to travel for the holidays again. Instead, everyone will want to come to your house. For the best results, season the turkey the day before roasting it. While the turkey rests in the fridge, lightly curing, you'll be getting other things done. For suggestions on creating an entire holiday feast, see page 236.

tools | small frying pan | large roasting pan | roasting rack | chef's knife | bulb baster or brush | instant-read thermometer

FOR THE SPICE RUB

1 Tbsp fennel seeds

¾ tsp red chili flakes

3 Tbsp Madras or other curry powder

2 Tbsp sugar

1 Tbsp sweet paprika

1 Tbsp kosher salt

1 turkey (14–18 lb/7–9 kg)

⅓ cup (3 fl oz/80 ml) olive oil

To make the spice rub, toast the fennel seeds in a small frying pan over medium heat until lightly browned and fragrant, about 1 minute. Transfer to a blender or mortar, add the chili flakes, and pulse or grind with a pestle until the mixture is finely ground. Place the mixture in a small bowl and stir in the curry powder, sugar, paprika, and salt.

Pull off and discard any lumps of fat from the cavity of the turkey and remove the giblets and neck. (Save the giblets for the gravy, if desired.) Rinse the turkey inside and out and pat dry with paper towels.

In a small bowl, stir together the spice rub and olive oil. Cover the whole turkey with the spice mixture, massaging it thoroughly all over the skin and inside both the neck and body cavities. Refrigerate for at least 4 and up to 12 hours.

Remove the turkey from the refrigerator about 2 hours before you begin to roast it to allow the bird to temper, or lose its chill, which helps it cook more evenly. Preheat the oven to 325°F (165°C).

Place the turkey breast side up on a rack in large roasting pan and place in the oven. Roast the turkey, basting every 20 minutes with the pan drippings, until an instant-read thermometer inserted in the thickest part of the breast registers 160°F (71°C); start checking the temperature after about 2½ hours.

Transfer the turkey to a platter and let rest for 30 minutes in a warm place. This allows the juices within the bird to redistribute, which results in a moist and tender turkey. Reserve the drippings in the roasting pan to make gravy (right).

When the gravy is ready, carve the turkey and serve with the gravy.

Gravy

preparation **10** minutes | cooking **15** minutes | **12** servings

This gravy—an essential feature of any holiday meal—uses the simpler method of thickening with cornstarch slurry instead of roux. Prepare it while the turkey rests.

tools | medium saucepan | degreasing cup or large glass measuring cup | wooden spatula

Place the turkey roasting pan with the drippings over 2 burners and turn the heat to medium-high. Add 6¾ cups (54 fl oz/1.7 l) of the stock to the roasting pan and bring to a brisk simmer. Deglaze the pan, stirring and scraping with a wooden spatula to loosen the caramelized bits from the bottom, about 5 minutes.

Remove from the heat and pour the liquid into a degreasing cup in batches as needed. Let sit for a minute to allow the fat to rise, then pour off the liquid, discarding the fat. (If you don't have a degreasing cup, pour the liquid into a large glass measuring cup, let sit for a minute, then carefully spoon as much fat as possible from the top of the liquid.) Transfer the degreased liquid to a medium saucepan. Place over medium-high heat and simmer briskly for 5 minutes.

In a small bowl, stir the remaining ¼ cup (2 fl oz/60 ml) chicken stock into the cornstarch to make a slurry. Gradually stir the slurry into the gravy. Cook until the gravy thickens, 3–4 minutes. Season to taste with salt and pepper.

Pour the gravy into a warmed gravy boat or pitcher and pass at the table.

7 cups (56 fl oz/1.75 l) chicken stock (page 216)

¼ cup (1 oz/30 g) cornstarch (cornflour)

Kosher salt and freshly ground pepper

Puff Pastry Chicken Potpie

preparation **20** minutes | cooking **45** minutes | Makes **two** 9-inch (23-cm) pies

There are countless types of chicken potpie, from versions with cornmeal or Cheddar cheese crusts to those with bell peppers (capsicums), corn, or eggplant (aubergine) in the filling. Our recipe uses vegetables that are available year-round. This recipe will yield two 9-inch (23-cm) pies, so you can freeze the second for later, or feed a crowd.

tools | medium saucepan | small saucepan | 2 baking sheets | two 9-inch (23-cm) pie pans | chef's knife | paring knife | large metal spoon | wooden spoon

2 boneless, skinless chicken breasts

2 boneless, skinless chicken thighs

2 Tbsp olive oil

2 cups (8 oz/250 g) diced yellow onion

1 cup (4 oz/125 g) peeled, sliced carrots

1 cup (5 oz/155 g) diced celery

2 cups (10 oz/315 g) peeled, diced Yukon gold potatoes (about ¾-inch/2-cm dice)

2 cups quartered, stemmed button mushrooms

3 cups (24 fl oz/750 ml) chicken stock (page 216)

1 tsp finely chopped fresh sage

2 tsp finely chopped fresh thyme

2 tsp finely chopped celery leaf

Kosher salt and pepper

2 Tbsp butter

3 Tbsp flour

⅓ cup (3 fl oz/80 ml) heavy (double) cream

2 sheets frozen puff pastry

Preheat the oven to 400°F (200°C). Dice the chicken breasts and thighs into large (¾-inch/2-cm) dice. Set aside.

Heat the olive oil in a medium saucepan over medium heat. Add the onion, carrots, and celery. Sauté the vegetables until slightly softened, 4–5 minutes. Add the potatoes and mushrooms and sauté, stirring often, for 3–4 minutes. Add the stock and bring to a boil. Lower the heat to medium-low and add the chicken pieces. Bring to a gentle simmer. Using a large metal spoon, skim off any fat or scum that has risen to the top. Add the sage, thyme, celery leaf, 2 tsp salt, and several grindings of pepper. Simmer for 10 minutes.

Meanwhile, make a roux by melting the butter over low heat in a small saucepan. Add the flour and stir constantly with a wooden spoon to mix thoroughly. Cook, stirring constantly, for 5 minutes. Do not allow the roux to brown. Add the cream and stir vigorously until the mixture thickens. Season to taste with salt and pepper. Stir the roux into the chicken and vegetable mixture and simmer gently for 5 minutes. The chicken mixture should thicken slightly and not look runny. Check the potatoes for doneness; they should be cooked through, but not mushy. Taste and adjust the seasoning with salt, pepper, sage, thyme, and celery leaf. Remove from the heat. The dish can be prepared to this point up to 1 day in advance, refrigerated, and brought back to room temperature before baking.

Divide the chicken and vegetable mixture evenly between two 9-inch (23-cm) pie pans, leaving ½ inch (12 mm) space at the top so that the pastry will not become soggy. Let the mixture cool. Remove the prepared puff pastry from the freezer 10 minutes before using it to let it thaw. Cut a 9-inch (23-cm) round from each sheet of puff pastry. Cover each pie with a pastry round, pinching the edges of the pastry over the edge of the dish with your thumb and forefinger to secure the pastry to the dish. Make several incisions in the center of the pastry with a paring knife to allow steam to escape.

Place the pies on baking sheets and bake until the pastry is golden brown, about 15 minutes. Let cool for 5 minutes before serving.

Duck with Tart Cherry and Port Sauce

preparation **10** minutes | cooking **25** minutes | resting **10** minutes | **4** servings

Tart cherries deliciously complement the smoky flavor of duck breast and add fruity flavor notes to a port wine sauce. For a stress-free dinner party, make the sauce a day in advance and store it, covered, in the refrigerator, until the duck is ready.

tools | cast-iron frying pan | saucepan | baking sheet | chef's knife

If using the hazelnuts, preheat the oven to 350°F (180°C). Spread the hazelnuts on a baking sheet and toast until golden and fragrant, 10–12 minutes. Let cool slightly, then wrap in a clean kitchen towel and rub gently to remove the skins. Chop coarsely and set aside.

Meanwhile, to make the cherry-port sauce, combine the cherries, vinegar, port, and stock in a saucepan. Simmer the mixture over medium heat until reduced by half, 10–12 minutes. Remove from the heat and set aside.

Trim any extra skin hanging over the edges of the duck breasts. Turn the breasts skin side up and make 4 shallow incisions diagonally across the breast skin. The slices should be about ⅛ inch (3 mm) deep into the skin only; take care not to cut into the breast meat. Create a crosshatch pattern by making a second set of 4 diagonal incisions in the opposite direction. Season the duck breasts liberally with salt and pepper on both sides.

Heat a cast-iron frying pan over medium-high heat. Add the olive oil. When the oil is very hot, add the duck breasts, skin side down. Reduce the heat to medium-low. Cook without turning until the skin is nicely browned and plenty of fat is rendered, 10–12 minutes. Reduce the heat to low, turn the duck breasts over, and cook until an instant-read thermmeter inserted into the center of a duck breast reads 140°F (60°C) for medium-rare, 4–5 minutes more. For medium to well-done, cook the duck until it registers 160°–165°F (71°–74°C), 5–10 minutes more. Transfer the duck breasts to a platter and let rest, loosely covered with foil, for 10 minutes.

While the duck rests, reheat the cherry-port sauce. Cut each duck breast into thin slices and arrange the slices on 4 warmed plates. Spoon the sauce over the duck slices and sprinkle with the hazelnuts, if using. Serve at once.

Note: For even better flavor, season the duck breasts 1 or 2 days in advance and store them, covered, in the refrigerator. In early summer, substitute 2 handfuls of fresh Bing cherries for the dried tart cherries: Roast for 10 minutes in a 350°F (180°C) oven, pit if desired, and serve warm with the duck.

¼ cup (1 oz/ 30 g) hazelnuts (filberts) (optional)

FOR THE CHERRY AND PORT SAUCE

2 Tbsp dried tart cherries or cranberries

1 Tbsp sherry vinegar or red wine vinegar

½ cup (4 fl oz/125 ml) ruby port

2½ cups (20 fl oz/625 ml) prepared veal stock or chicken stock (page 216)

4 boneless duck breasts, skin on, about 6 oz (185 g) each

Kosher salt and pepper

Sole with Brown Butter and Capers

preparation **10** minutes | cooking **15** minutes | **2** servings

Petrale sole has a sweet and mild flavor that pairs well with tart lemon, briny capers, and sweet butter. Seek out the freshest fish you can find, since its quality will shine through in a simple dish such as this. Because it's ready in a flash, this is another good weeknight recipe. Serve with sautéed spinach (page 163) and mashed potatoes (page 178).

tools | large and small sauté pans | small frying pan | chef's knife | slotted spoon or skimmer | wide spatula

2 lemons

½ cup (2½ oz/75 g) flour

2 Tbsp (½ oz/15 g) fine-grind cornmeal

¼ tsp ground cayenne pepper

2 sole fillets, preferably petrale, about 6 oz (185 g) each

Kosher salt and freshly ground black pepper

1 Tbsp olive oil

4 Tbsp (2 oz/60 g) butter

½ shallot, finely diced

1 Tbsp chopped fresh chives

1 Tbsp capers, rinsed and patted dry, fried if desired (right)

Peel and segment the lemons with a chef's knife (page 233).

On a plate, stir together the flour, cornmeal, and cayenne. Season each fillet on both sides with salt and pepper and dredge the fish in the flour mixture to coat, shaking off any excess. Heat the olive oil in a large sauté pan over medium heat. Add the fillets and cook, turning once, until golden brown, 3–4 minutes per side. Use a wide spatula to turn the delicate fish. Transfer to individual plates and keep warm in a low (200°F/95°C) oven.

In a small sauté pan over medium heat, melt the butter. Add the shallot with a pinch of salt and sauté until the butter foams. Lower the heat slightly and continue to cook until the butter browns, 2–3 minutes. Add the lemon segments to the butter and swirl the pan to heat them through. Remove the pan from the heat and promptly spoon an equal amount of the lemon–brown butter sauce over each fish fillet. Sprinkle the fish with the chives and capers and serve at once.

fried capers Heat 2 Tbsp olive oil in a small frying pan over medium heat. When the oil is hot, add several of the capers. As they cook, they will open, lighten in color, and float to the top. After 2 minutes, remove the capers from the oil with a slotted spoon or skimmer and let drain on paper towels. Repeat in batches until all the capers are fried. The fried capers will keep for up to 2 days, covered. Before using, recrisp them in a 300°F (150°C) oven for 3 minutes.

Sea Bass with Fennel and Bacon

preparation **10** minutes | cooking **25** minutes | **4–6** servings

Roasting a side of fish is a clever way to entertain: presenting a whole fillet at the table in the vessel it was roasted in always brings on oohs and aahs.

tools | baking dish | small sauté pan | chef's knife

Preheat the oven to 350°F (180°C). In a small sauté pan over medium heat, fry the bacon until browned but not completely crisp, about 3 minutes. Transfer to paper towels to drain.

Arrange half of the fennel in a single layer in a shallow baking dish. Season the fish with salt and pepper on both sides. Place the fish on top of the fennel and place the remaining fennel on top of the fish. Sprinkle with the bacon. Roast the fish until the surface is slightly firm to the touch and the center is just opaque, 18–25 minutes, depending on the thickness of the fish. Let the fish rest for a few minutes before serving directly from the baking dish.

4 thick slices bacon, cut into 1-inch (2.5-cm) pieces

5 or 6 wild fennel tops or 1 trimmed fennel bulb, cut into thick slices

1 whole sea bass or halibut fillet, about 2 lb (1 kg)

Kosher salt and pepper

2 Tbsp extra-virgin olive oil

Halibut with a Bread Crumb Crust

preparation **10** minutes | cooking **20** minutes | **6** servings

Slow roasting may take a little longer, but it results in extremely moist and tender fish. Serve with spicy Italian-style cauliflower (page 158) or braised red cabbage (page 158).

tools | large baking dish | baking sheet | chef's knife

Preheat the oven to 400°F (200°C). In a bowl, toss the bread crumbs with 1 Tbsp olive oil, 1 tsp of the garlic, and the wine. Spread the crumbs on a baking sheet and toast until lightly browned, about 8 minutes. Lower the oven temperature to 325°F (165°C).

Meanwhile, stem the arugula. In a bowl, combine ½ cup (4 fl oz/125 ml) olive oil with the parsley, arugula, oregano, marjoram, vinegar, and the remaining 1 tsp garlic. Season the herb sauce with salt and pepper.

Lightly oil a large baking dish. Arrange the halibut fillets in a single layer, season with salt and pepper, and roast for 8 minutes. Sprinkle the fish with the toasted bread crumbs and continue roasting until the fish is just opaque in the center and the crumbs are crisp and golden, 12–15 minutes longer. Transfer the fish to individual plates, drizzle with the herb sauce, and serve at once.

1 cup (2 oz/60 g) coarse fresh bread crumbs (page 215)

Extra-virgin olive oil

2 tsp minced garlic (divided)

1 Tbsp dry white wine

1 bunch arugula (rocket)

¼ cup (⅓ oz/10 g) minced parsley

1 Tbsp *each* minced fresh oregano and marjoram

2 tsp red wine vinegar

Kosher salt and pepper

6 skinless halibut fillets, about

Salmon with French Lentils

preparation **20** minutes | cooking **30** minutes | **4** servings

The combination of lentils and salmon is a classic French brasserie offering. Serve this autumnal dish with a dry but fruity white such as a Viognier, Pinot Blanc, or dry Riesling. In the wintertime, you can cook the fish under the broiler (grill) instead of on an outdoor grill.

tools | medium saucepan | sauté pan | chef's knife | grill

FOR THE LENTILS

1 cup (7 oz/220 g) Puy lentils or French caviar lentils

4 sprigs fresh thyme

2 Tbsp butter

½ yellow onion, finely diced

1 carrot, peeled and finely diced

1 rib celery, finely diced

¾ tsp kosher salt, or to taste

1 tsp red wine vinegar

1 Tbsp extra-virgin olive oil

4 salmon fillets, about 6 oz (185 g) each

Extra-virgin olive oil

Kosher salt and pepper

Prepare a charcoal or gas grill for direct-heat grilling.

To make the lentils, while the coals are getting hot, rinse the lentils in cold water and place in a medium saucepan. Add 3 cups (24 fl oz/750 ml) water and the thyme, bring to a simmer over medium heat, and cook for 15 minutes.

Meanwhile, melt the butter in a sauté pan and sauté the onion, carrot, and celery over medium-low heat until slightly softened, about 5 minutes. Season with the salt. Add the vegetables to the lentils, stir, and continue to simmer until the lentils are tender, about 10 minutes more. Add the vinegar and olive oil. Stir once more, taste, and adjust the seasoning. Keep warm by covering and placing in a warm spot on the stove, perhaps over a pilot light.

When the coals have burned down to glowing embers covered with gray ash, spread them out under the grill. Rub the salmon fillets with olive oil and season with salt and pepper. Place the fish on the hot grill and cook on one side for 3–4 minutes, depending on the thickness. Turn and cook on the other side for 2–3 minutes longer for medium-rare (the center will still be slightly translucent). Remove the salmon from the grill. Spoon a small mound of lentils onto each serving plate and top with a salmon fillet. Drizzle with olive oil and serve at once.

lentils Lentils come in a wide range of colors, including brown, green, yellow, red, pink, and ocher. The town of Le Puy in eastern France is famous for its tiny, olive green lentils, known as lentilles du Puy, or simply French lentils. The prized lentils are harvested in summer and traditionally dried under the hot local sun. Unlike the more common brown lentils, which can become very soft and lose their shape when cooked, French lentils keep their lenslike profile and subtle flavor, making them a favorite for lentil side dishes and salads.

Mussels with Wine and Tomato

preparation **20** minutes | cooking **35** minutes | **4** main-course servings or **8** first-course servings

This dish, mussels quickly steamed in a broth made of stock and wine, is a twist on the French classic moules marinière. *Plan on using a pound (500 g) of mussels per person. Pair the shellfish with a crisp Italian white wine such as Pinot Grigio or Sauvignon Blanc and serve with bread—especially warm, buttery garlic bread.*

tools | large saucepan | chef's knife | ladle

In a large nonreactive saucepan, heat the olive oil over medium-low heat. Add the onions and garlic and sauté gently until slightly softened, 10–15 minutes. Do not allow the onions to brown. Add the tomatoes, thyme, and bay leaf, season with salt, reduce the heat to low, and simmer until the tomatoes become saucelike, about 10 minutes. Stir occasionally to prevent the mixture from browning. Add the wine, raise the heat to medium-high, and bring to a boil. Lower the heat to a simmer and cook until the wine is reduced by half. Add the chicken stock and clam juice and bring to a vigorous simmer.

Meanwhile, rinse the mussels thoroughly under cold water, pulling off any "beards" (see below) with your fingers. Discard any mussels that do not close to the touch. Add the mussels to the simmering tomato broth, cover, and steam until they open, 4–6 minutes, depending on their size. Stir the mussels once or twice while cooking to ensure that they cook evenly.

Use a large ladle to transfer the mussels to 4 large serving bowls, discarding any that failed to open. Distribute the broth evenly among the bowls. Drizzle the extra-virgin olive oil evenly over the bowls, sprinkle with the parsley, and serve at once.

> **mussels** For this dish, choose small blue mussels; larger, more tender Mediterranean mussels; or green-lipped mussels from New Zealand or China. When choosing mussels, select those with tightly closed shells (open shells can mean the mussel inside is deteriorating or dead). To store, place the mussels in a deep bowl and cover with a damp kitchen towel; refrigerate for up to 1 day. Before cooking, scrub the shells with a stiff-bristled brush under cold running water. Using a small knife or scissors, cut off the beard, a fibrous tuft at the edge of the shell often present in locally harvested wild mussels. Cultivated mussels, the variety you find today in most fish markets, have little or no beards and are easier to clean.

2 Tbsp olive oil

2 small yellow onions, cut into ½-inch (12-mm) wedges

1 clove garlic, very thinly sliced

1 cup (6 oz/185 g) canned diced tomatoes, drained

1 sprig fresh thyme

1 bay leaf

Kosher salt

1 cup (8 fl oz/250 ml) dry white wine

3 cups (24 fl oz/750 ml) chicken stock (page 216)

1 cup (8 fl oz/250 ml) bottled clam juice

4 lb (2 kg) mussels

3 Tbsp extra-virgin olive oil

2 Tbsp chopped fresh parsley

Wok-Glazed Sea Scallops

preparation **10** minutes | cooking **5** minutes | **2** servings

This bold and saucy stir-fry is quick to prepare and utterly delicious. Serve over steamed jasmine rice and accompany with bok choy (page 168).

tools | wok or large sauté pan | chef's knife

1 Tbsp cornstarch (cornflour)

2 Tbsp Asian black beans

1 Tbsp chopped fresh ginger

2 Tbsp *each* chopped garlic, Chinese rice wine, and peanut or grape seed oil

10 oz (315 g) sea scallops

1 cup (8 fl oz/250 ml) chicken stock

4 Tbsp (2 fl oz/60 ml) light soy sauce

Pinch of red chili flakes

2 Tbsp chopped cilantro (coriander)

Mix the cornstarch with 3 Tbsp water to make a slurry and set aside. Coarsely chop the black beans. In a small bowl, stir together the black beans with the ginger, garlic, and wine. Set aside. Heat a wok or large sauté pan over high heat. Add the oil and heat for 1 minute. Add the scallops and stir-fry to brown them, stirring vigorously, for 1 minute. Remove the scallops from the wok and set aside. Add the black bean mixture to the wok and stir until fragrant, 1 minute. Return the scallops to the wok and add the stock, soy sauce, chili flakes, cilantro, and cornstarch slurry. Stir, then cook until the sauce is nicely thickened and the flavors are balanced, about 2 minutes. Serve at once.

Fried Rice with Prawns

preparation **10** minutes | cooking **7** minutes | **4** servings

This is the perfect dish to throw together when you have leftovers. Roast chicken, shredded pork, diced ham, or your favorite vegetables could all be substituted for the prawns.

tools | wok or large frying pan | chef's knife | paring knife

4 cups (1¼ lb/625 g) cooked rice

1 green (spring) onion

1 cup (7 oz/ 220 g) cooked prawns

2 Tbsp peanut oil

2 Tbsp soy sauce

1 tsp chili oil

½ tsp Asian sesame oil

Freshly ground pepper

2 eggs, lightly beaten

Cook the rice and let cool or let cold leftover rice come to room temperature.

Thinly slice the green onion on the diagonal. If needed, peel and devein the prawns (page 67).

Heat the peanut oil in a wok or large frying pan over medium heat and add the rice, green onion, prawns, soy sauce, chili oil, sesame oil, and pepper to taste. Sauté, stirring often, until the onion is softened, about 5 minutes. Add the eggs and stir quickly to disperse and cook evenly. As soon as the eggs are set, remove the rice from the heat and serve at once.

Roasted Crab with Garlic and Fennel

preparation **15** minutes | cooking **30** minutes | **2** servings

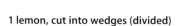

We suggest that when you eat this dish, you cover your table with newspapers, not a tablecloth, and set out cloth napkins or kitchen towels, finger bowls, and lemon wedges. Have fun, get messy, and then just throw the newspaper away.

tools | large roasting pan | small saucepan | medium sauté pan | stockpot | chef's knife | tongs

Bring a stockpot of water to a boil and add half of the lemon wedges and the kosher salt. Cook the crabs one at a time, adding them head first and cooking for 4 minutes each, or 1 minute for blue crabs. Drain the crabs, let them cool, and clean and crack them (see below). Break the bodies in half and set aside.

Preheat the oven to 425°F (220°C). Cut all the stalks from the fennel bulbs, reserving a handful of the green fronds. If the fronds do not look fresh, discard them, but otherwise mince enough of the best-looking ones to measure about 2 Tbsp and set aside. Cut the fennel heads in quarters. Toss the fennel with olive oil and a pinch of salt. Heat a medium sauté pan over medium heat and lightly sauté the fennel quarters until they begin to turn golden brown, about 5 minutes per side. Transfer the fennel quarters to a large roasting pan and stir in the potato pieces and crab halves.

Melt the butter in a small saucepan, add the garlic, and sauté gently for 5 minutes. Pour the butter mixture over the crab, potatoes, and fennel. Roast until the edges of the crab just begin to turn golden brown, 5–6 minutes, or 3–4 minutes for blue crabs.

Arrange the crab and vegetables on a serving platter. To create a fragrant crab sauce, set the roasting pan with its juices on 1 or 2 burners over very low heat. Pour the Pernod into the pan and stir to combine with the pan juices and garlic, about 1 minute. Pour the crab sauce over the crab and vegetables, garnish with the minced fennel fronds, if using, and the remaining lemon wedges, and serve at once.

1 lemon, cut into wedges (divided)

¼ cup (2 oz/60 g) kosher salt, plus a pinch

2 live Dungeness crabs, about 1½ lb (750 g) each, or 4 blue crabs

2 fennel bulbs, with stems and fronds still attached, if possible

Olive oil for tossing

4 or 5 small new potatoes, boiled until tender and cut in half

½ cup (4 oz/125 g) butter

Cloves of 1 head garlic, minced

¼ cup (2 fl oz/60 ml) Pernod

> **cleaning and cracking crab** To clean a crab, pull off and discard the eyes and mouth parts. Pull off the top shell and reserve it. Remove and discard the gills, which are the white feather-shaped pieces on each side of the body above the legs. Pull out and discard the firm, crooked white intestine along the center of the back. Turn the crab on its back and pull off the small triangular breast plate at the top. Spoon out and reserve, if desired, the white and yellow "butter" in the body. Reach inside the reserved top shell and pull out the crab butter in the corners. This can be added to a dish for extra crab flavor. Use the flat side of a chef's knife, a lobster and crab cracker, or a mallet to gently crack the shells on the legs.

Pasta, Pizza, and Risotto

We know that this chapter will get a lot of use. These brilliant Italian dishes are staples we rely on again and again in our own dinnertime repertoire. Take, for example, pasta carbonara or spaghetti with tomato sauce: where would we be without them on nights when we haven't planned out dinner? The ingredients come from the pantry, so a delicious hot meal is only minutes way. We hope you delight in the several pizza ideas we provide and invent some of your own topping combinations. Similarly, once you master making risotto, flavor possibilities are as limitless as your imagination.

Pasta Puttanesca

preparation **10** minutes | cooking **25** minutes | **4–6** servings

Fiery pepper flakes are the hallmark of this classic pasta dish from Naples. It's a good recipe to have in the suppertime rotation—quick and easy, and very flavorful.

tools | medium saucepan | large pot | chef's knife | colander

¼ cup (2 fl oz/60 ml) olive oil

2 Tbsp minced garlic

1 can (28 oz/875 g) diced tomatoes

½ cup (2 oz/60 g) pitted black olives, coarsely chopped

3 Tbsp coarsely chopped anchovies

2 Tbsp capers, rinsed and chopped

1½ tsp kosher salt, or to taste

¼ tsp red chili flakes, or to taste

¼ cup chopped fresh parsley

1 lb (500 g) linguine, fedelini, spaghettini, or other long pasta

Parmesan cheese for grating (optional)

Heat the olive oil over low heat in a medium saucepan. Add the garlic and sauté until softened and just starting to turn golden, about 5 minutes. Drain the tomatoes and add to the saucepan. Add the olives, anchovies, capers, salt, and chili flakes. Simmer gently over medium-low heat until the sauce is reduced by about one-third, 15 minutes. Taste and adjust the seasoning with salt. Add the parsley.

Meanwhile, bring a large pot of water to a boil. Add the pasta and cook until al dente, tender but firm, according to the package directions. Drain the pasta thoroughly and add to the warm sauce. Toss the pasta vigorously until it is evenly coated with the sauce. Season once more to taste, and serve the pasta at once in warmed bowls. Pass the Parmesan at the table, if you like.

capers Caper bushes grow wild throughout southern France and around the Mediterranean. Before they can flower, the small, olive green buds are harvested and preserved in salt or a vinegar brine. Pleasantly tangy, capers add a piquant bite to dishes. Salt-packed capers have a slightly more pungent flavor and are worth seeking out. They should be rinsed and drained before using. Capers labeled "nonpareils," from the south of France, are the smallest and considered the best.

Spaghetti with Quick Tomato Sauce

preparation **10** minutes | cooking **20** minutes | **2** servings

Here is a basic tomato sauce to enjoy with pasta for a simple lunch or supper. Use perfectly ripe tomatoes in midsummer when they are in season. For variations, add rinsed chopped capers, pitted and chopped olives, or ricotta cheese, or garnish the dish with warm toasted bread crumbs (page 215).

tools | medium sauté pan | large pot | chef's knife | box grater or vegetable peeler | colander

Heat the olive oil in a medium sauté pan over medium-low heat. Add the garlic, basil, and marjoram and sauté gently for about 1 minute until fragrant. Add the tomatoes, stir well, and season with salt and pepper. Add the sugar and chili flakes. Lower the heat and cook until the mixture has a nice saucelike consistency and you like the way it tastes, 10–15 minutes.

Meanwhile, bring a large pot of water to a boil. Add the spaghetti and cook until al dente, tender but firm, according to the package directions. Drain thoroughly, reserving a few tablespoons of the pasta cooking water.

Return the pasta to the pot, season with salt, and add the tomato sauce. Add the reserved pasta cooking water as needed to loosen the sauce, and then add the arugula. Mix well and drizzle with the extra-virgin olive oil. Transfer the pasta into warmed pasta bowls and serve with the cheese.

3 Tbsp olive oil

1 Tbsp finely chopped garlic

2 Tbsp chopped fresh basil

1 Tbsp chopped fresh marjoram or parsley

2 cups (12 oz/375 g) chopped canned tomatoes

Kosher salt and pepper

Pinch of sugar

Pinch of red chili flakes

½ lb (250 g) spaghetti

Leaves from 1 small bunch of arugula (rocket), coarsely chopped

2 Tbsp extra-virgin olive oil

Freshly shaved or grated pecorino Romano or Parmesan cheese for serving

Pasta Carbonara

preparation **10** minutes | cooking **20** minutes | **2** servings

You can make this pasta in a pinch, as we often do, when you need a good supper for the two of you and haven't planned ahead. It requires just a few pantry staples.

tools | sauté pan | large pot | chef's knife | box grater | colander | wooden spatula | tongs

½ lb (250 g) spaghettini, fedelini, or other long pasta

1 Tbsp olive oil

3 thick slices bacon, diced

2 eggs

¼ tsp freshly grated nutmeg (optional)

Kosher salt

Chopped fresh parsley for serving (optional)

Pecorino Romano or Parmesan cheese for serving

Freshly ground pepper

Bring a large pot of water to a boil. Add the pasta and cook until al dente, tender but firm, according to the package directions. While the pasta cooks, heat the olive oil in a medium sauté pan over medium heat and add the bacon. Sauté until browned and slightly crisp, 3–5 minutes. Pour off all but 1½ Tbsp of the fat. (Discard or save for another use.) Set aside the pan with the bacon and reserved fat.

In a small bowl, beat the eggs with a fork to loosen them, add the nutmeg, if using, and season with a little salt. Drain the pasta, reserving ¼ cup (2 fl oz/60 ml) of the pasta cooking water for use later, and season with salt. If the bacon pan has cooled down, warm it up again and add the pasta to the warm bacon in the pan. Using tongs, thoroughly toss the pasta with the bacon and its fat, taste, and season with salt, if needed. Turn off the heat and, working quickly, add the egg mixture to the pasta and toss thoroughly. (The heat of the noodles and the pan will cook the egg just enough to thicken the sauce; the burner should be turned off to avoid scrambling the eggs.) If the sauce seems too dry, add 1 or 2 Tbsp of the reserved pasta cooking water and toss again. Sprinkle with parsley, if using. Divide the pasta among warmed shallow bowls, and grate cheese and coarsely grind pepper over each serving. Eat at once.

Note: This recipe includes semicooked egg. For more information, see page 226.

Orecchiette with Broccoli Rabe

preparation **10** minutes | cooking **15** minutes | **4** servings

We use orecchiette, or "little ears," for this dish because the shape holds the braised greens and fruity olive oil well. Other chunky shapes of pasta such as penne or fusilli will also work well in this recipe.

tools | medium sauté pan | large pot | chef's knife | colander | wooden spatula

Bring a large pot of water to a boil. Trim the large stems from the broccoli rabe and chop the rest—the leaves, tender stems, and flowering buds—into 1-inch (2.5-cm) pieces. Heat 2 Tbsp of the olive oil in a medium sauté pan over medium heat. Add the broccoli rabe, salt and chili flakes to taste, and garlic along with a few splashes of water to help the greens cook. Reduce the heat to low and cook, stirring frequently, until the broccoli rabe is tender, 6–10 minutes. Turn off the heat.

Add the pasta to the boiling water and cook until al dente, tender but firm, according to the package directions. Drain well, reserving 2 Tbsp of the pasta cooking water. Return the pasta and the reserved pasta cooking water to the pot. Season the pasta with salt and the remaining 1 Tbsp olive oil, or more to taste. Stir in the broccoli rabe and mix thoroughly. Taste again, adjust the seasoning with salt, and transfer the pasta to a warmed serving bowl. Sprinkle with the bread crumbs and serve at once.

2 large bunches broccoli rabe, about 1½ lb (750 g)

3 Tbsp extra-virgin olive oil, or to taste (divided)

Kosher salt

Pinch of red chili flakes

1 Tbsp chopped garlic

1 lb (500 g) orecchiette pasta

½ cup (2 oz/60 g) toasted bread crumbs (page 215)

the broccoli family The availability of this family of vegetables seems to grow every year. Delicious on its own or tossed with your favorite pasta, broccoli rabe is a versatile green that has nutty, sweet, and bitter notes. It's a leafy green with long, thin stems topped with broccoli-like florets. Don't confuse it with broccoflower, a hybrid of broccoli and cauliflower that looks like a pale green head of cauliflower, or broccolini, a new hybrid of broccoli and Chinese kale with long, juicy stems similar to asparagus but topped with small flowering buds.

Fettuccine with Peas and Asparagus

preparation **20** minutes | cooking **10** minutes | **4** servings

Sweet English peas and asparagus are abundant in the spring. For this pasta, these two flavors are paired with fragrant basil and mildly sweet Meyer lemons. If Meyer lemons aren't available, you can use regular lemons, but reduce the quantities of juice and zest; regular lemons are more tart in flavor than mild Meyers.

tools | small sauté pan | large pot | paring knife | box grater or citrus zester | citrus reamer | colander | vegetable peeler

1 bunch thick asparagus (about 8 spears)

1 Tbsp butter or olive oil

²/₃ cup (5 fl oz/160 ml) heavy (double) cream

Minced zest and juice of 1 or 2 Meyer lemons

Kosher salt and pepper

³/₄ cup (4 oz/125 g) freshly shelled English peas

1 lb (500 g) fresh fettuccine (page 143)

Leaves from several sprigs fresh basil

Shaved or grated Parmesan or pecorino cheese for garnish

To prepare the asparagus, snap off the tough woody ends of the spears and, if the skin is fibrous, peel it starting from just below the tips. With a sharp paring knife, cut the asparagus on the diagonal into pieces about ⅛ inch (3 mm) thick. In a small sauté pan, melt the butter over medium heat. Add the asparagus and sauté for 2 minutes. Reduce the heat to low, add the cream, and heat until warm. Add lemon zest, salt, and pepper to taste. Do not allow the mixture to boil.

Bring a large pot of water to a boil. Add the peas and cook for 30 seconds. Add the pasta and cook until the pasta is tender and rises to the surface, 30 seconds– 5 minutes, depending on freshness. Stir occasionally so that the noodles cook evenly. Drain the pasta and peas, reserving a few tablespoons of the cooking water.

Return the pasta and peas to the pot and season with salt. Pour the asparagus-cream mixture over the pasta and toss to coat thoroughly. Add the reserved pasta cooking water as needed to loosen the sauce. Tear some of the basil leaves into pieces and add along with lemon juice to taste and additional salt to taste to balance the flavors. Serve at once in warmed pasta bowls sprinkled with additional torn basil leaves and pepper, garnished with cheese.

Linguine with Clams

preparation **15** minutes | cooking **10** minutes | **2** servings

Once you've measured out the ingredients, this satisfying pasta is very quick to put together and gorgeous to look at. We find that thin noodles glistening with parsley-infused broth and trapping a mosaic of tiny clam shells pleases the eye as much as the palate. Choose baby clams if they are available, for their sweet, flavorful, and tender meat. Provide extra plates for discarding the shells as you devour the clams.

tools | sauté pan | large pot | box grater | colander | ladle | tongs

Rinse the clams under cold water and rub away any dirt with your fingers. The clams should glisten and feel clean. Discard any clams that do not close to the touch.

Bring a large pot of water to a boil. Add the linguine and cook until al dente, tender but firm, according to the package directions.

While the pasta cooks, heat the olive oil in a sauté pan over medium heat. Add the clams, garlic, and wine, if using. Cover and steam until the clams begin to open, 3–5 minutes. For clams that do not open, try to open them by inserting the flat end of a pair of tongs between the shells. If they open easily, return them to the pan. Discard any clams that do not open easily.

Drain the linguine thoroughly and add to the pan with the clams. Season the linguine liberally with salt and mix in a generous drizzle of olive oil. Toss. Divide the linguine between warmed plates. Ladle the clam mixture over the pasta, neatly tucking the clam shells into the pasta. Moisten each bowl of pasta with the clam juices. Drizzle with more olive oil and sprinkle the lemon zest and parsley on top. Serve at once.

1 lb (500 g) fresh clams such as littleneck or Manila, preferably baby clams

½ lb (250 g) dried linguine

1 Tbsp olive oil

1 large clove garlic, peeled and left whole

¼ cup (2 fl oz/60 ml) dry white wine (optional)

Kosher salt

Extra-virgin olive oil

1 tsp grated lemon zest

1 Tbsp chopped fresh parsley

clams The best clams for this classic pasta are Manila clams or littlenecks. Pick the smallest ones you can find; they are the most tender. Always buy clams from a reputable fish merchant. In the case of littlenecks, which are hard-shelled clams, look for even-colored, firm, tightly closed shells. If a shell has opened slightly, tap it; it should immediately close tightly. If it does not, the clam is dead and should be discarded. Scrub the shells under running water to clean them thoroughly before cooking.

Fettuccine with Roquefort and Lemon

preparation **10** minutes | cooking **20** minutes | **4** servings

Even though the pasta sauce is made with cream and blue cheese, this dish is light and fragrant. Reserving a little of the pasta cooking water to add to the pasta and sauce at the end keeps the sauce from becoming heavy and cloying.

tools | saucepan | large pot | box grater | colander | wooden spoon

1 cup (8 fl oz/250 ml) heavy (double) cream

¼ cup (1½ oz/45 g) crumbled Roquefort cheese

1 lb (500 g) fresh or dried fettuccine

Kosher salt

Grated zest of 1 lemon

Freshly grated nutmeg

Freshly ground pepper

Bring a large pot of water to a boil. Meanwhile, warm the cream in a saucepan over medium-low heat and add the Roquefort. Mash the cheese with a wooden spoon until it is fully incorporated into the cream. When the mixture is warm and uniformly blended, remove it from the heat and set aside. Do not allow it to boil.

Add the pasta to the boiling water, stir it to prevent sticking, and cook until al dente, tender but firm, 30 seconds–5 minutes for fresh pasta, depending on freshness, or according to the package directions for dried pasta. Drain well, reserving ½ cup (4 fl oz/125 ml) of the pasta cooking water.

Return the pasta to the pot and season liberally with salt. Pour the cream mixture over the pasta and toss to coat thoroughly, adding a little of the reserved pasta cooking water as needed to loosen the sauce. Add the lemon zest and season to taste with nutmeg and pepper. Taste and adjust the seasoning. Serve at once in warmed pasta bowls.

Bolognese Sauce with Tagliatelle

preparation **20** minutes | cooking **2** hours **45** minutes | **6–8** servings

Bolognese, the classic meat sauce from Bologna, Italy, benefits from being prepared a day ahead to give the flavors a chance to marry. This shouldn't keep you from eating it the same day it's made, though. It's just that any leftovers will be especially good! Fresh fettuccine can be used in place of the tagliatelle

tools | 2 large pots | chef's knife | box grater | colander | wooden spatula

Heat the olive oil in a large nonreactive pot over medium heat. Add the onion and sauté, stirring often, for 5 minutes. Reduce the heat to low, cover, and cook, stirring occasionally, until softened, 20 minutes longer. Add the carrot, celery, and bacon and cook for 10–15 minutes. The bacon should be rendered of its fat and starting to brown. Add the garlic, 2 tsp salt, and pepper to taste and cook until fragrant, about 1 minute.

Raise the heat to medium, add the beef, veal, and pork, and stir vigorously with a wooden spatula to break up the meat. Cook, stirring occasionally, until the meat is lightly browned, about 10 minutes. Add the mushrooms, tomatoes, chicken and beef stocks, wine, and chili flakes. Stir well and reduce the heat to low. Simmer, uncovered, for 2 hours, stirring occasionally. Check the sauce frequently: it should remain at a gentle simmer and not come to a boil. When ready, the sauce should look glistening and deep in color, and taste rich.

Bring a large pot of water to a boil. When the sauce is just about ready to serve, add the pasta to the boiling water and cook until it is tender and rises to the surface, 30 seconds–5 minutes, depending on freshness. Drain, reserving a few tablespoons of the pasta cooking water.

Return the pasta to the pot, season with salt, and ladle in the Bolognese sauce. Add the reserved pasta cooking water as needed to loosen the sauce. Stir in the cream, taste for salt, and adjust the seasoning. Divide the pasta among warmed pasta bowls, sprinkle with the parsley and Parmesan, and serve at once.

> **fresh pasta** Bolognese sauce is traditionally served over fresh wide pasta called tagliatelle. You can also use dried pasta, but it won't have the same silky texture that complements this rich, creamy sauce so well. Look for fresh pasta at well-stocked supermarkets and Italian delis. While dried pastas can take more than 10 minutes to cook, fresh pastas are usually ready in less than 5 minutes, and really fresh homemade pasta cooks in less than 1 minute. Cooked fresh pastas won't have the same al dente texture as dried pastas, but they too should not be cooked until mushy.

¼ cup (2 fl oz/60 ml) olive oil

1 large onion, finely diced

1 carrot, peeled and finely diced

1 small rib celery, finely diced

3 slices bacon, finely minced

1 Tbsp finely chopped garlic

Kosher salt and pepper

1 lb (16 oz/500 g) ground (minced) beef sirloin

½ lb (8 oz/250 g) ground (minced) veal

½ lb (8 oz/250 g) ground (minced) pork

1 cup (3 oz/90 g) chopped button mushrooms

2 cups (16 fl oz/500 ml) basic tomato sauce (page 213)

1 cup (8 fl oz/250 ml) chicken stock

1 cup (8 fl oz/250 ml) beef stock

2 cups (16 fl oz/500 ml) dry red wine

Pinch of red chili flakes

2 lb (1 kg) fresh tagliatelle or fettuccine *(left)*

⅔ cup (5 fl oz/160 ml) heavy (double) cream, warmed

¼ cup (⅓ oz/10 g) chopped fresh parsley

Freshly grated Parmesan cheese

Penne with Sausage and Greens

preparation **20** minutes | cooking **20** minutes | **4** servings

The addition of potatoes and greens gives this classic sausage-and-tomato sauce a satisfying heartiness. You can use any greens you may have on hand, or you can use fresh flat-leaf parsley leaves.

tools | large sauté pan | large pot | small saucepan | chef's knife | box grater | colander | vegetable peeler

1 cup (5 oz/155 g) peeled and finely diced yellow-fleshed or waxy potatoes such as Yukon gold or creamers

Kosher salt

1 lb (500 g) penne, ziti, or small pasta shells

2 Tbsp olive oil

1 small yellow onion, finely diced

2 sweet or spicy Italian sausages, about 7 oz (220 g) total weight, casings removed and meat crumbled

2 small cloves garlic, chopped

1 cup (8 fl oz/250 ml) basic tomato sauce (page 213)

Pinch of red chili flakes

Handful of arugula (rocket) or red mustard greens, patted dry

Grated Parmesan cheese for serving

Bring a small saucepan of water to a boil. Add the potatoes and a pinch of salt, lower the heat to medium, and simmer just until tender, 6–9 minutes. The potatoes should retain their shape without falling apart. Drain and set aside to cool.

Meanwhile, bring a large pot of water to boil. Add the pasta and cook until al dente, tender but firm, according to the package directions.

While the pasta is cooking, heat the olive oil in a large sauté pan over medium heat. Add the onion and sauté until golden, 5–7 minutes. Add the sausage, stir well, and cook for 3 minutes. Add the garlic, tomato sauce, chili flakes, and cooked potatoes. Taste and adjust the seasoning with salt and chili flakes.

Drain the pasta thoroughly, reserving a few tablespoons of the pasta cooking water. Add the pasta and the reserved pasta cooking water to the sauce. Toss well, taste, and adjust the seasoning with more salt or chili flakes, if desired. Immediately before serving, fold in the greens. Serve in warmed bowls. Pass the Parmesan at the table.

Pizza Four Ways

preparation **20** minutes | cooking **10** minutes | each pizza serves **1**

Instead of presenting traditional soup-to-nuts courses at a dinner party, surprise guests with a series of delicious homemade pizzas. Provide an array of toppings from the choices below, or invent your own. Each recipe below will top one 8-inch (20-cm) pizza crust; on page 219 you'll find a recipe for 6 rounds.

tools | chef's knife | box grater | pizza peel | pizza stone | zester

Pizza Bianca This is a modern version of a wintery classic. *Pizza bianca* means "white pizza"; the name refers to the lack of tomato sauce. *Pizza bianca* is graced with three cheeses: ricotta, fresh mozzarella, and Fontina. We like to add a chiffonade of sweet escarole leaves, lemon zest, and garlic to decorate the rich canvas of cheese. Add chili flakes in place of the pepper if you like a little spice. If escarole is not available, use radicchio or Belgian endive (chicory/witloof).

Place a pizza stone in the oven and preheat to 500°F (260°C). Lightly flour a wooden pizza peel and place the dough round on it. Scatter the cheeses evenly over the dough. Avoid placing too much cheese in the center of the pizza; the cheese will flow toward the center during baking. Scatter the escarole generously in an even layer on top of the cheese. It will shrink during baking. Sprinkle the lemon zest, garlic, salt to taste, and olive oil over the pizza. Slide the pizza from the wooden peel onto the stone in the oven and bake until the crust is crisp and the toppings are cooked, 10 minutes or longer, depending on your oven. Use the peel to transfer the pizza to a wooden board, top with pepper, if using, and serve at once.

Flour for dusting

One 8-inch (20-cm) pizza dough round (page 219)

1 oz (30 g) fresh mozzarella cheese, torn into small pieces

1 oz (30 g) Fontina cheese, grated

2 tablespoons fresh ricotta

Handful of inner escarole (Batavian endive) leaves, thinly sliced

Zest of ¹/₂ lemon, finely chopped

1 small clove garlic, minced

Kosher salt

1 Tbsp fruity extra-virgin olive oil

Freshly ground pepper (optional)

Pizza Margherita This simple classic can be served year-round. Our secret is to use high-quality organic canned tomatoes, lightly chopped and mixed with olive oil, salt, and a pinch of sugar. Use the best mozzarella you can find and the best extra-virgin olive oil you have on hand.

Place a pizza stone in the oven and preheat to 500°F (260°C). Drain the tomatoes, reserving 1–2 Tbsp of the juices, and coarsely chop them, leaving a few large chunks. Toss the tomatoes and the reserved juice together with the sugar, olive oil, and ¹/₄ tsp salt. Lightly flour a wooden pizza peel and place the dough round on it. Scatter the mozzarella evenly over the dough. Scatter the chopped tomatoes liberally over the mozzarella, trying to avoid putting too many in the center of the pizza. Sprinkle with more salt. Slide the pizza from the wooden peel onto the stone in the oven and bake until the crust is crisp and the toppings are cooked, 10 minutes or longer, depending on your oven. Use the peel to transfer the pizza to a wooden board. Scatter the basil leaves on top of the pizza and serve at once.

1¹/₄ cups (8 oz/250 g) canned whole tomatoes

Pinch of sugar

2 Tbsp extra-virgin olive oil

Kosher salt

Flour for dusting

One 8-inch (20-cm) pizza dough round (page 219)

1¹/₂–2 oz (45–60 g) fresh mozzarella cheese

Several fresh basil leaves

continued >

Grilled Eggplant Pizza Fresh herbed bread crumbs give this summertime pizza a fabulous crunchy texture. The lacy layer of bread crumbs will absorb flavors from the tomatoes, garlic, herbs, and Parmesan. For a salty kick, sprinkle with chopped rinsed capers before baking.

1 Japanese or Italian eggplant (aubergine)

1 Tbsp olive oil

Kosher salt and pepper

Flour for dusting

One 8-inch (20-cm) pizza dough round (page 219)

2 oz (60 g) fresh mozzarella cheese

1 ripe red tomato, sliced ⅛ inch (3 mm) thick

3 Tbsp fresh bread crumbs (page 215)

2 tsp chopped fresh oregano

2 tsp chopped fresh parsley

1 small clove garlic, minced

1 Tbsp grated Parmesan cheese

1 Tbsp extra-virgin olive oil

Place a pizza stone in the oven and preheat to 500°F (260°C). Preheat the broiler (grill). Slice off the stem end of the eggplant and cut the eggplant into slices ¼ inch (6 mm) thick. Brush both sides of each slice with the olive oil and lightly season with salt. Place the eggplant on a broiler pan and broil (grill) for 2 minutes, turn the pieces over, and broil for 2 minutes more. Let cool slightly, then cut on the diagonal into strips 1½ inches (4 cm) wide. Season with pepper.

Lightly flour a wooden pizza peel and place the dough round on it. Tear the mozzarella into bite-sized pieces. Scatter the mozzarella evenly over the dough. Arrange the tomato slices evenly on top of the mozzarella. (If the tomato is large you may have too much.) Layer and intersperse the eggplant with the tomato and mozzarella. In a bowl, stir together the bread crumbs, oregano, parsley, and garlic. Sprinkle the bread crumb mixture liberally over the pizza. Sprinkle the pizza with the Parmesan, season with ½ tsp salt, and drizzle with the extra-virgin olive oil. Slide the pizza from the wooden peel onto the stone in the oven and bake until the crust is crisp and the toppings are cooked, 10 minutes or more, depending on your oven. Use the peel to transfer the pizza to a wooden board and serve at once.

Pizza Quattro Stagione Each quadrant of this pizza, available at nearly every pizzeria in Rome, is topped with a different ingredient: artichoke hearts, prosciutto, button mushrooms, and capers. And although it's debatable whether these four staples accurately represent the "four seasons" suggested by the name, we still think it's a charming idea. You can vary this recipe with your own favorite ingredients. We like to sprinkle fresh arugula leaves over the entire pizza to bring "the seasons" together.

Flour for dusting

One 8-inch (20-cm) pizza dough round (page 219)

1 oz (30 g) fresh mozzarella cheese, torn into ½-inch (12-mm) pieces

4 button mushrooms, brushed clean and thinly sliced

¼ tsp kosher salt

1 Tbsp capers, rinsed and coarsely chopped

3 marinated artichoke hearts, quartered

2 paper-thin slices prosciutto

Handful of arugula (rocket) leaves

1 Tbsp extra-virgin olive oil

Place a pizza stone in the oven and preheat to 500°F (260°C). Lightly flour a wooden pizza peel and place the dough round on it. Scatter the cheese evenly over the dough. Arrange the mushroom slices evenly over one-quarter of the pizza. Season with the salt. Scatter the capers evenly over a second quarter and arrange the artichoke hearts on top of the third quarter. Leave one-quarter empty; that one is for the prosciutto.

Slide the pizza from the wooden peel onto the stone in the oven and bake until the crust is crisp and the toppings are cooked, 10 minutes or more, depending on your oven. Use the peel to transfer the pizza to a wooden board. Drape the prosciutto slices on top of the final quarter. Scatter the arugula leaves over the entire pizza, and drizzle with the olive oil. Serve at once.

Risotto Milanese

preparation **10** minutes | cooking **40** minutes | **4–6** servings

This dish, the classic accompaniment to osso buco (page 100), relies on the best ingredients: deep orange-red saffron, good homemade stock, and true Parmesan cheese.

tools | small baking dish | large saucepan | large pot | chef's knife | box grater | ladle

Preheat the oven to 375°F (190°C).

Put the saffron in a small baking dish and toast for 3 minutes; this will deepen its color and awaken its flavor.

Melt 4 Tbsp (2 oz/60 g) of the butter in a large pot over low heat. Add the onion, cover, and cook, uncovering to stir often, until the onion is soft but not browned, 10–12 minutes.

Meanwhile, crumble half the saffron into the stock in a large saucepan. Bring to a full boil over high heat, then turn off the heat.

Add the rice and remaining saffron to the onion and stir to coat. Stirring constantly, add 1 cup (8 fl oz/250 ml) of the stock. Season with the salt and continue stirring over medium-low heat until the stock is absorbed. Add a ladleful of stock and stir until it is absorbed. Repeat this process, gradually adding the stock until the rice is creamy but al dente, about 20 minutes. If the rice seems dry or sticky, add a splash more stock.

Stir in the remaining 1 Tbsp butter and taste and adjust with salt, if necessary. Sprinkle the Parmesan on top and serve at once on warmed plates or bowls.

> **risotto with peas and prosciutto** Follow the instructions above but omit the saffron. After 10 minutes of stirring stock into the risotto, add 2 cups (10 oz/315 g) shelled fresh English peas. Continue adding stock until the risotto is creamy but al dente and the peas are tender. To serve, stir in 1 tsp minced fresh parsley and 1 tsp minced fresh mint, and garnish liberally with strips of prosciutto or serrano ham.
>
> **risotto with pumpkin and sage** Follow the instructions above but omit the saffron. Just before cooking the risotto, sauté 2 cups (10 oz/315 g) diced peeled fresh Sugar Pie, Cheese, or other eating pumpkin in olive oil until just tender. After 15 minutes of stirring stock into the risotto, add the sautéed pumpkin and 2 tsp minced fresh sage. Continue adding stock until the risotto is creamy but al dente and the pumpkin is completely tender.

¾ tsp loosely packed saffron threads

5 Tbsp (2½ oz/75 g) butter (divided)

1 small yellow onion, finely diced

8 cups (64 fl oz/2 l) chicken stock (page 216)

1¾ cups (12 oz/375 g) Arborio rice

1 tsp kosher salt

⅓ cup (1½ oz/45 g) freshly grated Parmesan cheese

Vegetables

Here is a group of recipes we gathered to help you through the year of changing seasons and to celebrate the availability of so much wonderful fresh produce. When we were growing up, it seemed that carrots, peas, and spinach were the only choices. Now, thanks to a green-market revolution, we truly have a wealth of options. This chapter contains some of our absolute favorites: fragrant braised fennel and nutty caramelized Brussels sprouts. As in other chapters, some of these recipes can stand alone as a main course. Try summery ratatouille with a garden salad and crisp warm bread.

Asparagus Mimosa

preparation **15** minutes │ cooking **15** minutes │ **4–6** servings

Chopped hard-cooked egg resembles the fluffy yellow-and-white mimosa flower, hence, the name of this recipe. The mimosa flower blooms in springtime, which is also the best season for asparagus. Serve this dish for an alfresco brunch to celebrate the return of longer days and milder weather.

tools │ large pot │ baking sheet │ chef's knife │ tongs │ vegetable peeler │ whisk

2 hard-cooked eggs (page 214)

½ cup (1 oz/30 g) coarse fresh bread crumbs (page 215)

¼ cup (2 fl oz/60 ml) extra-virgin olive oil, plus 1 Tbsp

Kosher salt and pepper

1 shallot, finely chopped

2 tsp champagne vinegar

1½ lb (750 g) thick asparagus

Preheat the oven to 375°F (190°C). Peel the eggs, chop finely, and set aside.

Toss the bread crumbs with the 1 Tbsp olive oil and salt to taste, spread on a baking sheet, and toast until golden, 10–12 minutes.

In a nonreactive bowl, combine the shallot with the vinegar and salt and pepper to taste. Let the shallot stand in the vinegar for 5 minutes. Whisk in the ¼ cup olive oil, taste, and adjust the seasoning with salt and pepper.

To prepare the asparagus, snap off the tough woody ends of the spears and then trim the ends neatly. Using a vegetable peeler, peel the spears lengthwise, starting from beneath the tip, to expose the tender, light green flesh and remove the fibrous exterior. Bring a large pot of salted water to boil and blanch half of the asparagus (to avoid overcrowding) for about 1 minute. Remove the asparagus from the water with tongs and spread on a baking sheet to cool. Repeat to cook the remaining asparagus.

Toss the asparagus spears with the vinaigrette to coat, taste, and adjust the seasoning. Arrange the spears on a serving platter.

Sprinkle the chopped egg over the asparagus, followed by the bread crumbs. Pour any remaining vinaigrette over the asparagus, if desired, and serve.

Ginger Carrot Salad

preparation **10** minutes | cooking **10** minutes | marinating **1** hour | **6** servings

These carrots can accompany a main dish or be served as part of an antipasto platter with thin slices of your favorite salami, hard cheese, cucumber salad (page 156), and warm marinated olives (page 58). For the best flavor, look for small, slender young carrots with tops still attached to indicate freshness—but remove the tops as soon as you get them home to prevent them from drawing moisture from the carrots.

tools | large sauté pan | small sauté pan | baking sheet | chef's knife | citrus reamer | mortar and pestle (optional) | vegetable peeler

Trim the carrots, leaving ¼ inch (6 mm) of the green stem intact, and then peel. Heat 2 inches (5 cm) of water in a large sauté pan. Add 2 tsp of the vinegar and the salt and bring to a simmer. Taste the water: it should have a mildly acidic, salted flavor. This gives a sparkle to the carrots as they cook. Add the carrots and simmer until tender but still firm, 7–8 minutes. Drain the carrots and let cool in a single layer on a baking sheet.

Place the cumin and caraway seeds in a small sauté pan over medium heat and toast, shaking the pan so that they heat evenly, until fragrant, just 20 seconds. Coarsely grind the seeds with a mortar and pestle, or chop firmly using a sharp chef's knife.

In a shallow serving bowl, toss the carrots with the lemon juice, ½ teaspoon of the ginger, the cayenne, the remaining 2 tsp vinegar, the ground cumin and caraway, and the olive oil until well coated. Taste and adjust the seasoning with additional salt, ginger, or lemon juice. Sprinkle with the chopped cilantro. Let marinate at room temperature for 1 hour before serving.

Note: The carrots will keep, refrigerated, for 1–2 days.

2 bunches of slender, young carrots

4 tsp champagne vinegar or sherry vinegar (divided)

1 tsp kosher salt

¼ tsp cumin seeds

¼ tsp caraway seeds

1 tsp fresh lemon juice

¾ tsp peeled and minced fresh ginger

¼ tsp ground cayenne pepper

2 Tbsp extra-virgin olive oil

2 Tbsp chopped cilantro leaves (fresh coriander)

Cucumber Salad

preparation **10** minutes | **2–4** servings

Serve this refreshing salad as part of a summertime supper, with toasted bagels and slices of smoked salmon for brunch, or with ginger carrot salad (page 155) and sautéed spinach (page 163) for a colorful antipasto course. For a touch of heat, add a pinch of ground cayenne pepper with the curry powder.

tools | chef's knife | vegetable peeler

2 English (hothouse) cucumbers

Kosher salt

2 Tbsp crème fraîche or sour cream

¼ cup (2 fl oz/60 ml) plain yogurt

¼ tsp curry powder

Leaves from 6 sprigs cilantro (fresh coriander), chopped

Peel the cucumbers, cut in half lengthwise, and scrape out the seeds with a spoon. Cut crosswise into uniform slices about ⅛ inch (3 mm) thick. Season the cucumbers with salt and combine in a serving bowl with the crème fraîche, yogurt, and curry powder. Garnish with the cilantro and serve.

Peas with Lemon, Tarragon, and Shallots

preparation **15** minutes | cooking **10** minutes | **4** servings

If tiny fresh, sweet garden peas are available, by all means use them. The spring season for fresh-shelled peas is short and their sweetness is fleeting. Luckily, frozen peas are an acceptable substitute here, making this a year-round dish.

tools | sauté pan | chef's knife | citrus reamer | citrus zester

1 Tbsp butter

1 Tbsp olive oil

2 shallots, minced

2 cups (10 oz/310 g) fresh or frozen English peas

2 tsp finely chopped fresh parsley

1 Tbsp chopped fresh tarragon

1 tsp finely chopped lemon zest

1½–2 tsp fresh lemon juice

Kosher salt

Heat the butter and olive oil in a sauté pan over medium heat. When the butter has melted, sauté the shallots until softened but not browned, about 5 minutes. Add the peas, 2 Tbsp water, the parsley, tarragon, lemon zest, and lemon juice, and salt to taste. Cook until the peas are heated through, 3–5 minutes. Serve at once.

Stuffed Zucchini

preparation **15** minutes | cooking **20** minutes | **6–8** servings

Serve stuffed zucchini as a side dish, as an appetizer before a pasta dinner, or with a garden salad for a light lunch on a sunny day.

tools | large baking pan | large pot | chef's knife | box grater | colander

Bring a large pot of salted water to a boil. Add the whole zucchini and reduce the heat to a simmer. Simmer the zucchini just until tender, 10–15 minutes. Drain and let cool.

Preheat the broiler (grill). Lightly oil a large baking pan. In a bowl, stir together the ricotta and ¼ cup Parmesan with the flour, salt and black pepper to taste, the cayenne, and the lemon zest. Slice the zucchini in half lengthwise and scoop out the seeds with a small spoon. Place the zucchini in the prepared baking pan. Season with salt and pepper and fill with the cheese mixture to form soft mounds. Sprinkle with the pecorino Romano cheese. Place under the broiler until the cheese is warm and starts to brown slightly, 5–7 minutes. Remove from the broiler, chop the basil leaves, and sprinkle on top. Serve warm.

> **seeding zucchini** The method of seeding zucchini is the same as for cucumber. Cut the vegetable in half lengthwise, then draw a small spoon (a melon baller is perfect for this) down the length of the vegetable, scooping out the seeds.

4 zucchini (courgettes), each 4–5 inches (10–13 cm) long

Olive oil for greasing

1 cup (8 oz/250 g) fresh ricotta

¼ cup (1 oz/30 g) freshly grated Parmesan

1 Tbsp flour

Kosher salt and black pepper

Pinch of ground cayenne pepper

Pinch of grated lemon zest

2 Tbsp freshly grated pecorino Romano or Parmesan

Leaves from 1 large sprig fresh basil

Spicy Italian-Style Cauliflower

preparation **15** minutes | cooking **25** minutes | **4–6** servings

This caramelized cauliflower has an appealing texture and spiciness that can convert even those who swear they don't like cauliflower. Try this technique with broccoli, too.

tools | large sauté pan | chef's knife | citrus zester

1 head cauliflower, about 2 lb (1 kg)

3 Tbsp olive oil, or as needed

½ tsp kosher salt

3 Tbsp capers, rinsed and chopped, or to taste

2 tsp finely chopped lemon zest

3 cloves garlic, minced

¼ tsp red chili flakes, or to taste

3 Tbsp finely chopped pitted black or green olives

Remove the outer leaves of the cauliflower and trim off the stem end. Cut the cauliflower into ½-inch (12-mm) slices from the top to bottom, using the entire head, florets and stalks. The cauliflower will break up as you slice it, leaving you with pieces of varying sizes and shapes. Heat the olive oil in a large sauté pan over medium heat. (You may need to cook the cauliflower in batches.) When the oil is hot, add the cauliflower. Allow it to sizzle and begin to brown, stirring often so it does not scorch. When the cauliflower begins to soften slightly, after 3–4 minutes, add the salt, capers, lemon zest, garlic, chili flakes, and olives. Continue cooking, stirring often, until the cauliflower is golden brown and the other ingredients have caramelized and the flavors have melded, 10–15 minutes. As you stir, scrape the pan with your spoon to loosen the caramelized bits that have stuck to the bottom. Taste and adjust the seasoning with chili flakes, capers, and salt. Serve at once.

Braised Red Cabbage

preparation **10** minutes | cooking **35** minutes | **4** servings

Braised cabbage is an essential comfort food for autumn, winter, and even a chilly early spring. Serve with roast turkey (page 116), or duck (page 121).

tools | large saucepan | chef's knife | paring knife or vegetable peeler | wooden spatula

1 red cabbage

3 Tbsp butter or olive oil

4 shallots, thinly sliced

2 tsp sugar

2 Tbsp cider vinegar

½ cup (4 fl oz/125 ml) dry red wine

Kosher salt and pepper

1 firm but ripe large pear

Cut the cabbage in half lengthwise. Cut out the core and slice the cabbage thinly.

Melt the butter in a large saucepan over medium heat. Add the shallots and sauté, stirring constantly, until they are tender but not browned, 3–5 minutes.

Add the cabbage, sugar, vinegar, and wine and season to taste with salt and pepper. Cover, reduce the heat to low, and braise slowly for about 25 minutes. The cabbage should deepen in color and be tender, but with a slightly toothy texture. Peel the pear and cut in half lengthwise, removing the stem. Scoop out the core with a round measuring spoon and dice the pear. Add to the cabbage and cook for 5 minutes more. Taste and adjust the seasoning with salt and pepper. Serve warm.

Celery Root Rémoulade

preparation **15** minutes | **4** servings

This dish can wear a lot of hats. Serve it with a combination of salad greens or sliced apples at a picnic or brunch, or as an accompaniment to sliced prosciutto, salami, cured or smoked fish, roasted crab (page 129), or roast chicken (page 112). One of our favorite ways to eat celery root rémoulade is as a late-night supper with marinated beets (see page 90) or perfectly ripe avocado wedges. The flavor of the dish improves as it sits, so it can be made a day or two in advance.

tools | chef's knife or mandoline | citrus reamer | vegetable peeler or paring knife | whisk

To make the dressing, combine the vinegar, lemon juice, salt, and olive oil in a small nonreactive bowl. Whisk in the mustard, mustard seeds, and cream until well blended.

Carefully peel the outer skin of the celery root with a vegetable peeler or sharp paring knife. Slice the bulb lengthwise into thin slices, then stack the slices and slice again to make julienne (thin matchstick shapes). Put the celery root in a serving bowl, salt lightly, and mix well. Pour the dressing over the celery root and toss with your hands. Taste and adjust the seasoning. Refrigerate for 1–2 hours, or until ready to serve. Serve chilled or at room temperature.

> **celery root** Also known as celeriac, celery root is a knobby, round winter vegetable that contributes a subtle celery flavor to purées when cooked and a crisp crunch to salads when used raw.

FOR THE DRESSING

2 Tbsp champagne vinegar

2 tsp fresh lemon juice

½ tsp kosher salt

½ cup (4 fl oz/125 ml) olive oil

1 Tbsp Dijon mustard, or to taste

2 tsp yellow or black mustard seeds

⅓ cup (3 fl oz/80 ml) heavy (double) cream

1 medium celery root (celeriac), about 1 lb (500 g)

Kosher salt

Ratatouille

resting **45** minutes | preparation **20** minutes | cooking **65** minutes | **8** servings

Ratatouille is Provence's velvety mélange of colorful summer vegetables. Some think that it's better served the day after it is made, once the flavors have had a chance to marry. We think it's great hot or cold, and it's delicious when folded into scrambled eggs. Choose smaller eggplants for better flavor.

tools | large baking dish | large frying pan | chef's knife | colander | vegetable peeler

1 lb (500 g) eggplant (aubergine)

Kosher salt

5 small zucchini (courgettes)

1 red bell pepper (capsicum)

1 yellow bell pepper (capsicum)

1 large yellow onion

4 large, ripe tomatoes, peeled

6–8 Tbsp (3–4 fl oz/90 ml–125 ml) extra-virgin olive oil

1 bay leaf

1 tsp finely chopped garlic

4 sprigs fresh thyme

Freshly ground black pepper

Ground cayenne pepper

Fresh basil leaves for serving

Preheat the oven to 375°F (190°C). Peel the eggplant's skin and cut the flesh into 1-inch (2.5-cm) chunks. Lightly season with ½ tsp salt, place in a colander, and weight down with a plate and a 1-lb (500-g) can or something of similar weight. Let the eggplant drain for 45 minutes. Cut the zucchini into 1-inch (2.5-cm) chunks. Seed and derib the red and yellow bell peppers and cut into 1-inch (2.5-cm) squares. Cut the onion and tomatoes into large dice.

Pat the eggplant dry with paper towels. Heat 4 Tbsp (2 fl oz/60 ml) of the olive oil in a large frying pan over medium heat and sauté the eggplant until lightly browned, 10–15 minutes depending on moisture content. Transfer the eggplant to a large baking dish. Add the zucchini and bell peppers to the same frying pan, along with additional oil if necessary to prevent the vegetables from sticking. Season with salt and sauté until the vegetables are slightly softened, about 2 minutes. Transfer to the baking dish. Add the onion and tomatoes to the baking dish. Add the bay leaf, garlic, and thyme and season generously with salt, black pepper, and cayenne. Stir all the vegetables together.

Cover the dish with foil and bake for 30 minutes (the foil will cause the vegetables to cook in their own steam). Remove the foil and continue to bake until the ratatouille has thickened and you like the way it tastes, about 20 minutes longer. Serve warm or cold with freshly torn basil leaves as a finishing touch.

Sautéed Kale with Golden Raisins

preparation **15** minutes | cooking **25** minutes | **4** servings

Kale is a delicious green available in the fall, winter, and early spring. Cooking time can depend on the age and tenderness of the plant. Cook these greens a little longer if they are mature; if using tender, young kale, cook it a little less.

tools | small saucepan | large sauté pan | chef's knife | salad spinner

In a small saucepan, combine the raisins with water to cover and add the red wine vinegar. Warm gently over low heat until the raisins are plump, about 5 minutes. Remove from the heat, drain, and set aside.

Meanwhile, remove the stems from the kale. Rinse and lightly dry the leaves, leaving a little water clinging to them. Chop the leaves into bite-sized pieces. Heat a large sauté pan over medium-low heat. Add the olive oil and a handful of kale to cover the bottom of the pan. Cook gently, adding more kale as it wilts and cooks down, until all of the kale has been added. Season with salt, reduce the heat to low, cover, and cook for 10 minutes. Uncover, add the raisins, and continue to cook until the excess moisture has evaporated and the kale is tender, about 10 minutes more. Stir in the cider vinegar and serve warm or at room temperature.

¼ cup (1½ oz/45 g) golden raisins (sultanas) or regular raisins

1 tsp red wine vinegar

2 bunches kale, about 2 lb (1 kg) total weight

3 Tbsp olive oil

Kosher salt

1½ Tbsp apple cider vinegar

Spinach with Chili and Garlic

preparation **10** minutes | cooking **4** minutes | **2** servings

Here's a quick-cooking vegetable side dish that makes a classic accompaniment for fish. Try it with the sole with lemon, brown butter, and capers (page 122), or with the salmon with French lentils (page 124).

tools | large sauté pan | chef's knife | salad spinner | tongs

Warm the olive oil in a large sauté pan over low heat. Add the pancetta and sauté gently until lightly golden but not crispy, 2–3 minutes. Add the garlic and sauté for 30 seconds, then add the spinach. Use tongs to lift and turn the spinach gently in the pan just until it is wilted. Don't overcook, or the spinach will become wet and soggy. Add the chili flakes and season with salt. Serve at once.

1 Tbsp olive oil

2 slices pancetta or 1 slice bacon, minced

½ tsp minced garlic

½ lb (250 g) medium spinach leaves, stemmed and patted dry

Pinch of red chili flakes

Kosher salt

Caramelized Brussels Sprouts

preparation **10** minutes | cooking **5** minutes | **2** servings

This oft-maligned vegetable is meltingly delicious when cooked right. For an autumn and winter treat, we like to separate Brussles sprouts into leaves and quickly sauté them until lightly caramelized. Sautéing in fruity olive oil brings out a sweet, nutty flavor.

tools | sauté pan | paring knife | wooden spatula

16 Brussels sprouts

2 Tbsp fruity olive oil

Kosher salt and pepper

Remove any loose fibrous outer leaves of the Brussels sprouts. Trim the bottom ends and remove the tiny cores with a sharp paring knife. Use your fingers to separate the individual leaves. If the inner core of leaves is too compact to separate, slice it into thin sections.

Heat the olive oil in a sauté pan over medium heat. When the oil is hot, add the Brussels sprout leaves. Season with salt and pepper. Sauté vigorously, stirring and tossing, until the leaves have softened and are beginning to crisp and brown slightly, about 5 minutes. Serve at once.

Roasted Winter Squash Crescents

preparation **10** minutes | cooking **30** minutes | **4–6** servings

Delicata squashes, recognizable by their distinct stripes and oblong shape, make their debut in late summer and are available until midwinter. Serve these crescents with roast turkey (page 116) or duck (page 121), paired with sautéed kale (page 163).

tools | baking sheet | chef's knife

3 medium delicata squash

¼ cup (2 fl oz/60 ml) olive oil

1 Tbsp brown sugar

1 tsp kosher salt

Freshly ground pepper

Preheat the oven to 350°F (180°C). Rinse the squash under cold water and pat them dry. Cut each squash in half lengthwise. Using a spoon, scrape out the seeds and discard. You should be left with 6 squash "boats," each smooth inside. Trim the ends of the squash, discard, and slice each squash half into slices ½ inch (12 mm) thick, making crescent shapes. Combine all the squash slices in a large bowl with the olive oil, brown sugar, salt, and pepper to taste and toss until well coated. Arrange the squash on 1 or 2 baking sheets in a single layer. Bake for 15 minutes, turn the pieces over, and bake until the flesh is golden and tender, about 15 minutes more. You should be able to pierce the flesh easily with a fork; if there is still slight resistance, bake for 5–10 minutes more. Serve warm.

Braised Fennel

preparation **15** minutes | cooking **50** minutes | **4** servings

As fennel cooks, its flavor deepening and its texture becoming velvety, its heady anise aroma fills your kitchen. This versatile autumn side dish complements a number of main courses, including brined pork chops (page 105), roast sea bass with bacon (page 123), and roast chicken (page 112).

tools | small sauté pan | small baking dish | chef's knife | mortar and pestle (optional)

Preheat the oven to 400°F (200°C). Put the fennel seeds in a small sauté pan and toast over low heat, shaking the pan frequently so that they toast evenly, until fragrant, 2–3 minutes. Crush and grind the seeds with a mortar and pestle, or chop firmly using a sharp chef's knife.

Cut all the stalks from the fennel bulbs, reserving a handful of the green fronds. If the fronds do not look fresh, discard them, but otherwise lightly chop enough of the best-looking ones to measure about ¼ cup (⅓ oz/10 g). Remove any bruised outer leaves from the fennel bulbs, then cut the bulbs into 1½-inch (4-cm) wedges and arrange them in a small, shallow baking dish. Drizzle the olive oil and wine on top of the fennel and sprinkle with salt and the fennel seeds. Add the stock and sprinkle the chopped fennel fronds over all, if using. Toss to coat evenly.

Cover the dish with foil and braise in the oven for 30 minutes. Remove the foil and continue cooking until the fennel is golden, another 15–20 minutes. The fennel should be tender when pierced with the tip of a knife. Serve warm.

> **gratinéed fennel:** About 10 minutes before the fennel has finished cooking, brush the top with 1 Tbsp melted butter and sprinkle with 3 Tbsp grated Parmesan for a gratinéed effect.

1 tsp fennel seeds

3 medium fennel bulbs, with stems and fronds still attached, if possible

2 Tbsp olive oil

½ cup (4 fl oz/125 ml) dry white wine

Kosher salt

¼ cup (2 fl oz/60 ml) vegetable stock (page 216) or water

Honey-Balsamic Sweet Potato Mash

preparation **10** minutes | cooking **50** minutes | **4** servings

Honey and balsamic vinegar give these sweet potatoes an alluring sweet-sour flavor. Serve with roast turkey (page 116) or chicken (page 112) or pork roast (page 106).

tools | chef's knife | food mill, ricer, potato masher, or fork

3 lb (1.5 kg) sweet potatoes

4 Tbsp (2 oz/60 g) butter

¼ cup (2 fl oz/60 ml) heavy (double) cream

1 Tbsp wildflower, lavender, or your favorite honey

2 tsp balsamic vinegar

½ tsp kosher salt

Freshly ground pepper

Preheat the oven to 400°F (200°C). Line a baking sheet with foil. Prick the sweet potatoes in a few places with a fork. Bake on the prepared sheet until very tender, 50–60 minutes.

Set the sweet potatoes aside to cool. When cool enough to handle, halve them lengthwise and scoop out the flesh into a large bowl. Discard the skins. For a velvety texture, pass the sweet potatoes through a ricer or food mill. For a more rustic texture, mash them with a potato masher or fork. Stir in the butter, cream, honey, vinegar, salt, and pepper to taste. Serve at once.

Stir-Fried Bok Choy

preparation **10** minutes | cooking **7** minutes | **4** servings

Bok choy, also known as Chinese white cabbage, is a cousin of broccoli and has a nutty, spinachlike flavor—only mildly reminiscent of typical cabbage. To trim, just cut away the tough core. This dish is particularly delicious served with wok-glazed scallops (page 128).

tools | chef's knife | wok or large frying pan

1–2 Tbsp peanut or olive oil

2 cloves garlic, peeled and lightly crushed

½ tsp kosher salt

2 lb (1 kg) bok choy, trimmed and cut into slices ¼ inch (6 mm) thick

1 Tbsp Asian sesame oil

Heat a wok or large frying pan over medium-high heat until hot. Add the oil and garlic and stir-fry until the oil is perfumed, about 30 seconds. Add the salt and bok choy, raise the heat to high, and stir-fry for 2 minutes. Add 2 Tbsp water and continue to stir-fry until wilted and tender, another 4–5 minutes. Serve at once, drizzled with the sesame oil.

Celery Root Purée

preparation **10** minutes | cooking **30** minutes | **4** servings

Because it turns creamy when puréed, celery root makes a nice alternative to mashed potatoes. Serve with roast beef (page 98), roast pork loin (page 106) or chops (page 105).

tools | large saucepan | chef's knife | vegetable peeler | whisk

Peel the celery roots and potato and cut into 1-inch (2.5-cm) chunks. Put the vegetables in a large saucepan with the butter and add water just to cover. Bring to a simmer over low heat, cover, and simmer until the celery roots and potato are tender, about 30 minutes. Stir from time to time, adding more water, if necessary, to keep the celery roots and potato from sticking to the bottom of the pan.

Drain the vegetables and return to the saucepan. Whip with a whisk, stir in the cream, and season to taste with salt and pepper. Sprinkle with nutmeg and serve.

2 medium celery roots (celeriac)

1 medium yellow-fleshed potato such as Yukon gold or Yellow Finn

2 Tbsp butter

¾ cup (6 fl oz/180 ml) heavy (double) cream

Kosher salt and pepper

Freshly grated nutmeg for serving

Field Mushroom Salad

preparation **15** minutes | **4** servings

In this simple but elegant dish, raw mushrooms are sliced paper-thin and adorned with olive oil, lemon juice, and very fresh mint. We like to use Parmigiano-Reggiano as the finishing touch, but you could use Asiago, pecorino, or goat cheese. Serve the salad immediately or its delicacy will be lost.

tools | chef's knife | paring knife | citrus reamer | vegetable peeler

Right before you intend to serve the salad, use a dry cloth to brush any dirt off the mushrooms. Trim off the stems with a sharp paring knife. Place the mushrooms flat side down and thinly slice each cap. Spread the mushroom slices in a single layer on a large serving platter. Crush ½ tsp salt between your fingers to create a fine dust and sprinkle it evenly over the mushrooms. Drizzle most of the olive oil evenly over the mushrooms, reserving a little more for later, and do the same with the lemon juice. Pick the leaves from the mint sprigs, stack them, and finely slice them crosswise to make a chiffonade. When ready to serve, sprinkle the chiffonade on the mushrooms and use a vegetable peeler to shave thin curls of Parmesan on top. Drizzle the remaining olive oil over the mushrooms, sprinkle with more lemon juice to taste, taste for salt, and grind fresh pepper over all. Serve at once.

1 lb (500 g) cremini mushrooms

Kosher salt and pepper

3 Tbsp fruity extra-virgin olive oil (divided)

2 tsp fresh lemon juice, plus more to taste

Several sprigs fresh mint

Parmesan cheese for shaving

Roasted Radicchio with Pancetta

preparation **10** minutes | cooking **15** minutes | **4** servings

In this recipe, crisp radicchio is roasted until tender, while the pancetta wrapped around it turns crisp. It's an out-of-the-ordinary side dish or appetizer for the start of a hearty autumn or winter supper. Smoked bacon can be substituted for the milder unsmoked pancetta as long as it is very thinly sliced. If you have a fine aged balsamic vinegar, this is the time to use it—sparingly—as a condiment.

tools | baking sheet | chef's knife

1 medium head of radicchio (12–16 oz/375–500 g)

2 Tbsp extra-virgin olive oil

Kosher salt and freshly ground pepper

3 oz (90 g) very thinly sliced pancetta or bacon

2–3 tsp aged balsamic vinegar

Preheat the oven to 350°F (180°C). Slice the head of radicchio into wedges approximately 1 inch (2.5 cm) thick at the widest point. The core at the bottom of the radicchio should help keep each of the wedges intact. Place the wedges on a baking sheet, drizzle with the olive oil, and sprinkle with salt and pepper. Lightly wrap each wedge with a slice or two of pancetta (don't worry if the pancetta slices tear). Use all the pancetta pieces until each wedge is loosely wrapped, leaving some of the radicchio exposed to encourage even cooking. Rub the wrapped wedges in any olive oil that remains on the baking sheet and arrange them flat on the sheet.

Roast until the pancetta is completely rendered of its fat and crisp and the radicchio is a dark mauve and completely soft, 15–20 minutes. The edges of some of the radicchio wedges may be crisp. Drizzle the wedges with the balsamic vinegar and serve at once.

radicchio A variety of chicory native to Italy, radicchio is characterized by its variegated purplish red leaves and bitter taste. The sturdy raw leaves hold up well, and their assertive flavor is nicely matched with cheeses, cured meats, anchovies, olives, and capers. Crisp and brightly colored, radicchio grows in round or elongated heads. It complements many ingredients with its deep ruby red color and pleasantly bitter flavor.

Sides

Don't let the name of this chapter mislead you. We have been known
to crave one of these "sides" and create an entire meal around it. Side
dishes can be as inspiring as main courses—it's all in how you think
about them. Round out zucchini potato pancakes with an impromptu
buffet of olives, cheese, and prosciutto. Each of these recipes offers
its own delights of texture and flavor: tarragon-spiked twice-baked
potatoes, earthy mushroom rice pilaf, and smooth and comforting
soft polenta will each inspire a different mood.

Mushroom Rice Pilaf

preparation **10** minutes | cooking **45** minutes | resting **10** minutes | **4** servings

In this recipe, mild, nutty, gold chanterelle mushrooms give a rich, earthy flavor to pilaf. If chanterelles are not available, use another brown mushroom instead.

tools | saucepan | chef's knife | cheesecloth | kitchen string

1 sprig fresh lavender or thyme

8 Tbsp (4 oz/125 g) butter (divided)

1 yellow onion, finely chopped

1 clove garlic, minced

1 cup (3 oz/90 g) chanterelle mushrooms, chopped

1½ cups (10½ oz/330 g) long-grain rice

1½ cups (12 fl oz/375 ml) *each* vegetable stock (page 216) and beef stock (page 217)

1 tsp kosher salt and pepper

Wrap the lavender tightly in cheesecloth (muslin) and tie with kitchen string. Melt 6 Tbsp (3 oz/90 g) of the butter in a saucepan over medium heat. Add the onion and garlic and sauté until tender but not browned, about 10 minutes. Add the remaining 2 Tbsp butter, then the mushrooms, stir well, and cook, stirring often, until the mushrooms release their liquid and it is reabsorbed, about 10 minutes. Add the rice to the saucepan and reduce the heat to low. Stir constantly for 2 minutes to toast the rice lightly and ensure that each grain is thoroughly coated with butter and turns slightly opaque. Add the vegetable and beef stocks, the salt, and the lavender bundle. Cover and simmer for 25 minutes. Remove the lavender and let the rice stand, covered, for 10 minutes before serving. Transfer to a warmed serving dish, and pass the pepper mill at the table.

Potato Gratin

preparation **20** minutes | cooking **25** minutes | **4–6** servings

Thinly sliced potatoes are cooked gently in cream on the stove top, then finished in the oven for a golden gratinéed top. Warm up leftovers and serve for breakfast with fried eggs.

tools | baking dish | large saucepan | chef's knife or mandoline | paring knife | vegetable peeler

1½ tsp butter, at room temperature

2 lb (1 kg) Yukon gold or russet potatoes

2 small cloves garlic

1 cup (8 fl oz/250 ml) heavy (double) cream

1½ cups (12 fl oz/375 ml) half-and-half (half cream)

¾ tsp kosher salt

Freshly ground pepper

Preheat the oven to 400°F (200°C). Grease a 2-qt (2-l) baking or gratin dish with the butter. Peel the potatoes and, with a chef's knife or mandoline, cut them crosswise into slices about ⅛ inch (2 mm) thick. Place the potatoes in a large, heavy saucepan. Lightly crush the garlic cloves and add to the pan along with the cream, half-and-half, salt, and 10 or more twists of the pepper mill. Bring the mixture just to a boil over medium heat, then lower the heat and simmer, stirring occasionally, for 10–12 minutes. (This dish can be prepared up to this point in advance.) Transfer the potatoes and cream to the prepared dish and arrange the potatoes in layers. Bake until the potatoes are tender, about 15 minutes. Serve hot.

Crisp Rosemary Potatoes Two Ways

preparation **10** minutes | cooking **25–35** minutes | **4** servings

Boiling potatoes in salted water imbues them with seasoning and brings out their flavor, then roasting in a hot oven or frying in olive oil gives them crisp texture. Choose between these two cooking methods based on the other dishes you want to cook at the same time.

tools | large pot | baking sheet | cast-iron frying pan (optional) | chef's knife | colander | metal spatula

If you will be roasting the potatoes, preheat the oven to 400°F (200°C). Wash the potatoes, trim away any blemishes, and cut the unpeeled potatoes into irregularly shaped pieces about 1 inch (2.5 cm) thick. Bring a large pot of water to a boil and add the salt. Stir the water and add the potatoes. Lower the heat to a simmer. Cook the potatoes until they are tender and a bit "frayed" at the edges but still retain their shape, about 10 minutes. Don't worry if the skins start to peel away and a few bits of potato break off. Drain the potatoes well.

To roast the potatoes, toss them with the olive oil to coat. Arrange the potatoes in a single layer on a baking sheet, with space in between. Pick the leaves from the rosemary sprigs, coarsely chop, and sprinkle evenly over the potatoes. Bake for 10 minutes, then start turning the potatoes individually as they brown. Bake for 15 minutes more, occasionally rotating and flipping the potatoes so that they brown evenly on all sides. If the potatoes stick to the pan, loosen them with a metal spatula.

To panfry the potatoes, spread the parboiled potatoes on a baking sheet to cool. Heat the olive oil in a cast-iron frying pan over medium heat. In batches as needed, add a layer of potatoes and cook for 8 minutes, flipping the potatoes as needed so that they brown evenly. Continue cooking until the potatoes are golden on all sides, another 6–8 minutes.

Whichever method you choose, the potatoes can be served at once or held in a 250°F (120°C) oven for up to 20 minutes.

2 lb (1 kg) Yukon gold, Yellow Finn, or russet potatoes

2 tsp sea salt

¼ cup (2 fl oz/60 ml) olive oil

1 sprig fresh rosemary

Best Mashed Potatoes

preparation **10** minutes | cooking **20** minutes | **4** servings

There's no comfort food quite as comforting as mashed potatoes. All good cooks have a secret to their mashed potatoes, and here's ours: use an electric mixer to whip your mashed potatoes into a feathery lightness that your children and grandchildren (or nieces and nephews) will remember fondly. A balloon whisk also works well. Use half-and-half for the richest results and the greatest future nostalgia.

tools | large pot | chef's knife | paring knife | colander | vegetable peeler | electric mixer, whisk, or potato masher

2 lb (1 kg) russet potatoes, peeled and cut into chunks 1½ inches (4 cm) thick

Kosher salt and pepper

4 Tbsp (2 oz/60 g) butter

½ cup (4 fl oz/125 ml) half-and-half (half cream) or whole, low-fat, or nonfat milk

Put the potatoes in a large pot of cold water and season with salt. Over medium heat, bring the water to a boil, lower the heat slightly to maintain a vigorous simmer, and cook the potatoes until tender when pierced with a small knife, about 20 minutes. Drain the potatoes and return them to the pot. Let steam until dry. With an electric mixer, or by hand with a whisk or potato masher, beat in the butter. Beat in the half-and-half. Whisk vigorously until the potatoes are fluffy. Season to taste with salt and pepper and serve at once.

mashed potatoes with arugula and garlic In this variation, peppery arugula (rocket) and fragrant garlic imbue the mashed potatoes with a sweet and nutty flavor. Omit the half-and-half. Boil the potatoes as directed in the recipe above. While the potatoes cook, heat 1 Tbsp olive oil or butter over low heat and add 1 finely chopped garlic clove. Cook the garlic slowly, stirring constantly so that the garlic doesn't burn, about 10 minutes. Add ¼ lb (125 g) arugula leaves to the garlic and cook briefly until the arugula wilts slightly, about 2 minutes. After draining the potatoes and beating in the butter, coarsely chop the garlicky greens and stir them into the potatoes with any pan juices. Season to taste and serve at once.

mashed potatoes with mascarpone Mashed potatoes take on an ethereal quality with the addition of creamy Italian cheese. Follow the recipe for mashed potatoes, but use only 2 Tbsp half-and-half and add ¼ cup (2 oz/60 g) mascarpone cheese.

Potato Salad with Dijon Mustard

preparation **10** minutes | cooking **12** minutes | **4** servings

This dish belongs to the German school of potato salad, in which hot potatoes are tossed with dressing, so that the potatoes soak up its flavors. It makes a nice change from the usual baked or mashed potatoes, but it's still easy enough for an everyday supper. The best potatoes to use are so-called waxy potatoes, which hold their shape after cooking better than starchy baking potatoes. To dress the salad up for company, garnish it with fried sage leaves.

tools | small sauté pan | large pot | chef's knife | colander | slotted spoon | whisk

Cut the unpeeled potatoes into irregularly shaped pieces about 1 inch (2.5 cm) thick. Bring a large pot of water, lightly seasoned with salt, to a full boil over high heat. Add the potatoes and lower the heat to maintain a simmer. Cook until the potatoes are just tender but still retain their shape, 12–15 minutes. Drain the potatoes, transfer to a large bowl, and, while they are still warm, toss them with the wine and mustard seeds and season with salt.

While the potatoes are cooking, combine the shallots, vinegar, and 1 Tbsp salt in a nonreactive bowl and let stand for 5–10 minutes to soften the shallots. Whisk in the Dijon mustard, then drizzle in the olive oil while whisking to make a vinaigrette.

Toss the potatoes with the vinaigrette to mix thoroughly (don't worry if the potatoes break apart a bit during the tossing). Season with pepper and serve warm, with fried sage leaves arranged on top, if desired.

> **fried sage garnish**   Sturdy, flavorful fresh sage leaves become delightfully crisp when deep-fried. They pair very well with potatoes in any form. Pour peanut oil to a depth of about ½ inch (12 mm) into a small sauté pan and heat over medium heat until hot but not smoking. Pick the leaves from 1 bunch of fresh sage and pat dry. Place the sage leaves, a few at a time, in the oil and fry until they just begin to get crisp but have not begun to brown, 5–10 seconds. Remove with a slotted spoon and drain on paper towels. Repeat with the remaining sage leaves. The leaves will crisp as they cool.

4 lb (2 kg) Yellow Finn or Yukon gold potatoes

Kosher salt and pepper

½ cup (4 fl oz/125 ml) dry white wine

2 Tbsp mustard seeds, lightly toasted (page 61)

⅓ cup (2 oz/60 g) minced shallots

¼ cup (2 fl oz/60 ml) red wine vinegar

3 Tbsp Dijon mustard

¾ cup (6 fl oz/180 ml) olive oil

Fried sage garnish (*left;* optional)

Crispy Onion Rings

preparation **15** minutes | cooking **15–20** minutes | **2–4** servings

A buttermilk-and-flour batter creates a lacy, fragile coating that seals in the sweet onion flavor. These require close attention, so while one of you cooks the onion rings, the other should grill some burgers. Now that's teamwork.

tools | cast-iron frying pan | baking sheet | chef's knife | oil and candy thermometer | tongs

2 cups (16 fl oz/500 ml) well-shaken buttermilk

1 Tbsp finely chopped fresh parsley

½ tsp chopped fresh thyme

1½ cups (7½ oz/235 g) flour

2 tsp kosher salt

2 sweet onions, sliced ¼ inch (6 mm) thick and separated into rings

3 cups (24 fl oz/750 ml) grape seed or safflower oil

Pour the buttermilk into a small bowl and add the parsley and thyme. Combine the flour and salt on a plate. Dip the onions into the buttermilk mixture, then dredge in the flour and place on a baking sheet.

Pour the oil into a cast-iron frying pan and heat over medium heat to 300°–330°F (150°–165°C) on an oil/candy thermometer. Add the onion rings to the hot oil in small batches, being careful not to crowd the pan. Fry for about 3 minutes, turning once, or as needed so that they cook evenly. Adjust the heat as needed to maintain the temperature. Using tongs, transfer the onion rings to paper towels to drain and keep warm on a warm corner of the stove while you fry the next batch. Serve immediately.

Twice-Baked Potatoes with Tarragon

preparation **15** minutes | cooking **1** hour **15** minutes | **6–8** servings

These irresistible potatoes make a good side dish to serve with a main course that needs last-minute attention. You can get them ready in advance, hold the stuffed potatoes until you're ready, then put them back in the oven for 15 minutes to heat.

tools | saucepan | baking sheet | chef's knife | potato masher or large fork

4 medium russet potatoes, preferably organic

2 tsp olive oil

4 Tbsp (2 oz/60 g) butter

½ cup (4 fl oz/125 ml) milk

Kosher salt and ground pepper

3 Tbsp crème fraîche or sour cream

⅓ cup (½ oz/15 g) chopped fresh tarragon

Preheat the oven to 400°F (200°C). Prick the potatoes with a fork, rub with the olive oil, and sprinkle with 1 Tbsp water. Wrap each potato in foil and bake for 1 hour. Remove the potatoes from the oven and unwrap. Leave the oven on.

When the potatoes are cool enough to handle, halve them lengthwise. Scoop the flesh into a saucepan and set the skins aside. Mash the flesh with the butter, milk, and salt and pepper to taste. Reheat over low heat, stirring in the crème fraîche. Remove from the heat, adjust the seasoning, and stir in the tarragon.

Use a spoon to fill the potato skins with the mashed potato mixture, filling them evenly to the top. Place on a baking sheet and bake until golden on top, about 15 minutes. Serve at once.

Zucchini-Potato Pancakes

preparation **10** minutes | cooking **30** minutes | **10** small pancakes

These green pancakes can be served as a side or for brunch, lunch, supper, or a late-night snack. Cook them slowly so that they crisp on the outside and stay creamy inside. Serve with sour cream or plain yogurt, sliced prosciutto, and a salad of watercress.

tools | cast-iron frying pan | chef's knife | box grater | ladle | vegetable peeler

Shred the potato and zucchini into a bowl using the large holes of a box grater and place in a bowl. Add the onion and egg, season with the salt and pepper to taste, and mix well. The mixture will oxidize and brown slightly, so work quickly.

Heat 2 Tbsp of the oil in a large cast-iron frying pan over low heat. When the pan is hot enough to create a small sizzle, ladle the mixture into the pan to form several 3-inch (7.5-cm) pancakes, leaving some space around each pancake. Cook until golden on the bottom, 7–10 minutes. Using a spatula, turn the pancakes over until browned on the second side, about 6 minutes longer. Transfer to a plate and keep warm in a low (200°F/95°C) oven. Repeat with the remaining mixture, adding more oil if needed. Serve at once.

1 large russet potato, about ½ lb (250 g), peeled

1 large zucchini (courgette), about ½ lb (250 g), ends trimmed

⅓ cup (1½ oz/45 g) diced onion

1 large egg

1 tsp kosher salt

Freshly ground pepper

2–4 Tbsp grape seed, sunflower, or olive oil

Buttermilk Biscuits

preparation **15** minutes | cooking **15** minutes | **16** biscuits

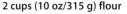

Our favorite recipe for buttermilk biscuits comes from our friend Marion Cunningham, author of the well-loved Fanny Farmer Cookbook. *We find ourselves baking these tender, flaky biscuits every time we make Grandmother's chicken (page 111).*

tools | baking sheet | chef's knife | whisk or fork

Preheat the oven to 425°F (220°C). Combine the flour, salt, baking powder, and baking soda in a bowl and stir to combine with a whisk or fork. Drop the shortening into the dry ingredients by spoonfuls, then use your fingers to work the shortening into the dry ingredients until the mixture forms fine, irregular crumbs that resemble soft bread crumbs. Add the buttermilk all at once and stir with a fork just until the dough comes together into a mass.

Place the dough on a lightly floured work surface and knead with your hands 12–14 times. Pat into an 8-inch (20-cm) square about ½ inch (12 mm) thick. Use a sharp knife to cut the dough into 2-inch (5-cm) squares. Arrange the biscuits with their edges touching on a large ungreased baking sheet. Bake until risen and golden, 15–20 minutes. Serve at once.

2 cups (10 oz/315 g) flour

½ tsp kosher salt

2 tsp baking powder

½ tsp baking soda (bicarbonate of soda)

½ cup (4 oz/125 g) solid vegetable shortening

⅔ cup (5 fl oz/160 ml) well-shaken buttermilk

Cheese Soufflé

preparation **10** minutes │ cooking **1** hour │ **2** main-course or **4** side-dish servings

Here is an old-fashioned recipe that deserves another look. Not only does it always impress guests at a dinner party, it also makes a satisfying meatless supper for two, paired with a green salad and a glass of white wine.

tools │ 2 saucepans │ soufflé dish │ box grater │ fine-mesh sieve │ rubber spatula │ stainless-steel or copper bowl (optional) │ whisk │ balloon whisk or electric mixer

5 Tbsp (2½ oz/75 g) butter, plus butter for greasing

5 Tbsp (1½ oz/50 g) flour, plus flour for dusting

1½ cups (12 fl oz/375 ml) milk

1 cup (8 fl oz/250 ml) heavy (double) cream

5 large eggs, separated

6 oz (185 g) Gruyère cheese, grated

⅛ tsp cream of tartar

Preheat the oven to 350°F (180°C). Butter and flour a 7½-inch (19-cm) diameter soufflé dish. In a large, heavy saucepan over medium-low heat, melt the butter. Stir in the flour and cook until the flour loses its raw taste, making a roux, 6–8 minutes. Do not let the roux get too brown; it should be just a light tan color. Remove the saucepan from the heat. Combine the milk and cream and slowly pour into the roux, beating constantly with a whisk until the mixture is thoroughly blended. Return the saucepan to very low heat and simmer, stirring occasionally, until the mixture thickens, about 10 minutes.

Put a saucepan with 2 inches (5 cm) of water over very low heat and bring to a bare simmer. Put the egg yolks in a stainless-steel bowl. Slowly strain the hot milk mixture through a fine-mesh sieve into the bowl with the yolks, whisking constantly until well blended. Add the cheese, then place the bowl on top of the saucepan of barely simmering water. Heat the mixture gently, stirring until the cheese is melted.

Place the egg whites in a stainless-steel bowl or copper bowl. Add the cream of tartar, unless you are using a copper bowl, in which case you can omit it. Whisk until stiff peaks form (page 234) With a wide rubber spatula, fold the whites gently into the yolk mixture, being careful not to deflate the whites by stirring too much. Pour the batter into the prepared dish (the dish will be about three-quarters full) and place in the oven.

Bake until the soufflé doubles in height and the top is a deep golden color, 40–45 minutes. Serve at once.

Holiday Stuffing

preparation **20** minutes | cooking **60** minutes | **6–8** servings

When it comes to stuffing, there are no rules. Use this recipe as a starting point and invent a holiday tradition for your own new family. This basic stuffing includes plumped currants and toasted almonds for contrast in texture and flavor, and cumin seeds for a savory depth. Minced giblets, golden brown caramelized sausage, and gently cooked greens are just a few of the ingredients you could add to create your own signature stuffing.

tools | small and medium saucepans | baking sheet | chef's knife | large baking dish

If the bread you are using is fresh, preheat the oven to 325°F (165°C). Place the bread cubes on a baking sheet and place in the oven to dry out, 10–15 minutes. Set aside. Raise the oven temperature to 375°F (190°C). Spread the almonds on a baking sheet and toast until golden and fragrant, 10–12 minutes. Coarsely chop and set aside. Leave the oven on.

Meanwhile, put the currants in a small saucepan, fill with water, and add the vinegar. Place over low heat and simmer until the currants are plump, about 10 minutes. Set aside.

Melt the butter in a medium saucepan over low heat. Add the onion, carrot, and celery and sauté until slightly softened, about 5 minutes. Add the sage, thyme, cumin seeds (if using), and stock, raise the heat to medium, and bring to a boil. Turn off the heat and let the mixture cool for 3 minutes.

Place the bread cubes in a large bowl. Pour the stock mixture over the bread. Add the almonds and currants, plus a little of their soaking liquid, and season with salt and pepper. Mix well. Spread the stuffing in a large baking dish and cover with foil. Bake for 30 minutes. Remove the foil and continue to bake until golden, about 20 minutes more. Alternatively, loosely fill the cavity of an 8- to 10-pound (4- to 5-kg) turkey with the mixture and roast immediately (see page 116). Serve the stuffing hot.

1 lb (500 g) peasant bread, day-old if possible, cut into ½-inch (12-mm) cubes

¾ cup (3 oz/90 g) whole natural almonds

⅓ cup (2 oz/60 g) dried currants

1 tsp red wine vinegar

3 Tbsp butter

1 small yellow onion, finely diced

1 small carrot, peeled and finely diced

1 rib celery, finely diced

1 tsp chopped fresh sage

½ tsp chopped fresh thyme

½ tsp toasted cumin seeds (optional)

1½ cups (12 fl oz/375 ml) chicken or vegetable stock (page 216)

Kosher salt and pepper

Polenta Two Ways

preparation **10** minutes | cooking **50** minutes | **4** servings

We have been making polenta for years—it's a staple in our home, and we hope it will become one in your household, too. You'll find it makes a nice change from the usual potatoes or rice. There are two methods for making polenta, one for "soft" polenta and the other for "hard." One of our favorite ways to serve soft polenta is with Bolognese sauce (page 143). Hard polenta is delightful with a simple warm tomato sauce (page 213) and a grating of your favorite cheese. The key to making good polenta is using fresh stone-ground cornmeal with an intense yellow hue and distinct corn flavor.

tools | baking dish or baking sheet | saucepan or pot | whisk

FOR SOFT POLENTA

¾ cup (4 oz/125 g) polenta

2 tsp kosher salt

3 Tbsp butter

A hunk of Parmesan cheese for serving

FOR HARD POLENTA

1½ cups (7½ oz/235 g) polenta

2 tsp kosher salt

3 Tbsp butter

To make soft polenta, bring 4½ cups (36 fl oz/1.1 l) water to a full boil in a heavy saucepan or pot over high heat. Lower the heat slightly and gradually add the cornmeal, whisking constantly until all the cornmeal is incorporated. Whisk often for the first 5 minutes, dispersing any lumps that appear. Lower the heat to a simmer and continue cooking, whisking every 5–10 minutes, for 20 minutes. Season the polenta with the salt, stir in the butter, and cook, whisking occasionally, until thick, smooth, and no longer grainy on the tongue, about 25 more minutes. Taste and adjust the seasoning with salt. Serve at once and pass the cheese at the table for grating on top.

To make hard polenta, bring 4½ cups (36 fl oz/1.1 l) water to a full boil in a heavy saucepan or pot over high heat. Lower the heat slightly and gradually add the cornmeal, whisking constantly until all the cornmeal is incorporated. Whisk often for the first 5 minutes, dispersing any lumps that appear. (Note that the larger amount of cornmeal used for making hard polenta may require more whisking than soft polenta in order to eliminate the lumps.) Lower the heat to a simmer and continue cooking, whisking every 5–10 minutes, for 20 minutes. Season the polenta with salt, stir in the butter, and cook for 20 more minutes, whisking occasionally. Taste and adjust the seasoning with salt. Pour the polenta into a baking dish or a baking sheet with a rim at least ½ inch (12 mm) high. Let cool completely. The polenta is now ready to cut into pieces and grill, roast, or fry. Hard polenta will keep several days wrapped and refrigerated and can be made in advance of serving.

polenta additions To vary the texture and the flavor, add ½ cup (2½ oz/75 g) diced onions and an extra pinch of salt during the second half of cooking. Also, cooked and chopped greens, such as kale or chard, turn polenta green and add flavor, vitamins, and interest to soft polenta. Stir greens into the polenta during the last 10 minutes of cooking.

White Beans and Sage

preparation **10** minutes | cooking **1¾–2¼** hours | **8–10** servings

White beans and sage go together like love and marriage. Serve this rustic Tuscan dish with grilled sausages, roast chicken (page 112), or a simple green salad and a chunk of your favorite cheese. Use leftovers to make bruschetta (page 64).

tools | deep sauté pan or pot | chef's knife | large metal spoon

Rinse and pick over the beans, discarding any misshapen or discolored beans. Place in a bowl, add water to cover by 3 inches (7.5 cm), and soak for at least 4 hours or up to overnight.

Drain the beans, rinse them with cold water, and place them in a deep sauté pan or pot. Add cold water to cover by 2 inches (5 cm) and bring to a gentle simmer over medium heat, skimming off any particles that rise to the top with a large spoon.

Add the olive oil, onion, garlic, bay leaf, and sage. Simmer for 20 minutes, stirring often so that the beans cook evenly. Add the tomato sauce and season with salt. Cook, uncovered, for 30 minutes, stirring occasionally to ensure even cooking and adding more water if necessary to keep the beans submerged. After 30 minutes, check the water level. The beans should still be submerged. Reduce the heat to low and continue to simmer gently, stirring occasionally, until the beans are tender but not falling apart, 45 minutes–1¼ hours, depending on the age of the beans. Add water if needed to keep the beans moist whille they cook.

Remove from the heat and let cool slightly. Remove the bay leaf and serve.

Note: The timing of bean cooking can vary greatly depending on the age of your dried beans. They may have been on a shelf or in a bin for 2 weeks or for 6 months, and there's no way to tell until you start to cook them. Be patient and taste-test the beans from time to time as they simmer until they are to your liking.

2 cups (14 oz/440 g) dried white beans such as cannellini, white runner beans, or butter beans

2 Tbsp extra-virgin olive oil

1 yellow onion, finely diced

2 cloves garlic, finely chopped

1 bay leaf

4 or 5 fresh sage leaves

1 cup (8 fl oz/250 ml) basic tomato sauce (page 213)

Kosher salt

Tuscan Farro

preparation **10** minutes | cooking **20** minutes | **4–6** servings

Farro, an ancient variety of wheat with a nutty flavor similar to that of wild rice, has a distinguished history in ancient Roman cuisine and has recently been enjoying a modern renaissance. Here, we combine the versatile grain with grilled broccoli rabe and shaved pecorino cheese. Using tomatoes, cucumber, or diced roasted butternut squash instead of the broccoli rabe will result in distinct and delicious variations.

tools | large pot | baking sheet | chef's knife | colander | vegetable peeler | grill

Sea salt

1½ cups (10½ oz/330 g) whole-grain farro

1 lb (500 g) broccoli rabe, tough ends trimmed

2 Tbsp olive oil

6 Tbsp (3 fl oz/90 ml) extra-virgin olive oil

1 Tbsp red wine vinegar or sherry vinegar

A hunk of pecorino Romano for shaving

Bring 4 cups (32 fl oz/1 l) water and 1 tsp sea salt to a boil in a large pot over high heat. Add the farro, stir once or twice, and cook, uncovered, until tender with a little resistance to the bite, 12–14 minutes. It should be neither too firm nor too soft. Drain the farro in a colander and immediately spread on a baking sheet to cool.

Meanwhile, prepare a charcoal or gas grill for direct-heat grilling (page 228). When the coals have burned down to glowing embers covered with gray ash, place the grill rack 5 inches (13 cm) from the fire. Toss the broccoli rabe with 1 Tbsp water, a pinch of salt, and the olive oil. Grill on one side for 2 minutes, then turn over and continue grilling until slightly charred and some of the leaves are crisp, another minute or two. Remove from fire, coarsely chop, and toss with the farro. Sprinkle with the extra-virgin olive oil and the vinegar. Season with salt, arrange on a warmed platter and, using a vegetable peeler, shave pecorino Romano over the top to garnish. Serve warm or at room temperature.

Spoon Bread with Sweet Corn

preparation **15** minutes | cooking **55** minutes | **4–6** servings

Spoon bread is a wonderful old-fashioned side dish that goes with just about anything, including pork chops (page 105), roast chicken (page 112), lamb (page 104), or grilled steak (page 67). You can replace the corn with sautéed sweet onions or wild mushrooms like morels or chanterelles. Buttermilk gives the dish a pleasant tang.

tools | medium pot | pie dish or baking dish | chef's knife | whisk

Preheat the oven to 425°F (220°C). Grease a glass pie dish or square baking dish with butter.

To shuck the corn, strip off the husks and the corn silk. Holding the ear by its tip, stand the cob on its end in a large bowl and use a sharp knife to slice the kernels off the cob into the bowl. Measure out 1 cup (6 oz/185 g) kernels and save the rest, if any, for another use.

In a medium nonreactive pot, bring 2⅔ cups (21 fl oz/660 ml) water and the salt to a boil over medium heat. Slowly pour the cornmeal into the water, whisking constantly to dissolve any lumps. Reduce the heat to medium-low and cook until the mixture becomes very thick and begins to pull away from the sides of the pan, 5–8 minutes. Stir in the butter, remove from the heat, and let cool slightly about 5 minutes. Meanwhile, in a bowl, whisk together the eggs, buttermilk, and cream until well blended. Add the egg mixture and corn kernels to the cornmeal mixture and stir until blended. Pour the batter into the prepared dish.

Bake until the top is golden brown and a skewer inserted in the center comes out clean, 35–40 minutes. The spoon bread will rise much like a soufflé. Serve at once.

Butter for greasing

1 or 2 ears white or yellow corn

1 Tbsp kosher salt

1 cup (5 oz/155 g) fine-grind cornmeal

2 Tbsp butter

4 large eggs

1 cup (8 fl oz/250 ml) well-shaken buttermilk

⅓ cup (3 fl oz/80 ml) heavy (double) cream

Tabbouleh

preparation **45** minutes | **6–8** servings

Bright-flavored ingredients like lemon juice, mint, and tomatoes make this bulgur salad particularly appealing. It is ideal picnic fare, as it is best at room temperature and it travels well. Serve with pita bread and hummus.

tools | chef's knife | citrus reamer | fine-mesh sieve

1 cup (6 oz/185 g) medium-grind bulgur

2 cups (2 oz/60 g) fresh parsley

1 cup (1 oz/30 g) mint

6 green (spring) onions

3 medium tomatoes

Juice of 1 lemon

⅓ cup (3 fl oz/80 ml) olive oil

Kosher salt and pepper

Put the bulgur in a large bowl and add cold water to cover generously (you want the bulgur to remain covered after it absorbs some of the water). Allow the bulgur to swell and soften for 30–40 minutes.

Finely chop the parsley and mint. Slice the green onions crosswise, including the tender green tops. Core and coarsely chop the tomatoes.

Drain the bulgur in a fine-mesh sieve, pressing out all the excess moisture with the back of a large spoon. If the bulgur still seems moist, wrap it in a clean kitchen towel and squeeze out the remaining water.

In a serving bowl, toss the bulgur with the parsley, mint, green onions, tomatoes, and lemon juice. Stir in the olive oil and season with salt and pepper. Serve.

Sautéed Apples

preparation **10** minutes | cooking **10** minutes | **4** servings

Choose sweet yet tart, firm apples, such as Sierra beauty, Braeburn, Fuji, Gala, or pippin. Sautéed apples accompany pork or turkey especially well, or try them with duck breasts (page 121) and use the duck fat in place of the butter to cook the apples.

tools | medium sauté pan | paring knife or vegetable peeler | wooden spatula

3 or 4 medium apples

1 Tbsp butter

¼ tsp kosher salt

Pinch of sugar

Peel the apples and cut into wedges ½–1 inch (12 mm–2.5 cm) thick, depending on the size of the apples. Trim away the seeds and cores.

Melt the butter in a medium sauté pan over low heat. Add the apple wedges and cook for 5 minutes, then sprinkle with the salt and sugar. Arrange and adjust the apples as they begin to soften to ensure that each wedge is cooking evenly, and continue to cook for 2–3 minutes more. Turn the apples over as they begin to color slightly. Raise the heat to medium to start browning the apples and sauté vigorously until evenly golden, about 2 minutes more. Keep the apples on the firmer side of doneness for a toothy yet soft texture. Serve at once, or set aside and reheat when ready to serve.

Desserts

We think of dessert not so much as a sweet afterthought, but as the crowning touch—balancing, complementing, and, in a sense, honoring the meal it follows. These varied dessert recipes represent some of our favorites, from lighter-than-light lemon angel food cake that melts in your mouth to little chocolate pots de crème in all their glorious silkiness. We often find perfectly ripe fresh fruit makes the best ending to a meal, and that instinct inspired the irresistible nectarine and blackberry crisp with a rich almond-butter topping and the chilled and creamy blueberry fool.

Blueberry Fool

preparation **10** minutes | cooking **10** minutes | chilling **1** hour | **4** servings

Fool is an English dessert of puréed fruit. The combination of tart berries and smooth cream is a memorable match for a warm summer night. A splash of crème de cassis, a liqueur made from black currants, brings out the flavor of the blueberries.

tools | medium saucepan | electric mixer | box grater or zester | rubber spatula

1 cup (4 oz/125 g) blueberries

3 Tbsp sugar (divided)

1 Tbsp crème de cassis

1 cup (8 fl oz/250 ml) heavy (double) cream

½ tsp vanilla extract (essence)

¼ tsp grated or minced lemon zest

Combine the blueberries with ⅓ cup (3 fl oz/80 ml) water in a saucepan over medium heat and simmer until the berries are tender, about 10 minutes. Add 2 Tbsp of the sugar and the liqueur and stir. Pour into a bowl, let cool, cover, and chill for 1–2 hours.

With an electric mixer on medium speed, whip the cream in a large bowl with the remaining 1 Tbsp sugar and vanilla until soft peaks form when the whisk is lifted. Fold in the blueberries and lemon zest gently with a rubber spatula.

Divide the fruit mixture evenly among chilled glasses or bowls (or, if desired, you can pipe it, using a pastry bag). The fool should be served quite cold; it can be chilled in its glass briefly before serving, if needed.

Mascarpone-Stuffed Figs

preparation **10** minutes | cooking **15** minutes | **2–4** servings

On a late-summer evening, the garden or terrace is the natural place to savor these luscious figs. If you have cause to celebrate, enjoy them with Champagne.

tools | baking dish | baking sheet | chef's knife | citrus zester | whisk

⅓ cup (2 oz/60 g) whole almonds with the skin

8 very ripe figs

½ cup (4 oz/125 g) mascarpone cheese, at room temperature

1 tsp orange zest strips

1 Tbsp lavender or wildflower honey

Preheat the oven to 350°F (180°C). Spread the almonds on a baking sheet and toast until fragrant, about 10 minutes. Coarsely chop and set aside.

Trim the stems from the figs and cut the figs in half lengthwise. Place in a shallow baking dish large enough to hold the figs in a single layer, with the cut sides of the figs facing up. Bake until the figs are swollen and heated through, about 15 minutes. Remove the figs from the oven. Reserve any fig drippings in the baking dish to garnish the figs.

In a medium bowl, whisk the mascarpone with the orange zest. Arrange the figs on individual plates and place a small dollop of the mascarpone mixture on each fig. Drizzle the figs with the honey along with any reserved fig juices. Sprinkle the almonds over the top and serve.

Almond Cookies

preparation **30** minutes | chilling **3** hours | cooking **8** minutes per batch | about **96** cookies

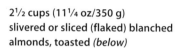

Delicate almond cookies are a nice treat for the cold months, when nuts are newly harvested. Serve these with hot cider at holiday time.

tools | baking sheets | chef's knife | electric mixer | parchment (baking) paper | wire racks

In a bowl, stir together the almonds and both flours; set aside.

In the bowl of an electric mixer fitted with the paddle attachment, beat the butter on medium speed until soft and creamy. Add the salt and powdered sugar and mix on medium-low speed until thoroughly combined, about 5 minutes, scraping down the bowl as necessary. Reduce the speed to low and add the egg; mix until blended. Add the flour mixture. As soon as the dough comes together, stop the mixer.

Scrape the dough onto a large sheet of plastic wrap. Using another piece of wrap to help shape the dough, gently press it into a rectangle about 4½ by 8 inches (11.5 by 20 cm) and about 1½ inches (4 cm) thick. Wrap the dough in plastic wrap and refrigerate until it is firm enough to slice, at least 3 hours or up to several days.

Preheat the oven to 400°F (200°C). Line 2 baking sheets with parchment (baking) paper.

Unwrap the dough, trim the edges to neaten them, and slice the dough length-wise into 3 logs each 1½ inches (4 cm) wide. Slice each log crosswise into square cookies ¼ inch (6 mm) thick. In batches as needed, arrange the squares ½ inch (12 mm) apart on the lined baking sheets.

Bake until lightly browned around the edges, about 8 minutes, switching racks and rotating the baking sheets halfway through for even baking. Let cool on the baking sheets until slightly set, then transfer the cookies to wire racks to crisp before serving them.

2½ cups (11¼ oz/350 g) slivered or sliced (flaked) blanched almonds, toasted *(below)*

1¼ cups (5 oz/155 g) cake (soft-wheat) flour

1 cup (5 oz/155 g) all-purpose (plain) flour

1 cup (8 oz/250 g) butter, slightly softened

¾ tsp kosher salt

2⅔ cups (11 oz/330 g) powdered (icing) sugar

1 large egg, at room temperature

> **toasting nuts** To toast nuts, spread them on a baking sheet and toast in a 350°F (180°C) oven for 7–15 minutes, depending on size. Shake the pan occasionally.

Nectarine and Blackberry Crisp

preparation **30** minutes | cooking **20** minutes | **4–6** servings

Nectarines and blackberries both enjoy a brief but glorious midsummer season. When they are available, you've got to make the most of them. A crisp is a very simple fruit dessert that lets delicious ripe fruit play the starring role. Serve with vanilla ice cream, if desired, to cap off a barbecue.

tools | large pot | baking sheet | 9-inch (23-cm) pie pan or baking dish | paring knife | slotted spoon | whisk

FOR THE TOPPING

Scant 1⅓ cups (7 oz/220 g) flour

⅓ cup (2½ oz/75 g) firmly packed brown sugar

⅓ cup (3 oz/90 g) granulated sugar

¼ tsp kosher salt

¼ tsp ground cinnamon

1 cup (5½ oz/170 g) whole almonds with the skin, toasted and coarsely chopped (page 199)

¾ cup (6 oz/185 g) cold butter

FOR THE FRUIT

5 or 6 ripe nectarines

1 cup (4 oz/125 g) fresh blackberries

Pinch of kosher salt

2 Tbsp granulated sugar

1 tsp balsamic vinegar

To make the topping, whisk together the flour, both sugars, the salt, and the cinnamon. Stir in the almonds. Cut the butter into small pieces and work into the flour mixture with your fingertips, rubbing and smearing, until the topping comes together and has a crumbly texture.

Preheat the oven to 350°F (180°C).

To prepare the fruit, bring a large pot of water to a boil and have a large bowl of ice water ready nearby. Immerse each nectarine into the boiling water for 4–5 seconds, depending on the ripeness, then remove it from the pot with a slotted spoon and plunge the nectarine into the ice water for several seconds. Use your fingertips to pull the skin off the nectarines; it should peel right off. Remove any stubborn bits of peel with a paring knife. Halve each nectarine and discard the pit. Slice each half into 3 wedges and place in a bowl. Add the berries, salt, and granulated sugar. Drizzle the vinegar over the fruit and toss to mix. Spoon the mixture into a 9-inch (23-cm) pie pan or a baking dish small enough so that the fruit comes nearly up to the top.

Sprinkle ¾ cup (4½ oz/140 g) of the topping over the fruit. Place the pan on a baking sheet to catch any drips and place the baking sheet in the oven. Bake until the topping is golden brown and the fruit juices have begun to bubble up the sides, 20–25 minutes. Remove from the oven and let cool slightly before serving.

Note: This recipe yields more topping than you will need, but is best made in larger quantities and stores very well tightly covered in the refrigerator or freezer for next time.

Strawberry Shortcakes

preparation **20** minutes | cooking **20** minutes | **6** servings

Fragrant berries paired with sweet cream and tender biscuits are the epitome of summer ease and remind us that simplicity never falls out of favor. Make the shortcake dough ahead, roll it out, and refrigerate it until you are ready to bake. Cut up the berries and marinate them before serving for the best flavor. Replace berries with other summer fruits that appeal to you, like peaches or nectarines, or a combination of fruits.

tools | baking sheet | paring knife | brush | citrus reamer | fine-mesh sieve (optional) | wooden spoon | balloon whisk or electric mixer | rolling pin | wire rack

To prepare the strawberries, roll them on paper towels to blot any excess moisture. Trim off the stem, remove the core, and trim away any unripe white areas or blemishes from each berry, then cut lengthwise into quarters. Sprinkle with the granulated sugar and add the orange juice and orange blossom water. Toss well and let sit for 30 minutes, stirring occasionally.

Meanwhile, make the shortcakes: Preheat the oven to 375°F (190°C). Combine the flour, granulated sugar, baking powder, and salt in a mixing bowl and stir with a fork. With the fork and your fingers, work the butter into the flour mixture until the butter is broken down into unevenly sized pieces, the largest as big as a pea. Pour in the 1 cup cream, letting it flow over all of the flour mixture. Mix quickly with a wooden spoon or an electric mixer on low speed just until the dough starts to come together. The dough should look and feel sticky in spots. Turn the dough out onto a lightly floured, cool work surface. Dust the top lightly with flour and, using a rolling pin, roll the dough out into a rectangle about 5 by 7½ inches (13 by 19 cm) and 1 inch (2.5 cm) thick. Using a sharp knife, cut into six 2½-inch (6-cm) squares. Arrange the squares on a baking sheet about 2 inches (5 cm) apart and brush the tops with the 1 Tbsp cream. Bake until risen and golden, 20–25 minutes. Transfer to a wire rack and let cool briefly.

Meanwhile, with a balloon whisk or an electric mixer on medium-low speed, gently whip the 1½ cups cream in a large bowl with the vanilla and 1 Tbsp powdered sugar until soft peaks form when the whisk is lifted. Cover and refrigerate until needed.

To serve, split each biscuit in half horizontally and place the bottom half on a dessert plate or in a shallow bowl. Spoon the strawberries and their juices on top. Place a dollop of whipped cream on top of the berries and top with the other half of the biscuit. Dust with powdered sugar, if desired, and serve.

FOR THE STRAWBERRIES

3 cups (12 oz/375 g) very ripe strawberries

¼ cup (2 oz/60 g) granulated sugar

¾ cup (6 fl oz/180 ml) fresh orange juice

2 tsp orange blossom water (optional)

FOR THE SHORTCAKES

2 cups (10 oz/315 g) flour

3 Tbsp granulated sugar

1 Tbsp baking powder

½ tsp kosher salt

5 Tbsp (2½ oz/75 g) cold salted butter, cut into ¼-inch (6-mm) pieces

1 cup (8 fl oz/250 ml) plus 1 Tbsp heavy (double) cream

1½ cups (12 fl oz/375 ml) cold heavy (double) cream

½ tsp vanilla extract (essence)

1 Tbsp powdered (icing) sugar, plus sugar for dusting (optional)

Ginger Cake with Hard Sauce

preparation **20** minutes | cooking **25** minutes | cooling **20** minutes | **8** servings

The unmistakable taste of fresh ginger shines through in this cake, which is extremely tender and flavorful, and stays moist stored at room temperature if well wrapped. If you prefer, try fruit preserves or ice cream with this cake instead of the hard sauce.

tools | 9-inch (23-cm) round cake pan | chef's knife | blender or box grater | fine-mesh sieve | skewer | whisk

1 large knob fresh ginger
(enough to make 3 Tbsp puréed)

1 cup (8 fl oz/250 ml)
dark molasses

1 cup (8 oz/250 g) sugar

1 cup (8 fl oz/250 ml) peanut
or canola oil

2½ cups (12½ oz/390 g) flour

1 tsp ground cloves

1 tsp ground cinnamon

1 Tbsp baking powder

½ tsp kosher salt

Hard sauce for serving (right)

Preheat the oven to 325°F (165°C). Use the edge of a spoon to scrape the skin from the ginger. Slice the ginger across the grain into ½-inch (12-mm) pieces. Pulse the ginger in a blender to purée, or use the finest rasps on a box grater to grate the ginger. Measure out 3 level Tbsp and put in a medium mixing bowl. Add 1 cup (8 fl oz/250 ml) cool water, the molasses, sugar, and oil. Mix vigorously with a whisk until the sugar is dissolved and the mixture is glossy. In a separate bowl, sift together the flour, cloves, cinnamon, baking powder, and salt. Add the flour mixture to the ginger mixture and mix thoroughly until the batter is smooth.

Pour into an ungreased 9-inch (23-cm) round cake pan. Bake until a skewer inserted in the center comes out clean, 25–35 minutes. Let the cake cool in the pan for 20 minutes, then turn out onto a serving plate. Serve at room temperature or still slightly warm, with hard sauce on the side.

hard sauce The traditional accompaniment to English plum pudding, hard sauce pairs well with any hearty autumn or winter dessert. Combine ½ cup (4 oz/125 g) butter at room temperature, ¾ cup (2½ oz/75 g) sifted powdered (icing) sugar, 1 Tbsp dark rum or brandy or 1 tsp vanilla extract (essence), and ⅛ tsp freshly grated nutmeg and mix well to blend. If desired, chill before serving.

Raspberry-Lemon Tart

preparation **30** minutes | cooking **10** minutes | chilling **2** hours | **8** servings

This tart is elegant enough to serve for a shower or fancy brunch, and both the tart shell and the lemon curd can be made ahead of time. When choosing raspberries, look for ones that are pretty, plump, and firm. Most important, smell the berries and choose the ones with the deepest perfume. To make the tart in winter, replace the berries with sliced mango.

tools | large pot | small saucepan | 9-inch (23-cm) tart pan | chef's knife | box grater | brush | citrus reamer | fine-mesh sieve | small spatula | stainless-steel bowl | whisk

Follow the directions on page 218 to make the tart shell.

To make the lemon curd, whisk together the whole eggs, egg yolks, and sugar in a large stainless-steel bowl. Whisk in the lemon zest, lemon juice, and salt. Set up a double boiler by putting 2 inches (5 cm) of water in a pot over low heat to create steam. Place the bowl with the egg mixture on top of the pot, not touching the water, and heat the eggs, whisking constantly to avoid scrambling them, until the mixture is thick enough to coat the back of a spoon, about 10 minutes. Remove the bowl from the heat and whisk in the butter. Strain the mixture through a fine-mesh sieve into a clean medium bowl, and place the bowl in a larger bowl filled with ice water. Whisk occasionally until the lemon curd is completely cool. Transfer the curd to a smaller container, cover, and refrigerate until completely cold, about 2 hours.

To assemble the tart, in a small saucepan, combine the raspberry jam with the kirsch and stir over medium heat until warm and liquid, 3–4 minutes. To strain out the seeds, pour the jam mixture through a fine-mesh sieve held over a bowl, pressing against the mixture with the back of a spoon. Brush a very thin layer of the jam mixture onto the back of the prebaked tart shell. Fill the shell with the chilled lemon curd and spread with a small spatula or the bottom of a large spoon, jiggling the shell gently so that the surface of the lemon curd is even. Gently spread out the berries on your work surface so you can see the condition of each berry. Discard (or eat) the imperfect ones. Place the remaining raspberries on top of the curd in one snug layer, with the bottoms of the raspberries facing upward. Refrigerate the tart until ready to serve.

Tart shell (page 218)

FOR THE LEMON CURD

3 large whole eggs

3 large egg yolks

½ cup (4 oz/125 g) sugar

¼ cup (½ oz/15 g) grated or minced lemon zest

½ cup (4 fl oz/125 ml) fresh lemon juice

¼ tsp kosher salt

4 Tbsp (2 oz/60 g) butter, cubed and slightly softened

⅓ cup (3 oz/90 g) raspberry jam

½ tsp kirsch

2 cups (8 oz/250 g) raspberries

Sabayon with Peaches

preparation **10** minutes | cooking **5** minutes | **4** servings

Sabayon, a frothy golden foam made with wine, seduces all who taste it. Halve the recipe to serve two—what could be more perfect for an anniversary dinner or Valentine's Day dessert? Silky fresh peaches are the perfect accompaniment and should be eaten immediately after slicing, before the flesh has a chance to oxidize and darken. Choose the ripest peaches you can find and serve the dessert in old-fashioned champagne saucers.

tools | pot | whisk

8 large egg yolks

6 Tbsp (3 oz/90 g) sugar

¾ cup (6 fl oz/180 ml) Champagne or sparkling wine

3 or 4 large perfectly ripe peaches, unpeeled and sliced into wedges

Combine the egg yolks and sugar in a large stainless-steel bowl. Whisk in the Champagne and place the bowl over a pot with 1–2 inches (2.5–5 cm) of gently simmering water. The pot should be deep enough so that the bottom of the bowl does not touch the water. Reduce the heat to low—you don't want to cook the egg, but simply create a light mist of steam below the bowl that will gently warm and thicken the egg. Whisk the egg mixture constantly until it thickens, 2–3 minutes. There should be no liquid left at the bottom of the bowl. Remove from the heat.

Arrange the peach slices in individual shallow bowls and spoon the warm sabayon on top.

using a double boiler   A double boiler is a set of two pans, one nested atop the other, with room for water to simmer in the bottom pan. Delicate foods such as chocolate and custards are placed in the top pan to heat them gently, or to melt them in the case of chocolate. The top pan should not touch the water beneath it, and the water should not be allowed to boil. A tight fit between the pans ensures that no water or steam can escape and mix with the ingredients in the top, which can cause melting chocolate to seize or stiffen. You can create your own double boiler by placing a heatproof mixing bowl or a slightly smaller saucepan over a larger one.

Chocolate Layer Cake

preparation **50** minutes | cooking **45** minutes | **8** servings

This chocolate cake is perfect for birthdays! The use of cake flour and sour cream makes this cake luscious and tender. Serve this with your favorite ice cream à la mode.

tools | two 8-inch (20-cm) cake pans | electric mixer | cake comb (optional) | icing spatula | skewer | wire rack | wooden spoon

Preheat the oven to 350°F (180°C). Butter and flour two 8-inch (20-cm) round cake pans. Melt the chocolate in the top of a double boiler (see note on opposite page) or in the microwave, then set aside to cool.

Sift the cake flour, sugar, baking soda, and salt together into a large bowl. Add the butter and the sour cream and beat for about 1 minute. Stir in the melted chocolate, then add the eggs, vanilla, and hot water and beat for 1 minute more.

Divide the batter between the prepared pans and jiggle the pans to even out the batter. Bake until a skewer inserted into the center comes out clean, 30–35 minutes. Remove from the oven and let cool in the pans on a wire rack for about 5 minutes, then turn the cakes out of the pans and let cool completely on the rack.

To fill and frost, place a cake layer flat side up on a serving plate and tuck 4 waxed paper strips under the sides to keep the plate clean. Using an icing spatula, put a large dollop of frosting in the center of the cake and spread it over the layer. Place the second cake layer on top, flat side down. Brush off any loose crumbs and apply a thin coating of frosting to the top and sides of the cake. Now frost the sides, sweeping upward and creating a rim of frosting above the top edge of the cake. Drop the rest of the frosting at 3 or 4 points on the top of the cake and spread it in a circular motion outward from the center, meeting the rim of frosting at a right angle. Smooth the top and any excess frosting that may have fallen down the sides. If desired, use a cake comb to create a pattern in the frosting. Remove the waxed paper and serve.

chocolate buttercream frosting Heat ¾ cup (6 fl oz/180 ml) milk in a saucepan over medium heat until small bubbles form around the edge. Meanwhile, combine 3 large egg yolks, 1 cup plus 2 Tbsp (3 oz/90 g) sifted powdered sugar, and ¼ tsp salt in a mixing bowl. Beat vigorously with an electric mixer until blended and smooth. Slowly pour the hot milk over the yolk mixture, stirring constantly with a spoon. Pour the mixture into the saucepan, add 3 oz (90 g) chopped unsweetened chocolate, and cook over medium-low heat, stirring constantly, until slightly thickened. Do not allow to boil. Remove from the heat, add 3 teaspoons vanilla extract (essence), and beat until the mixture is cool. When cool, begin beating in 1½ cups (12 oz/375 g) slightly softened butter, a tablespoon at a time, beating until smooth after each addition. If the frosting begins to separate, beat well.

Butter for greasing

4 oz (125 g) unsweetened chocolate

2 cups (8 oz/250 g) cake (soft-wheat) flour

1½ cups (12 oz/375 g) sugar

1 tsp baking soda (bicarbonate of soda)

1 tsp kosher salt

⅓ cup (3 oz/90g) butter, slightly softened

1 cup (8 oz/250 g) sour cream

2 large eggs

2 tsp vanilla extract (essence)

2 Tbsp hot water

Chocolate buttercream frosting (below)

Lemon Angel Food Cake

preparation **20** minutes | cooking **30** minutes | cooling **1** hour | **8** servings

Light and airy angel food cake requires a specialized angel-food cake pan, a tall, straight-sided tube pan that helps cook the delicate batter from the center as well as the outside and helps the cake rise high. Separating the eggs requires care. Don't let a drop of the broken yolk get mixed in with the egg whites, or this bit of fat will prevent them from whipping up properly. Also, make sure the bowl in which you whip them is spotlessly clean without a trace of grease, for the same reason.

tools | angel-food cake pan | serrated utility knife | electric mixer | citrus reamer | fine-mesh sieve | rubber spatula | skewer

1 cup (4 oz/125 g) cake (soft-wheat) flour

1½ cups (12 oz/375 g) granulated sugar (divided)

½ tsp kosher salt

2 cups (16 fl oz/500 ml) egg whites, from 12 to 13 large eggs, at room temperature (page 233)

½ tsp vanilla extract (essence)

2 tsp fresh lemon juice

1½ tsp cream of tartar

Powdered (icing) sugar for dusting

Fresh fruit for serving (optional)

Whipped cream for serving (optional)

Position a rack in the lower third of the oven and preheat to 350°F (180°C). Have ready at hand an ungreased 10-inch (25-cm) angel food cake pan. Sift the flour, ½ cup (4 oz/125 g) of the granulated sugar, and the salt together into a bowl. Set aside. In a large, spotlessly clean nonreactive bowl, combine the egg whites, vanilla extract, and lemon juice. Using an electric mixer, whip the egg white mixture with the whisk attachment on low speed for 1 minute. Add the cream of tartar and continue mixing on low speed for 30 seconds, then increase the speed to medium. Gradually sprinkle the remaining 1 cup (8 oz/250 g) granulated sugar into the egg whites and continue beating on medium speed until soft, drooping peaks form when the beater is lifted. The mixture should be voluminous but still moist.

Sift one-third of the flour mixture on top of the egg mixture and fold in with a rubber spatula. Scrape down the sides of the bowl to ensure thorough blending. Add the remaining flour mixture and quickly fold in, scraping the sides and bottom of the bowl.

Fill the angel food cake pan with the batter (the batter will begin deflating almost immediately, so work quickly). Gently smooth the surface of the batter with the spatula and bake for 30 minutes. To test for doneness, insert a long wooden skewer in the center; it should come out clean. If cake batter still clings to the skewer, bake for a few minutes longer, or until the skewer comes out clean.

Remove the cake from the oven and immediately invert the pan to cool upside down on its feet. If your pan does not have feet, invert it onto the neck of a full wine or similar bottle. Let the cake cool completely, then carefully run a long, thin knife around the inside and outside edges of the cake. Gently tap the pan to turn the cake out, using the knife if necessary to coax the cake out of the pan. Place the cake on your favorite serving platter. To slice the cake, use a serrated knife dipped in water to keep the cake from sticking to the knife. Dust with powdered sugar and serve with fresh fruit and whipped cream, if desired.

Chocolate Pots de Crème

preparation **20** minutes | cooking **30** minutes | chilling **2** hours | **6** servings

We use small ramekins for this recipe so these creams cook evenly and quickly. This makes the perfect amount of rich custard to complete a meal. if you like, finish these rich little chocolate puddings with a dollop of whipped cream on top.

tools | deep baking dish or roasting pan | medium saucepan | small ramekins or custard cups | chef's knife | large glass measuring cup | fine-mesh sieve | wooden spoon

Preheat the oven to 300°F (150°C). Heat the milk and cream in a medium saucepan over medium heat until you see small bubbles form along the sides of the pan. Add the chocolate; stir just to melt chocolate (do not let it cook). Set the mixture aside to cool slightly.

In a bowl, gently combine the egg yolks and sugar with a wooden spoon until the sugar is dissolved. Do not create too many bubbles as you mix; they will be hard to settle. Slowly pour the chocolate mixture into the egg yolk mixture, stirring constantly. Pour through a fine-mesh sieve into a large glass measuring cup. Spoon off any foam from the surface.

Arrange six ½-cup (4–fl oz/125-ml) ramekins or custard cups in a deep baking dish or roasting pan. Divide the chocolate mixture evenly among the ramekins, filling each partway. Fill the pan with water to reach about halfway up the sides of the ramekins and cover loosely with foil to prevent a skin from forming on the creams. Bake until the creams are just firm at the edges but still tremble in the center when gently shaken, about 30 minutes.

Remove the pan from the oven and carefully remove the ramekins from the water. Allow to cool completely before covering and refrigerating for at least 2 hours or overnight to set. Serve chilled, dolloped with whipped cream, if desired.

½ cup (4 fl oz/125 ml) whole milk

¾ cup (6 fl oz/180 ml) heavy (double) cream

3 oz (90 g) best-quality bittersweet chocolate, finely chopped

3 large egg yolks

⅓ cup (3 oz/90 g) sugar

Whipped cream for serving (optional)

Basic Recipes

The recipes that follow serve as building blocks for the other recipes in this cookbook, as well as other cookbooks. Although some of these items can be purchased for convenience, you'll find that your homemade dishes taste even better if you make these elements yourself. Some can be made ahead, perhaps on a quiet weekend day when you have some free time to devote to cooking, and kept on hand in the pantry until needed.

Crème Fraîche

preparation **5** minutes | cooking **5** minutes | standing **8** hours | **1** cup (8 fl oz/250 ml)

Crème fraîche is similar to sour cream but with a milder flavor. With a little advance planning, it's very simple to make at home.

tools | small saucepan

1 cup (8 fl oz/250 ml) heavy (double) cream

1 Tbsp buttermilk

Combine the cream and buttermilk in a small saucepan and warm over medium-low heat. Do not allow to simmer. Remove mixture from the heat, cover loosely, and let thicken and sour at warm room temperature until it suits your taste, 8–48 hours. Once it is as thick and flavorful as you want it, chill well before using.

Basic Vinaigrette

preparation **15** minutes | about **½** cup (4 fl oz/125 ml)

Simple, yet far superior in flavor to any store-bought vinaigrette. This keeps in a cool, dark cupboard for up to 1 week.

tools | chef's knife

2 Tbsp red wine vinegar

Kosher salt and pepper

1 small clove garlic (optional)

½ cup (4 fl oz/125 ml) extra-virgin olive oil

1 tsp Dijon mustard (optional)

Combine the vinegar and salt in a small jar with a tight-fitting lid or in a non-reactive bowl. If using the garlic clove, crush it lightly with the palm of your hand or the flat side of a chef's knife to release its flavor. Add to the vinegar and let stand for 10 minutes. Remove and discard the garlic. Add the olive oil and mustard, if using, then place the lid on the jar and shake vigorously, or whisk until the ingredients are blended. Season to taste with pepper.

Basic Mayonnaise

preparation **15** minutes | 1¾ cups (14 fl oz/430 ml)

Mayonnaise is not difficult to make, as long as you remember to drizzle the oil into the egg very slowly at first to help it combine, or emulsify. The flavor is outstanding.

tools | blender or food processor

Warm the uncracked egg in a bowl of hot tap water for 3 minutes. In a blender or food processor, combine the egg, mustard, lemon juice, salt, and pepper. Combine the vegetable and olive oils. With the motor running, slowly drizzle the combined oils into the blender (this should take several minutes) to make a thick mayonnaise. Stir in 1 Tbsp hot water.

Note: This recipe contains uncooked egg. For more details, see page 226.

> **spicy mayonnaise** Combine ½ cup (4 fl oz/125 ml) basic mayonnaise with the juice of ½ lemon, 1 tsp chili oil, ¼ tsp Tabasco (hot red pepper) sauce, and ¼ tsp ground cayenne. Blend well.

1 large egg

1 tsp Dijon mustard

1 tsp lemon juice or white wine vinegar

1 tsp kosher salt

¼ tsp pepper

¾ cup (6 fl oz/180 ml) vegetable oil

¾ cup (6 fl oz/180 ml) olive oil

Basic Tomato Sauce

preparation **15** minutes | cooking **45** minutes | 2½ cups (20 fl oz/625 ml)

This all-purpose sauce using good-quality canned tomatoes, perferably organic, can be used winter or summer in a wide variety of dishes.

tools | large pot | chef's knife | kitchen string

Tie the basil sprigs together with kitchen string. Heat the olive oil in a large, heavy nonreactive pot over medium heat. Add the onions and garlic and sauté until the onions are soft and translucent, about 15 minutes. Add the tomatoes, sugar, bay leaf, basil, and salt. Reduce the heat to low and simmer, uncovered, stirring occasionally, until you have a good sauce consistency, about 30 minutes. Taste and add more salt, if necessary. Remove the bay leaf and basil. The sauce will keep for up to 1 week covered in the refrigerator, or frozen for up to 1 month.

Notes: As a finishing touch, stir in 1–2 Tbsp fruity extra-virgin olive oil. In the height of summer, when flavorful fresh tomatoes are available, substitute 2 lb (1 kg) fresh tomatoes, peeled, seeded, and chopped (page 234), for the canned tomatoes.

3 sprigs fresh basil

3 Tbsp olive oil

2 yellow onions, finely chopped

3 cloves garlic, minced

1 can (28 oz/875 g) diced plum (Roma) tomatoes

1 tsp sugar

½ bay leaf

1 tsp kosher salt, or more to taste

Hard-Cooked Eggs, Perfected

preparation **5** minutes │ cooking **8** minutes

Smooth, creamy yolks and tender whites are the hallmarks of perfect hard-cooked eggs. We feel strongly that everyone should know how to cook these eggs, and we hope that once you learn how, you'll be inspired to use these perfect eggs to garnish foods such as asparagus, green beans, pizzas, crostini, and salads.

tools │ saucepan │ slotted spoon

3 or 4 fresh large eggs

Kosher salt

Prepare an ice bath by putting 2–3 cups (16–24 fl oz / 500–750 ml) water and ice in a large bowl.

In a saucepan, bring 1 qt (1 l) salted water to a full boil over high heat. Lower the eggs gently into the water with a slotted spoon and reduce the heat slightly to a gentle simmer; if cooked in boiling water, the eggs may crack against the pot. Exactly 8 minutes after adding the eggs to the water, remove them with the slotted spoon and plunge them into the ice bath to stop the cooking. When cool, after 30 seconds–1 minute, crack and peel the eggs. The shells will peel more easily after the ice bath.

Poached Eggs

preparation **5** minutes │ cooking **5** minutes │ **2** servings

Like hard-cooked eggs, poached eggs are an item that you'll find many uses for once you master the simple technique of preparing them.

tools │ pot or sauté pan │ paring knife │ ramekin │ slotted spoon

Kosher salt

4 large eggs

Put 2–3 inches (5–7.5 cm) of water in a shallow pot or large sauté pan. Season the water with salt and bring to a simmer over medium heat. One at a time, and working quickly, crack each egg into a small ramekin and carefully slip it into the water. Leave space around the eggs. Adjust the heat so that the water barely simmers. Poach the eggs gently for 3–5 minutes, depending on the desired doneness. Remove each egg from the water with a slotted spoon, and while the egg is still in the spoon, blot the bottom dry with a kitchen towel and trim off the ragged edges with a paring knife.

Fresh Bread Crumbs

preparation **10** minutes

There is really no substitute for freshly made bread crumbs. They lend texture and richness to many dishes such as pasta, sautéed greens, blanched asparagus, roasted fish. Do not substitute fresh bread crumbs for fine dry crumbs.

tools | food processor

Remove the crust from a French-style baguette. Cut or tear the interior crumb into 2-inch (5-cm) pieces. Put the bread in a food processor and pulse until you have irregular, fluffy, pea-sized pieces. Don't overpulse, or the crumbs will become too fine. Freeze freshly made bread crumbs wrapped in plastic for up to 2 weeks.

Stale peasant bread or baguette

Toasted Bread Crumbs

preparation **5** minutes | cooking **12** minutes | **1** cup (2 oz/60 g)

Toasted crumbs make a delightful savory topping to any number of dishes.

tools | baking sheet

Preheat the oven to 325°F (165°C). Toss the crumbs with the olive oil and salt.

Spread the crumbs on a baking sheet and bake until crisp and very golden, 12–15 minutes. Toasted bread crumbs may be stored for up to 3 days in a sealed jar. Reheat briefly in 300°F (150°C) oven right before needed.

1 cup (2 oz/60 g) fresh bread crumbs (above)

1 Tbsp olive oil

Pinch of kosher salt

Crostini

preparation **10** minutes | cooking **12** minutes | **30** crostini

Make crostini to serve with a topping as party food or to garnish a soup.

tools | baking sheets | serrated bread knife | brush

Preheat the oven to 350°F (180°C). Slice the baguette on the bias into 30 slices, each 2 inches (5 cm) in diameter (change the angle of the knife to make the slices wider if needed) and about ¼ inch (6 mm) thick. Place the slices on baking sheets, brush with the olive oil, sprinkle with salt, and bake until lightly golden, 12–15 minutes. Let the toasts cool slightly before using.

1 day-old baguette

1 Tbsp olive oil

Kosher salt

Chicken Stock

preparation **15** minutes | cooking **3** hours | about **3** quarts (3 l)

Using homemade chicken stock in your dishes will make them taste noticeably better. Ask your butcher for chicken backs and necks with a little meat left on them; these readily available and quite inexpensive ingredients make the best stock.

tools | stockpot | chef's knife | fine-mesh sieve | large metal spoon

5 lb (2½ kg) chicken backs and necks

1 yellow onion, quartered

2 carrots, peeled and cut in half

1 rib celery, cut in half

2 sprigs fresh parsley

1 sprig fresh thyme

½ bay leaf

1 tsp kosher salt (optional)

Combine the chicken parts with 4 qt (4 l) water in a large stockpot and bring to a boil. Reduce the heat to low and use a large spoon to skim off any gray foam that rises to the surface. Do not skim off the fat, however, as this locks in flavor as the stock cooks. Add the onion, carrots, celery, parsley, thyme, bay leaf, and salt (if using), reduce the heat to low, and simmer gently, uncovered, until the stock tastes rich and is a light golden color, about 3 hours. Strain the stock through a fine-mesh sieve and let cool completely. Skim off any fat from the surface. Use immediately or cover and refrigerate for up to 3 days (remove the hardened white fat from the surface after chilling) or freeze for up to 2 months.

Vegetable Stock

preparation **15** minutes | cooking **1** hour | about **3½** quarts (3½ l)

For an extra-fragrant vegetable stock, add half of a fennel bulb, thickly sliced. Or, for a flavorful summer stock, add fresh tomatoes, cut into quarters.

tools | stockpot | chef's knife | fine-mesh sieve

2 yellow onions, thickly sliced

1 leek, well rinsed and thickly sliced

2 carrots, peeled and coarsely chopped

2 ribs celery, coarsely chopped

3 or 4 sprigs fresh parsley

6 whole black peppercorns

1 bay leaf

2 sprigs fresh thyme

Combine all the ingredients with 4 quarts (4 l) water in a large stockpot and bring to a boil. Reduce the heat to low and simmer gently, uncovered, for 1 hour. Strain the stock through a fine-mesh sieve, pressing on the vegetables with the back of a spoon to extract as much liquid as possible. Discard the vegetables. You can use the stock immediately, refrigerate it for up to 3 days, or freeze it for up to 2 months.

Beef Stock

preparation **15** minutes | cooking **5½** hours | about **3** quarts (3 l)

Call the butcher a day in advance to ask for the meaty shank bones and beef knuckles you'll need to make a flavorful stock and ask him or her to cut them into 2-inch (5-cm) pieces to make the bones easier to handle.

tools | roasting pan | large stockpot | chef's knife | fine-mesh sieve | wooden spatula | large metal spoon

Preheat the oven to 425°F (220°C). Arrange the beef shanks and knuckles in a single layer in a heavy roasting pan and roast, turning once, until thoroughly browned, 20–25 minutes. Combine the roasted bones and 5 qt (5 l) water in a large stockpot and bring to a boil over high heat. Meanwhile, place the roasting pan with the drippings over 2 burners and turn the heat to medium-high. Add ⅓ cup (3 fl oz/ 80 ml) water to the roasting pan and bring to a brisk simmer. Deglaze the pan, stirring and scraping with a wooden spatula to loosen the browned bits from the bottom. Add the flavorful pan drippings to the pot.

When the stock reaches a boil, use a large metal spoon to skim off any gray foam that rises to the surface. Add the carrots, onions, celery, parsley, thyme, bay leaf, peppercorns, and salt, if using. Reduce the heat to low and simmer gently until the stock tastes rich and is a light caramel color, about 5 hours. Strain the stock through a fine-mesh sieve and let cool completely. Skim off any fat that has risen to the surface and refrigerate. Season to taste before using.

6 lb (3 kg) meaty beef shanks and knuckles

3 carrots, cut into 2-inch (5-cm) pieces

2 yellow onions, quartered

3 ribs celery, cut into 2-inch (5-cm) pieces

4 sprigs fresh parsley

2 sprigs fresh thyme

½ bay leaf

5 peppercorns

1 tsp kosher salt (optional)

Tart Shell

preparation **20** minutes | resting **60** minutes | cooking **20** minutes | **1** tart shell

This versatile tart shell can be prepared a day or two in advance of filling.

tools | 9-inch (23-cm) tart pan | chef's knife | box grater | wire rack

1 cup (5 oz/155 g) flour

1 Tbsp sugar

½ tsp kosher salt

¼ tsp grated lemon zest (optional)

½ cup (4 oz/125 g) cold butter, cut into ½-inch (12-mm) pieces

½ tsp vanilla extract (essence)

In a medium bowl, stir together the flour, sugar, salt, and lemon zest, if using. Work the butter into the flour mixture with your fingertips, pressing and blending, until the butter looks granular and the mixture begins to hold together. Combine 1 Tbsp water and the vanilla and work it into the flour-and-butter mixture with a fork until the ingredients are well combined and the pastry will hold together when pressed. Gather it into a ball and wrap it in plastic.

Let the dough rest for 30 minutes to allow the flour to absorb the moisture. Then, use your fingertips to press the pastry into the bottom and sides of a 9-inch (23-cm) tart pan, making sure it is distributed evenly. Cover and place the tart shell in the freezer for 30 minutes to firm.

Preheat the oven to 375°F (190°C). Remove the tart shell from the freezer and bake until light golden brown, 20–25 minutes. Let cool to room temperature on a wire rack before filling.

Pizza Dough

preparation **30** minutes | resting **40** minutes | enough for **6** individual pizzas

A good, crisp homemade dough and a choice of interesting toppings raise the pizza party to a new level. See page 147 for topping ideas and baking instructions.

tools | baking sheet | instant-read thermometer | pizza peel | pizza stone | stand mixer with dough hook | rolling pin

Combine the water, yeast, vinegar, and 3 Tbsp olive oil in the bowl of a stand mixer fitted with the dough hook. Mix on low speed until just blended, about 30 seconds. Add 1 cup (5 oz/155 g) of the flour and mix on low speed for 30 seconds. In a separate bowl, stir together the remaining 3 cups (15 oz/470 g) flour, the sugar, and salt until well blended. Add the flour mixture to the wet dough mixture in 3 batches, beating on low speed after each addition until thoroughly combined. When all the flour has been added, raise the mixer speed to medium and mix for 2 minutes more. The dough should pull away from the sides of the bowl, come together in a ball, and feel soft to the touch.

Place the ball of dough in a well-oiled bowl and turn it several times to coat the surface lightly with oil. Cover the bowl with a clean kitchen towel. Let the dough rest at room temperature for 30 minutes.

Divide the dough into 6 equal pieces and roll each piece into a smooth ball. Place the balls on a baking sheet and cover with a damp kitchen towel. Allow the dough to rest for 10 minutes. Use immediately or refrigerate for up to 4 hours.

If you've chilled the dough, take it out of the refrigerator about 30 minutes before using it to bring it to room temperature. Using your hands and a rolling pin, roll and stretch each ball into an 8-inch (20-cm) round (don't worry if they're not perfectly round).

1¼ cups (10 fl oz/310 ml) warm water (100°–110°F/38°–43°C)

2 envelopes (2½ tsp each) active dry yeast

2 tsp red wine vinegar

3 Tbsp olive oil, plus oil for greasing

4 cups (1¼ lb/625 g) flour, plus flour for dusting

2 tsp sugar

1 Tbsp kosher salt

Legumes and grains

A wide variety of grains and legumes awaits the adventurous cook who ventures beyond the world of white rice and canned beans. And it is a journey every cook should make, as these foods help form the foundation of a healthful diet.

Legumes—beans, peas, and lentils—are nutritious and economical foods. Some people avoid cooking them because the relatively lengthy preparation seems off-putting. Hard as small pebbles, dried beans require rehydrating to soften them. This is done by soaking before cooking. Depending on your schedule, you can choose a long- or quick-soak method *(right)*. Lentils and certain other dried legumes, such as split peas, do not require soaking and cook quickly in comparison to beans. Canned beans can be used in place of soaked beans: simply rinse well and drain before using, and be aware that they may be saltier than home-cooked beans. Or look for beans in jars; these are better quality than canned.

When shopping for dried beans, find a market with good turnover. Natural-foods stores and ethnic markets will often have the widest variety. Though they may seem to keep forever, old beans will not taste as good as fresh ones. Dried legumes can be stored in an air-tight container in a cool, dry cupboard for up to 1 year, but are best used within 2 or 3 months of purchase.

Grains may be used in virtually every course of a meal and at any time of day: as breakfast cereals or savory side dishes; to add both flavor and texture to salads, soups, stews, casseroles, and stuffings; and as the basis of or embellishment to desserts and baked goods. When planning a meal, consider making a grain side dish such as barley, bulgur, or wholesome brown rice as a change from the more common potato or white rice. All these grains are packed with fiber as well as nutrients.

Whole grains or cracked grains made from whole grains are rich in oil, which goes rancid over time. These grains are therefore perishable. Store whole and cracked grains in airtight containers in the refrigerator for up to 6 months. Polished grains can go into the cupboard for up to a year.

SOAKING BEANS

To rehydrate beans for cooking, put them in a pot or bowl with water to cover generously. Let soak at room temperature for at least 4 hours or up to overnight. The longer they soak, the more quickly they will cook. Add more water if needed to keep the beans covered. Drain and rinse before proceeding with a recipe.

To speed the rehydration process, you can use the quick-soak method. Put the beans in a pot with enough water to cover them by 3 inches (7.5 cm). Place over medium-high heat and bring to a rapid simmer. Adjust the heat to simmer the beans vigorously for 2 minutes. Do not boil. Remove the beans from the heat, cover, and let cool in the liquid for 1 hour. Drain and proceed with a recipe.

Some cooks say never to salt beans while they simmer for fear of toughening them.

Fruits and vegetables

When selecting fruits and vegetables, use all your senses, not just your eyes. Deep, bright color is one indication that produce is ripe, but nowadays many fruits and vegetables have been bred to look good, with little regard for flavor, and are picked too early so that they can be shipped long distances without bruising.

Use your nose and fingertips to judge smell and texture, and if possible ask for a taste. Being able to taste before you buy is one of the best reasons to shop at a farmers' market. Don't be shy about asking the greengrocer or farmer for advice about what's ready to eat and what will keep for a few days. Fruits like berries, peaches, and melons and vegetable-fruits like tomatoes should have distinct fragrances. Fruits that are meant to be tender, like mangoes or avocados, should give when pressed, rather than feeling rock hard, and crisp vegetables, such as cucumbers or green bell peppers (capsicums), should never be soft or wrinkled.

Storing fruits and vegetables

Many—though not all—vegetables and some fruits are best stored in the refrigerator. See the chart on pages 222–23 for details. Keeping these foods cool will extend their life, but don't let them get too dry or too cold. The refrigerator's crisper drawers are designed to create a temperate, humid climate that's ideal for fresh produce, and in newer fridges the drawers can be adjusted specifically for fruits or for vegetables.

In general, store fruits and vegetables unwashed and dry (to discourage mold) in perforated paper or plastic bags to increase their temperature and humidity slightly. Again, see exceptions in the chart. Keep fruits and vegetables away from the back wall of a refrigerator, which is the coldest part and can cause light freezing.

Like cooking times in a recipe, the time frames for storage given in the chart are merely estimates. Fresh produce may last for a shorter or longer time. Use your senses to determine whether an item is still fresh, and when in doubt, discard it.

WASHING PRODUCE

Always wash produce before cooking or eating it. Many fruits and vegetables have traces of dirt, dust, bacteria, fungus, or chemicals that can be rinsed off. Even when you don't plan to eat the peel, if you are going to use a knife to cut through a fruit or vegetable, wash the fruit or vegetable first. (Select organic or pesticide-free fruit when you plan to eat the peel.)

Scrub sturdy fruits and vegetables with your hands under slightly warm running water—not hot, but a few degrees above room temperture. Warm water cleans better and helps bring out the flavors of fruits and vegetables, especially if they've been refrigerated. An exception is salad ingredients that should be crisp; wash these in cold water. Pat produce dry with paper towels or a kitchen towel, or spin salad greens dry in a salad spinner so as not to dilute the dressing with excess water.

apples	Refrigerate for 2–6 weeks. Keep away from other fruits and vegetables, as they give off ripening gases.
avocado	Store at cool room temperature, or enclose in paper bag with banana for quicker ripening. After cutting, press plastic onto surface and store in refrigerator. Keep pit in place to slow exposure to air and discoloration.
bananas	Store at cool room temperature or enclose in paper bag for ripening. Best flavor when speckled brown. Skin will turn black in the refrigerator (can still eat flesh).
shelling beans	(Cranberry and cannellini beans, flageolets) Refrigerate in plastic bag for 1 week.
beets	Separate tops from roots and refrigerate tops in perforated plastic bag for 2 days, roots for 3 weeks. Scrub with soft brush.
bell peppers (capsicums)	Store at cool room temperature or refrigerate in paper bag for 5 days.
blackberries	Spread in single layer (not touching), cover with dry paper towel and plastic, and refrigerate for 1–2 days. Wash just before using by placing in colander and immersing in warm water.
bok choy	Refrigerate in perforated plastic bag for 1–2 days.
broccoli	Refrigerate in plastic bag for 4 days.
broccoli rabe	Wrap in damp paper towels and plastic and refrigerate for 4 days.
Brussels sprouts	Refrigerate in plastic bag for 1 week.
butternut and winter squashes	Hard-shell squash will keep in a cool, dark cupboard for a few months. Refrigerate only after cooking.

cabbage	Wrap tightly in plastic and refrigerate for 1 week.
carrots	Remove tops and refrigerate in plastic bag for 1 week. Scrub with a soft brush. Refresh limp carrots by soaking in ice water.
cauliflower	Refrigerate in plastic bag for 1 week.
celery	Wash and refrigerate in plastic bag for 2 weeks. Refresh limp ribs by soaking in ice water.
celery roots (celeriacs)	Wrap in plastic and refrigerate for 1 week.
chicories	(Belgian endive, curly endive, escarole, frisée, green endive, radicchio) Refrigerate in plastic bag for 5 days.
citrus fruits	Store at cool room temperature or refrigerate for longer storage, 1–2 weeks. Citrus won't ripen after harvest. Scrub with soft brush if using zest.
corn	Refrigerate in plastic bag for 1–2 days. Best eaten right after purchase, before sugars turn to starch.
cucumber	Refrigerate in paper bag for 1 week. Scrub with soft brush to remove wax.
eggplant (aubergine)	Store at cool room temperature or refrigerate in paper bag for 5 days.
fennel bulbs	Wrap in plastic and refrigerate for 3 days. Scrub with soft brush.
figs	Spread in single layer, not touching, cover with dry paper towel and plastic, and refrigerate for 3 days. Wash just before using by placing in colander and immersing in warm water.
grapes	Wash, wrap in paper towel and perforated plastic bag, and refrigerate for 1 week.

green beans	Wash and refrigerate in plastic bag for 4–5 days.
green onion	Remove rubber bands and wilted leaves, store in plastic bag for 5 days.
herbs	Put stems in glass of water, cover with plastic, and refrigerate for 3–4 days.
kale	Refrigerate in plastic bag for 5 days.
leeks	Remove tops, wrap in damp paper towels and plastic bag, and refrigerate for 1 week. Slice in half lengthwise and separate layers to wash out grit.
lettuces and salad greens	(Butter [Boston], oak leaf, red leaf, green leaf, and romaine [cos] lettuces; arugula [rocket], young dandelion greens, garden cress, mâche.) Refrigerate in plastic bag for 2 days–1 week, depending on sturdiness. Wrap tender leaves like dandelion in damp paper towel.
mushrooms	Layer on dry paper towels in paper bag and refrigerate for 5–7 days. Wipe delicate wild mushrooms clean with brush or damp cloth, or briefly rinse button mushrooms.
onions, shallots, and garlic	Store in cool, dark cupboard for several weeks or months. Keep away from potatoes, which cause onions to spoil. Green sprouts indicate age and bitterness.
parsnips	Wrap in paper towels, put in a plastic bag, refrigerate for up to 1 month.
peaches and nectarines	Handle gently to avoid bruising. Store at cool room temperature, set stem down and not touching, or place in paper bag for quick ripening. Refrigerate when ripe.
pears	Handle gently to avoid bruising. Store at cool room temperature, set stem up and not touching, or place in paper bag for quick ripening. Refrigerate when ripe.
peas, English	Refrigerate in plastic bag for 3 days. Best eaten right after purchase, before sugars turn to starch.
potatoes	Store in cool, dark cupboard for 2 weeks. Their starches turn to sugar in the refrigerator. Scrub with soft brush.
raspberries	Spread in single layer, not touching, cover with dry paper towel and plastic, and refrigerate for 1–2 days. Wash just before using by placing in colander and immersing in warm water.
spinach	Refrigerate in plastic bag for 3 days. Wash by immersing in warm water and lifting out, letting grit sink. Repeat with fresh water until water remains clean.
strawberries	Spread in single layer, not touching, cover with dry paper towel and plastic, and refrigerate for 1–2 days. Wash just before using by placing in colander and immersing in warm water.
sweet potatoes	Store in cool, dark cupboard for 1–2 weeks. Their starches turn to sugar in the refrigerator. Scrub with soft brush.
Swiss chard	Wrap in damp paper towel and plastic bag and refrigerate for 3–5 days.
tomatoes	Handle gently to avoid bruising. Store at cool room temperature, stems down and not touching, for 2–3 days if ripe. Place in paper bag with banana for quick ripening. Tomatoes lose their flavor and texture in the refrigerator.
turnips	Refrigerate for up to 1 week in plastic bag.
watercress	Put stems in glass of water, cover with plastic, and refrigerate for 3–4 days.
zucchini (courgettes) and summer squashes	Refrigerate in plastic bag for 2–3 days.

Meat and poultry

The best way to avail yourself of first-rate meat and poultry is to make friends with a butcher. Although some butchers put on a gruff air, many are secretly pleased to be asked for advice and can teach you a lot about the food you're buying and how to cook it.

When buying meat and poultry, as with any ingredient, it's worth paying more for better quality. If you care about the food you're putting on your table, it's only logical to care about the animal that has provided it. We love nothing more than a good steak or chop or roast chicken, but we also want to know that the cow or pig or bird was treated well, fed a wholesome and natural diet, not given unneeded hormones, and slaughtered humanely. Seek out meat and poultry labeled "organic," "free range," or "natural," and ask the butcher to tell you about where the meat came from and how it was raised.

A wide array of beef, pork, lamb, and veal cuts are available, and the choice can seem overwheming. One simple way to divide up cuts is into tender and tough. Tender cuts come from the less-exercised part of the animal. Using beef as an example, that means the short loin, sirloin, and ribs. Tougher cuts, that is, well exercised and with more connective tissue, include chuck and round. Lamb shanks and pork shoulder are other examples of tougher cuts. Whatever cut you're looking for, check its marbling before you buy it. Marbling refers to the little streaks of fat running through the meat that help keep it moist. The more marbling, the more tender and juicy the meat will be. This streaking is also an indication that the meat is of a superior grade. Look for small flecks or thin "streams" of fat, rather than large deposits or broad white "rivers."

When shopping for chicken, look for plump (but not necessarily big) birds or parts with even coloring, whether pale yellow or ivory. The skin coloration depends on what the bird was fed. Chicken is highly perishable. If poultry ever has an off smell, don't buy it or eat it.

When cooking meat and poultry, take it out of the fridge a little ahead of time to let it temper, or come to room temperature. This will help it cook more evenly. Seasoning well ahead of cooking time will deepen flavors—this is why our recipes sometimes call for

FOOD SAFETY

Meat and poultry are highly perishable foods that carry bacteria. They need to be handled with care in the kitchen to avoid the possibility of food-borne illness. When you bring meat or poultry home from the market, store it in the wrapper it came in, with additional wrapping if needed, and cook it within 3 days. If you are on the verge of going beyond that time, freeze it for later use. These foods should not sit out for more than 2 hours at most, or less time on a warm day. Always defrost frozen meat in the refrigerator rather than at room temperature (this can take several hours, depending on the size of the cut) and don't freeze it again after thawing (see page 29 for details).

When working in the kitchen, make sure that you prevent cutting boards and utensils used for raw meat and poultry from touching other foods to avoid cross-contamination.

marinating or brining hours ahead when possible. Brining, or soaking meat in a salt solution, adds moisture and flavor to lean cuts.

One of the keys to cooking meat and poultry is browning. It contributes flavor and gives the finished dish eye appeal. Don't rush this stage of cooking, and you'll be richly rewarded. As you cook meat and poultry and turn it in the pan or on the grill, use tongs rather than piercing it with a fork. Piercing will release juices, resulting in a drier finished dish. Overcooking also results in dryness. Use a thermometer or your instincts rather than recipe times, which are just estimates. While chicken and ground (minced) meat in particular need to be cooked through for safety reasons, a rare steak is safe from bacteria as long as the surface is seared brown, and even pork chops taste best if there is a touch of rosiness in the center. Unless you have particular health concerns, we recommend cooking tender, lean cuts of meat only to medium-rare.

DONENESS TEMPERATURES FOR MEAT AND POULTRY

TYPE OF MEAT	DONENESS TEMPERATURE	DESCRIPTION
Ground (minced) meat	160°F (71°C) for medium	Center meat is no longer pink.
Beef and lamb	135°F (57°C) for rare	Interior is red and shiny. Meat's texture is soft when pressed.
	145°F (63°C) for medium-rare	Rosy pink interior, juicy, meat has give when pressed.
	160°F (71°C) for medium	Pink only at center, pale, meat has slight give when pressed.
	170°F (77°C) for well done	Evenly brown throughout, no traces of red or pink, moist but no juices. Meat feels firm to the touch.
Veal and pork	145°F (63°C) for medium-rare	Rosy pink interior, juicy, meat has give when pressed.
	160°F (71°C) for medium	Pink only at center, pale pink juices, meat has slight give when pressed.
	170°F (77°C) for well done	Evenly brown throughout, no traces of red or pink, moist but no juices
Whole chickens	180°F (82°C) in thigh	Legs will move easily in sockets. When thigh is pierced, juices will run clear. Juices in cavity are clear, not pink.
Chicken breasts	170°F (77°C)	Meat becomes opaque and firm throughout.
Chicken drumsticks, thighs, and wings	180°F (82°C)	Meat releases easily from the bone.
Stuffing	165°F (74°C)	Check the temperature of stuffing cooked inside a whole bird.

Note: Since the temperature of larger cuts of meat or whole birds continue to rise by 5°–15°F (2°–7°C) as they rest after cooking and before slicing, plan to remove these foods from the oven a few degrees below ideal temperature. The larger the cut, the more the temperature will rise. Allow a resting period before slicing any meat or poultry to let the juices redistribute.

Eggs and dairy

A common kitchen ingredient, the egg is as much a staple as sugar, flour, and salt. But unlike its counterparts, the egg can both be eaten alone and play a role in countless dishes. Eggs are nutritional powerhouses, supplying protein; vitamins A, D, and E; and essential minerals such as iron, calcium, and zinc.

Milk is also highly nutritious and has been a part of the human diet for thousands of years, whether from a cow, a goat, a sheep, or even a yak. Rich in protein and now commonly fortified with vitamins A and D, milk sustains us, and also gives us the gifts of yogurt, cheese, butter, and ice cream.

As with all ingredients, it is important to choose and store eggs and milk with care. Buy organic eggs from free-range chickens, which have been allowed access to the outdoors and fed a wholesome diet. Refrigerate eggs and keep them for up to 5 weeks past the sell by date stamped on the carton. There is no nutritional difference between brown eggs and white ones; the color of the egg simply depends on the breed of chicken.

Choose organic milk and yogurt. They are pricier than conventional products, but they taste better and, when used in cooking and baking, will also make your food taste better. Choose whole or low-fat milk for cooking and baking, rather than nonfat, which is thin and lacks flavor. Store milk in the coldest part of the fridge for about 5 days after the sell-by date. (Date estimates are usually conservative, so give older milk a whiff to see if it's still good.)

As a general rule, choose unsalted butter. Salt is added to butter both as a seasoning and as a preservative. If you buy unsalted butter, it is likely to be fresher, since its shelf life is shorter. Using unsalted butter also allows you to season the dishes you use it in to suit your taste. Organic butter is widely available now, and European-style butter is growing in popularity. The latter contains less water and more milkfat than ordinary butter, and may be slightly fermented for a more savory butter flavor. It's a great choice, but bear in mind that it may behave differently in baked goods because of its lower water content—the recipe may require more liquid for balance.

Fish and shellfish

With the growing awareness of the benefits to be derived from eating fish and shellfish, more and more kinds of fish are turning up on menus and in markets. The problems that result from over-fishing and pollution are also gaining recognition, so it's important to be an informed fish buyer.

To find the best-quality fish, start with a reliable fishmonger or the seafood department of a well-stocked market with frequent turnover. Use your eyes and nose to help you discern quality and freshness. All fish should look moist and bright and have a fresh, clean scent reminiscent of the sea. Steer clear of discoloration, dryness, or an off odor. The fishmonger should be able to answer any questions you have about the seafood, including its origin and whether it is fresh or defrosted frozen. (Flash-frozen fish or shellfish—frozen on board the ship soon after being caught, rather than sitting in the hold for a day or two and then in the market for even longer—can in fact be better than some "fresh" fish.)

Fish and shellfish are highly perishable and won't keep for long. It's best to buy seafood on the day you plan to cook it. Most bivalves in the shell—clams, mussels, and oysters—as well as crabs and lobsters are still alive at the time of purchase and should be kept alive until you're ready to cook them. You can tell if a bivalve is alive by tapping the shell; the shell should close. At the market, pass over any that don't. (Shells that don't open after cooking are also a bad sign, although some can just be a little stubborn.) Hurry home with your purchase and keep it fresh nestled in a mound of ice in the fridge before cooking it as soon as you can.

The most important thing to know about cooking fish and shellfish is that it is easy to overcook these delicate foods. The rule of thumb when cooking fish is to allow 10 minutes per pound (500 g) at 350°F (180°C), but even this timing may be a little long if you are cooking salmon or tuna to a desirable medium-rare, still rosy in the center. With shellfish such as prawns, a change of color from gray to pink is a good indication of doneness, while the shells of bivalves such as mussels or clams will open when they are cooked.

ENDANGERED FISH

A number of the most popular kinds of fish are now considered endangered because of over-fishing or pollution. These include Chilean sea bass, swordfish, orange roughy, and cod. Lists of endangered fish occasionally change and can be reviewed online with resources such as Monterey Bay Aquarium's Seafood Watch (www.mbayaq.org/cr/seafoodwatch.asp). Because so many kinds of fish are available, there is no need to purchase endangered fish. Ask the fishmonger about types to substitute.

Another current concern is the mercury content in fish. Fish high in mercury include lean fish such as swordfish, tilefish, king mackerel, and shark. These fish should not be eaten by pregnant women those who may become pregnant, nursing mothers, or young children.

The skilled cook

Among the most important things a novice cook can learn is how to choose the correct cooking method for the ingredients at hand. In other words, knowing the best way to apply heat to any food is as critical to success as choosing the food itself. And usually there is more than one good way to cook most foods. This section will give you an overview of the various cooking methods, to help you understand why a recipe was written the way it was.

Tender, delicate foods like a fish fillet, a chicken breast, or a rib steak can be cooked quickly over high heat so that they don't have time to dry out. A tough cut of meat, like the well-exercised leg, needs to cook for a long time to become tender, but you can use liquid and gentle heat to keep it moist in the process. A sturdy vegetable can stand up to boiling. The different ways we apply heat to food can be grouped according to the quality of the heat used.

Quick and hot: grilling and broiling

Grilling over an open fire has a long history, reaching back millennia to when our ancestors first discovered that cooked food tasted better than raw. Nowadays, the fire is usually in a contained charcoal or gas grill, but grilling is still appreciated for the excellent flavor it delivers. To start a fire in a charcoal grill, pile the coals in a cylindrical metal chimney starter, light them using wadded-up newspaper, and let them burn until they have a light coating of gray ash, about 30 minutes. For direct grilling, spread the coals evenly in the grill and place the rack over them. If using a gas grill, preheat the grill for about 15 minutes before adding the food. For indirect grilling, pile all the coals on one side of the grill so that you can place the food on the other side and cover the grill to cook food more slowly.

In broiling, the heat comes from a heat element above the food, rather than below, but the effect is similar. If you don't have a grill, you can always substitute a broiler. If your broiler rack is adjustable, place it so the food is about 4 inches (10 cm) away from the heat source, or farther for thicker items to allow them to cook through. You can also broil foods for a couple of minutes to brown them.

Quick and hot: sautéing

Sautéed foods are quickly cooked over medium-high or medium heat in a small amount of fat such as oil or butter. Small pieces of food, like chopped onion or shrimp, are tossed or stirred in the pan; larger items like cutlets are turned rather than tossed. Sautéing gives the outside of a food a flavorful brown coating without overcooking the inside. Like grilling, sautéing is considered a dry-heat cooking method because it does not involve liquid.

Foods for sautéing should be relatively thin. For thicker pieces of meat or poultry, pound them with a meat mallet to flatten them to a uniform thinness. Pat foods dry before cooking if needed. Moisture will cause hot fat to spatter, and will interfere with browning.

When you first add the food to the pan, put its best-looking side down for larger pieces (like a chicken breast). Let it brown a little before you start to stir and toss. Larger pieces of food are usually ready to turn when they are golden brown on the underside. For the best appearance, turn large pieces only once; you can turn smaller pieces more often.

Quick and hot: deep-frying

Although deep-frying has gotten a bad rap in recent years, the truth is that if you do it right the food will not absorb too much oil and become greasy. And the results of immersing pieces of food in hot oil are incomparably delicious. The key is heating the oil to a high temperature and keeping it constant. At a high temperature, the oil will evaporate the water in the food instantly, turning it into steam that will prevent any oil from seeping into the food. If the oil temperature is too low, there will be no outward push and the food will absorb the oil instead. If the oil gets too hot, it will smoke and impart a bitter flavor. (And if oil is allowed to get extremely hot, it will burst into flame—so watch the temperature carefully.)

Try to keep the temperature as constant as possible. Each time you add food to the oil, the temperature will drop. Cooking food in small batches will prevent big drops in temperature and food from sticking together. Let the oil regain its correct temperature between each batch. Having foods at room temperature before frying also prevents a large drop in temperature.

Quick and hot: boiling and blanching

Boiling in water is an intense cooking method best suited to lobsters and crabs, sturdy vegetables, and dried pastas—and not much else. Most other foods need more gentle handling when cooking in a liquid (see simmering, poaching, and steaming, opposite). Partially cooking a food in boiling water is called blanching (when boiled for less than 2 minutes) or parboiling (cooking food halfway). Blanching and parboiling are useful for sturdy vegetables that you want to sauté for color and flavor, but that wouldn't become tender throughout with just a quick sautéing. Blanching also sets a bright color in green vegetables, loosens thin skins for easy peeling, and lessens strong flavors (garlic, bacon) that might overpower some dishes.

You can tell that water is at a full rolling boil if you stir it and it doesn't stop bubbling. A moderate boil can be stopped by stirring. When you need to time boiling or blanching carefully, start counting from when the water returns to a boil after you've added the food. This may take a little while, especially when cooking larger items like whole lobsters.

Hot and slow: roasting and baking

Roasting and baking don't demand a lot of attention or effort from the cook, and produce concentrated flavors. The term "baking" is commonly used for breads, cakes, pies, and the like, but when applied to meats, poultry, seafood, and vegetables, the terms "baking" and "roasting" are nearly interchangeable. Both refer to cooking in the dry heat of an oven. Baking foods are sometimes covered; roasting foods are always uncovered and typically cook at relatively high temperatures. This high heat releases the natural sugars in vegetables and fruits, leaving them tender on the inside and caramelized and sometimes even crisp on the outside. All meats, but especially lean meats, need a more watchful eye when roasting, as they will dry out if cooked for too long. Brining lean cuts, or soaking them in a salt or salt-and-sugar solution, can also counteract the drying effects of roasting and add good flavor.

Some recipes call for tying or trussing whole poultry or roasts into a compact shape, to hold in stuffing or make an attractive presentation when carving at the table. Trussing is not strictly necessary, and poultry thighs cook more evenly when the bird is not trussed.

BOILING AND BLANCHING TIPS

● When boiling pasta or potatoes, use a large pot and plenty of water. This helps the food tocook evenly, preventing sticking in the case of pasta. (Stirring also prevents sticking.)

● You can salt boiling water before adding the food, but for the best control over seasoning, do it after draining. If you wish to salt cooking water, do it after the water has come to a boil. Adding salt raises the boiling temperature of water, so salted water takes longer to come to a full boil.

● Recipes will often instruct you to "boil to reduce" a liquid. This means to let the liquid evaporate away, resulting in a thicker consistency and more concentrated flavor.

● When blanching, have ready a large bowl of ice water. Plunge the food into it to halt the cooking. Move the food quickly from the hot water to the cold water with tongs or a slotted spoon so that it does not continue cooking longer than desired.

ROASTING AND BAKING TIPS

● Use an oven thermometer to make sure the oven has reached the correct temperature before you put the food in. This will ensure good browning and better flavor.

● There should be room in the pan for the food to fit comfortably and air to circulate.

● Foods to be roasted should be allowed to "temper," or stand at room temperature to take the chill off. This encourages even cooking.

● Foods to be roasted should be patted dry and, in general, lightly oiled before they go into the oven. This helps encourage browning.

● Let roasted meat and poultry rest before carving to allow the juices to distribute evenly. Depending on its size, the food's temperature will rise 5°–15°F (3°–9°C) as it rests.

● When a recipe instructs you to simmer, keep an eye on the pot. You may need to stir and adjust the heat from time to time to keep the liquid from coming to a boil.

● Poaching is ideal for cooking eggs, chicken, fish, fruits such as pears, and other delicate foods that need careful treatment to prevent them from breaking apart or overcooking.

● Because it is a gentle cooking method, steaming is well suited to delicate foods like seafood and tender vegetables. It helps a food to retain its shape, color, flavor, and texture better than boiling, simmering, or even poaching.

● If food must steam for a long time, check periodically to make sure that the water has not boiled away completely, and add more boiling water as needed.

● Steam can scald you like boiling water, so take care when uncovering a pan.

● When braising, you don't cover the food with liquid. The pot will be covered, creating a moist and steamy cooking environment. For stewing, the liquid should just cover the food.

● Stews and braises should simmer very gently, never boil, which would toughen meat or poultry. The easiest way to keep the heat gentle and even is to put the pot in the oven at about 325°F (165°C).

● In a braise, the liquid should reduce to a saucelike consistency. To help it along, remove the food from the liquid when tender and simmer the liquid to reduce and thicken it.

● A final step in a stew or braise is to use a large spoon to skim the clear fat from the surface of the liquid. If you plan to serve the dish in a day or so, you can simply cool and chill it. The fat will solidify, making it easier to scrape off.

Gentle and slow: simmering, poaching, and steaming

These three "moist" cooking methods share a lot in common. All involve water, and each is gentler than the last. Simmering is boiling slowed down, with smaller bubbles around the pan edges that disappear when you stir. Where boiling might cause a food to toughen, simmering firms it nicely (in the case of meat) or makes it tender (in the case of vegetables). Poaching is simmering in slow-motion: big bubbles occasionally break the surface of the liquid. Steaming lets food gently cook in a steamy vapor.

These moist-heat cooking methods, unlike dry-heat grilling and roasting, do not involve browning. Foods remain pale in color and more delicate in flavor, which is desirable for some dishes.

The term "steaming" is sometimes used to describe cooking some foods, such as mussels and clams, in a small amount of simmering liquid in a covered pan. But generally it means to cook food over boiling or simmering water in a covered pan. You can use a steamer insert or basket, which will turn almost any saucepan into a steamer. In a pinch, you can also use a metal colander. In all cases, the steaming water in the pan must not touch the bottom of the rack or basket.

Gentle and slow: braising and stewing

These long, slow cooking methods give the cook plenty of time to do other things while the food cooks, and results in some of the world's most tender and meltingly delicious dishes. Braising is used for some sturdy leafy greens and especially for tough cuts of meat. In the case of meat, first you sear the food to brown it and add flavor, then you immerse it partway in liquid, cover, and cook very gently on the stove top or in the oven. The flavors meld together, even more so if allowed to sit until the next day. Stewing is similar but uses more liquid and smaller pieces of meat, and the food may cook uncovered or partially covered.

When browning foods before braising and stewing, the goal is to add attractive color and good flavor without cooking the foods through. Since they will cook in liquid for a good deal of time, you don't want to toughen it up. Use medium-high to high heat and use tongs to brown the food on all sides.

Other techniques

Chopping, mincing, and dicing

Even a task as simple as chopping has some basic rules to it. Keep the fingers of the hand holding the food tucked under so that you don't cut them. When cutting up food in order to cook it, try to cut the pieces into roughly the same size, so that they will cook at an even rate. "Mince" means to chop an item into very fine pieces. It's often used for herbs and garlic. First chop the item roughly, then gather it into a pile. Holding down the knife tip with your free hand, use the knife in a rocking motion to firmly and quickly cut the food to size. The term dice refers to neat cubes ranging in size from ¼ inch (6 mm) to ½ inch (12 mm). To dice an item, first slice it lengthwise as thick as you want the dice to be. Turn the slices 90 degrees and slice them lengthwise again. Now cut the strips crosswise into dice.

Dicing onion

Here's a trick that will make your life easier whenever you cook. Cut the onion lengthwise through the root end, then peel it. Place one of the halves flat side down. Make a series of horizontal slices as thick as you want the final dice, up to but not through the root end. (The root will help hold the onion layers together while you cut.) Now make a series of vertical slices, again not cutting through the root end. Last, make a series of crosswise slices to dice the onion.

Preparing garlic

To loosen cloves from a head of garlic, place the head, root end up, on a cutting board and press down on it firmly with the heel of your palm. To loosen the skin from a single clove for peeling, place the clove under the flat side of a chef's knife and press firmly with the heel of your palm. Slice the garlic in half lengthwise and remove any green sprout. (This sprout tastes bitter and means the garlic is past its prime.) Chop or mince as described above.

Preparing chilies

Use a little caution when cutting spicy chili peppers. Slice in half lengthwise to expose the seeds and white membranes, where the spiciness resides. Cut out the membranes and seeds, reserving them if you want to be able to adjust the heat of a dish. Be careful not to

touch your face as your work; the chili's oils can burn your eyes or lips. Wash your hands, knife, and cutting board with hot soapy water when you're through. If working with very spicy chilies, you can wear rubber gloves for more protection.

Preparing bell peppers

To slice or dice a bell pepper (capsicum), slice off the top and bottom, then make a lengthwise cut and open up the pepper into a flat rectangle. Cut out the membranes and seeds. These are not spicy as in a chili, but they're not desirable in a dish, either. Slice or dice the pepper.

To roast and peel a bell pepper, place it under the broiler 4–6 inches (10–15 cm) from the heat source and turn occasionally until charred black on all sides. Don't let the flesh burn. Seal the pepper in a bag and let steam until cool enough to handle. Peel off the charred skin, then cut open the pepper and remove the membranes and seeds.

Grating and shredding

Grating is the process of reducing a food, such as lemon zest or Parmesan cheese, into tiny particles using the finest rasps of a box grater. Using the large holes of the box grater, for Cheddar cheese, carrots, or potatoes, is called shredding. You can also shred and grate foods using a mandoline or food processor fitted with the right disk.

Segmenting citrus

Citrus can be peeled and segmented with a knife to remove all of the tough membrane and bitter white pith. First remove a slice from the top and bottom of the fruit, cutting deep enough to expose the colorful flesh. Standing the fruit on a cut side, follow the curve of the fruit with the knife to remove all the peel and white pith. Holding the fruit over a bowl to catch the juices, cut on either side of each segment to free it from the membrane, letting it fall into the bowl.

Separating eggs

Separating the yolks from the whites is easier to do when eggs are cold. Carefully crack each egg and, holding it over a bowl, pass the yolk back and forth between the shell halves, letting the white fall into the bowl. Be careful not to pierce the yolk with a jagged edge of eggshell. Drop the yolk into a separate bowl, and transfer the white to a third bowl so that you are cracking each new egg over an empty bowl.

Peeling and seeding tomatoes

Tomato skins tend to come off and curl up during cooking and can impart an annoying texture in some dishes. The following trick for peeling tomatoes also works for peaches and other thin-skinned fruit. Bring a pot of water to a boil. Using a sharp knife, cut a shallow X in the bottom end of each tomato. Have ready a bowl of ice water. Immerse the tomatoes in the boiling water (in batches if needed to avoid crowding) and blanch them for 15 seconds to loosen the skins; then, using a slotted spoon, transfer them to the ice water to stop the cooking. Peel the tomatoes with your fingers or a small knife. To seed, slice the tomatoes in half crosswise (lengthwise for plum/Roma) and lightly squeeze and shake, using your finger if needed to help dislodge the seeds and pulp.

Dredging and coating

Dredging, or completely coating pieces of fish, meat, or poultry in seasoned flour or bread crumbs, slows the escape of moisture during sautéing or frying and helps create an appealing golden crust. One of the most common ways to dredge a fillet is to drag both sides through the dry ingredient in a shallow bowl. Shaking the foods in a large zippered plastic bag with the flour is a quick, tidy way to dredge. Always dredge just before cooking; if left to sit, the coating will soak up moisture and become gummy. Shake off the excess flour before you put the food in the pan.

Whipping egg whites

For billowing clouds, use room-temperature egg whites, which can incorporate more air during whipping than cold ones. A copper bowl also increases volume through a chemical reaction with the egg white, or cream of tartar in a stainless-steel bowl can be used for the same effect. Whip the whites vigorously with a balloon whisk or with an electric mixer on high speed. The egg whites will become foamy, increase in volume, and go from translucent to opaque. As the volume increases, stop from time to time and turn the whisk or beaters upright to see whether the egg whites are forming peaks. Gentle peaks that slump to one side are "soft" peaks, while shiny peaks that hold a pointy shape are called "stiff" or "hard" peaks. Don't whip egg whites past the stiff-peak stage; overwhipped whites become lumpy and lose their sheen, and they don't blend into batters as well.

Sifting flour

Sifting aerates flour to make light, evenly textured cakes or cookies. It is also used to combine dry ingredients so that a leavener, such as baking powder, is distributed evenly. If you don't have a specialized flour sifter, simply pass the ingredients through a fine-mesh sieve. (For smaller amounts, stir the ingredients with a whisk.) Always follow a recipe exactly when it comes to sifting. Unless instructed otherwise, sift flour after measuring, since this will make a difference in the amount of flour used. See page 32 for general directions on measuring flour and other dry ingredients.

Folding

Folding is a way of combining a delicate mixture with a heavier one without deflating the delicate mixture. In a large mixing bowl, scoop the lighter mixture on top of the heavier one and, using a wide, flat spoon or rubber spatula, cut down through both of the mixtures to the bottom of the bowl. Using a sweeping motion, bring the spatula up along the side of the bowl farthest from you, lifting up some of the mixture from the bottom of the bowl and "folding" it over the top one. Give the bowl a quarter turn and repeat until the two mixtures are just blended, usually six or seven times. A few streaks can remain. Be careful not to overdo it, which can deflate a batter and affect the final results of the baked good.

Zesting and juicing citrus

Citrus zest, the colored portion of the peel, is rich in aromatic and flavorful oils. Choose organic fruit for zesting and scrub the fruit well to remove any wax or residue. Use only the thin outer layer of the rind, taking care not to include the bitter white pith. You can remove zest with a zester, a tool designed to remove it in thin strips. A vegetable peeler or a paring knife can also be used, but will produce pieces that are short, wide, and irregular. Or, you can remove zest with the fine rasps of a box grater. Thin-skinned fruits that are heavy for their size yield the most juice. Before juicing, roll the fruit firmly against a hard surface to loosen up and break the membranes inside. Halve the fruit crosswise and then extract the juice with a handheld reamer. You can also use a countertop mechanical press or an electric citrus juicer. Before juicing citrus, remove any seeds from the fruit with the tip of a sharp knife, or set a sieve over a bowl to catch the seeds.

Entertaining basics

Now that you're married, you may find yourselves increasingly interested in entertaining. As you and your friends grow older and settle down, socializing by spending an evening out on the town may give way to having friends over for dinner. You may also begin to invite family for the holidays. In some people's hands, a dinner party can seem effortless. But the truth is that throwing a great party always requires advance planning.

The goal of planning is to make the event a pleasure both for your guests and for yourselves. If you're not in the habit of entertaining, start off slowly, inviting two or four friends over for dinner. The more people you invite, the simpler the food should be. When choosing a date and time for your party, make sure you allow yourself time to prepare: if you work all week, Saturday night is a better choice than Friday night, since you will have all of Saturday to get ready (and Sunday to recover!). Give yourself at least a week between inviting and hosting—or longer for a more elaborate party.

Consider how you'd like to serve dinner, based on the occasion or style you want to set for the party and on the limitations of your space. Be creative: If you have a small dining table, you can serve food buffet style and let guests sit on the sofa and chairs to eat, or on a patio or porch. If this is the plan, you'll need to choose dishes that won't need to be cut with a knife, which is difficult when a dinner plate is balanced precariously on your lap. If you decide on a sit-down dinner, you can serve a few dishes at the same time, family style, and let guests help themselves, or you can serve dinner restaurant style: one course at a time, plated, for a more formal feel—or to work with a small table that won't accommodate several serving dishes. This decision of serving style will help determine which recipes you choose.

Planning a menu

You'll often hear it said that you should not try out a dish for the first time on guests. This is wise advice. Practice first on yourself, to make sure that you're familiar with the recipe and that it turns out the way you expect in the amount of time you expect. You can choose from the outset to serve dishes you are already comfortable making, or plan a test run in advance of the party.

For a novice cook, coming up with a menu may seem daunting, but you'll soon discover that one decision will lead into the next. We've created several menus for special occasions using the recipes in this book: turn to pages 240–43 for ideas. To come up with your own menu, consider the ambience you would like to create at your party: very casual and festive, or more calm and refined. Luckily, most recipes can be dressed up or down, served on more casual earthenware or plated on your best china. Think in general about the combination of flavors, colors, textures, and ingredients you'd like to combine that feel appropriate to the mood and occasion you wish to create. The seasonality of ingredients is also important: check with the greengrocer or at a farmers' market for guidance so you don't get your heart set on serving fresh salsa when tomatoes are out of season, bland, and mealy. If you are not sure where to begin, start with the main dish and work from there to select a starter, side, and dessert.

Elements of the table

Whether your party is casual or formal, you do not need to be an interior designer to create an attractive, inviting table. When in doubt, err on the side of simplicity: start with white and then add a few accents of color. Avoid overdecorating, and you will find that the flatware and glassware will add plenty of sparkle to the scene.

A casual table setting reflects the easygoing style of the meal to come. Select a no-frills tablecloth or place mats, and use matching or complementary colors of cotton napkin. Everyday flatware, dishes, and glassware are appropriate, and can be augmented with a few special pieces.

Following traditional table-setting guidelines might seem at odds with the spirit of a casual dinner. But these conventions, far from being arbitrary rules of style, are intended to make the meal a more comfortable and enjoyable experience for your guests.

For each guest, put a napkin on top of or to the left of the plate, folded side facing the plate, allowing space to its right for the forks. Arrange all flatware in the order in which it will be used, starting

MAKE A SEATING CHART

Decide the seating for a dinner party in advance and either tell guests where to sit or make simple place cards to let people know where to go; this may sound fussy, but in fact it spares the guests any confusion and awkwardness about finding a seat at the table.

For the most traditional seating arrangement, begin by placing yourselves, as the hosts, at the head and foot of the table. A female guest of honor sits to the right of the male host, and a male guest of honor to the right of the female host. Drawing a plan of the table will help you work out the seating for larger parties. Use a pencil and move guests around as needed until you have a plan that feels right. For the best conversations, mix up guests by age and sex, try to pair guests with common interests, and, if possible, avoid seating couples together. They see each other all the time!

from the outermost item. To the right of the napkin, put a salad fork if you are serving an appetizer or salad course. A larger, main-course fork goes to the right of the salad fork. The knife should be placed to the right of the plate, its blade facing inward. (Imagine yourself picking up the utensils and eating, with fork in left hand and knife in right, and you'll see how these positions make sense.) If you are serving soup, set the soup spoon to the right of the knife, since most people hold the spoon with their right hand.

Next, set the water glass directly above the knife. Place a white wineglass to the right of the water glass, and a red wineglass to the right of the white wineglass. Bread plates, butter knives, dessert implements, or teaspoons may make an appearance at formal meals. Guests can put bread directly on their dinner plate or on the tablecloth; forks or spoons for dessert can be brought out along with the dessert, and teaspoons with the tea or coffee.

Staying organized

As the main elements of your dinner party begin to take shape, it is important to keep track of all the little organizational details and special touches that will bring everything together. Make two lists, Shopping and Tasks. Organize the shopping list into categories. Try to arrange the tasks list in chronological order so you do not forget last-minute items. It is also helpful to work out a basic cooking and serving timetable to keep everything on track. Recruiting help is a good idea for dinner parties of eight or more (including yourselves), and will give you more time with your guests.

Putting it all together

Your most important task is to make your guests feel at ease. When the doorbell starts ringing, make sure you get out of the kitchen to greet them warmly, take coats and offer drinks, and introduce guests to one another if they are not already acquainted. Ideally you should plan not to be working on dinner right when guests are due to arrive, but if one of you needs to attend to last-minute details, the other can devote him- or herself to your friends or family.

With a good plan in hand, you can use the recipes in this book to create a delightful evening for friends or a cheery holiday meal for family. Put all the elements together, and you can't go wrong, so have fun and enjoy your party.

SET THE MOOD

● Lighting, music, and flowers help create a mood and ambience for a gathering, and should be planned ahead of time.

● For evening parties, use a combination of electric lights and candlelight to flatter everyone's appearance and create an inviting ambience. Scent-free, dripless regular or votive candles, such as beeswax candles, are good choices. The aroma of scented candles can come into conflict with the food, especially if you want to place the candles on the dining table.

● Music should complement the occasion or theme. Select it in advance, so it is easy to manage during the party. Set the volume low at first, to keep the music from competing with conversation. You can always raise the volume as the party gets livelier.

● If you plan to decorate the table with flowers, keep in mind that tall bouquets block guests' views across the table. Try smaller bouquets, or flowers floating in shallow bowls of water.

EXPECT THE UNEXPECTED

● Even at the most well-organized dinner party, accidents and unanticipated problems are bound to occur. The key is to stay calm and let the evening flow naturally while you deal with the situation discreetly.

● The most important thing to remember is that a party is all about enjoyment, and guests take their cue from the host. If your dinner plan is not unfolding the way you expected, have a sense of humor about it. If a side dish burns, simply omit it from the meal. If something doesn't turn out perfectly, just smile and pretend it's all come out just the way you planned. Don't apologize, and don't make a fuss, and likely no one will notice anything amiss.

A Valentine's Day Menu

MENU

Rib-Eye Steak with Pan Jus • 94

Tossed Green Salad • 82

Ginger Carrot Salad • 155

Blueberry Fool • 196

SERVES 2

Wine pairing: Côtes du Rhône

TIMELINE

UP TO 4 HOURS BEFORE SERVING
Make Blueberry Fool and refrigerate.

UP TO 2 HOURS BEFORE SERVING
Make Ginger Carrot Salad and hold at room temperature.

30 MINUTES BEFORE SERVING
Make Tossed Green Salad.
Make Rib-Eye Steak with Pan Jus.

Note: To serve two, cut the recipes for Tossed Green Salad and Blueberry Fool in half, and the recipe for Ginger Carrot Salad to one-third.

First Anniversary

MENU

Gazpacho • 72

Crab Cakes • 69

Tomato, Mozzarella, and Basil Salad • 84

Raspberry-Lemon Tart • 205

SERVES 2

*Wine pairing: California Sauvignon Blanc
or a French Sancerre (white or rosé)*

TIMELINE

UP TO 2 DAYS BEFORE SERVING
Make Gazpacho and refrigerate.
Make tart shell for Raspberry-Lemon Tart.

UP TO 4 HOURS BEFORE SERVING
Make lemon curd for Raspberry-Lemon Tart.
Shape Crab Cakes and refrigerate.

30 MINUTES BEFORE SERVING
Assemble tart and refrigerate.
Make Tomato, Basil, and Mozzarella Salad and hold at room temperature.

JUST BEFORE SERVING
Sauté Crab Cakes.

Note: To serve two, cut the recipes for Gazpacho and Tomato, Mozzarella, and Basil Salad in half, and plan for leftover Raspberry-Lemon Tart.

Open House

MENU

Spicy Almonds • 58

Warm Marinated Olives • 58

Gazpacho • 72

Roasted Radicchio with Pancetta • 170

Shrimp with Parsley-Garlic Butter • 67

mandarin oranges or tangerines

SERVES 12

Wine pairing: chilled rosé

TIMELINE

UP TO 1 WEEK BEFORE SERVING
Make Spicy Almonds and refrigerate.

UP TO 2 DAYS BEFORE SERVING
Make Gazpacho and refrigerate.

30 MINUTES BEFORE SERVING
Marinate Warm Marinated Olives.
Take Spicy Almonds out of refrigerator.
Put Radicchio in oven.

JUST BEFORE SERVING
Sauté Warm Marinated Olives.
Slide Shrimp with Parsley-Garlic Butter under
broiler (grill).

Dinner Party

MENU

Marinated Goat Cheese • 61

Caesar Salad with Garlic Croutons • 88

Sea Bass with Fennel and Bacon • 123

Blueberry Fool • 196

SERVES 6

Wine pairing: Viognier

TIMELINE

UP TO 2 DAYS BEFORE SERVING
Make Marinated Goat Cheese.

UP TO 4 HOURS BEFORE SERVING
Make 2 recipes Blueberry Fool and refrigerate.

1 HOUR BEFORE SERVING
Make Sea Bass up to step of roasting.

30 MINUTES BEFORE SERVING
Make 2 recipes Caesar Salad up to step of tossing.
Put Sea Bass in oven.

JUST BEFORE SERVING
Toss Caesar Salad.

New Year's Eve Dinner

MENU

Gougères • 61

Winter Chicory Salad • 83

Rack of Lamb • 103

Roasted Winter Squash Crescents • 164

Crisp Rosemary Potatoes • 177

Pots de Crème • 211

SERVES 6

*Wine pairing: Champagne or sparkling wine
with Gougères; Pinot Noir with Rack of Lamb*

TIMELINE

UP TO 1 DAY BEFORE SERVING
Make Gougères and hold wrapped at room temperature.
Make Pots de Crème and refrigerate.

1 HOUR BEFORE SERVING
Sear lamb rack and apply coating; parboil potatoes.

50 MINUTES BEFORE SERVING
Roast squash and hold warm.
Turn up oven temperature for lamb.

30 MINUTES BEFORE SERVING
Make 2 recipes Winter Chicory Salad and hold at room temperature.
Put lamb rack in oven.
Sauté 2 recipes Crisp Rosemary Potatoes and hold warm.

Sunday Brunch

MENU

Zucchini-Basil Frittatas • 51

Asparagus Mimosa • 152

Roasted Beet and Feta Salad • 90

Strawberry Shortcakes • 201

SERVES 4

Wine pairing: Fumé Blanc

TIMELINE

UP TO 1 DAY BEFORE SERVING
Make biscuits for Strawberry Shortcakes and hold wrapped at room temperature.
Roast beets.

UP TO 2 HOURS BEFORE SERVING
Prepare strawberries for Strawberry Shortcakes.

1 HOUR BEFORE SERVING
Make Asparagus Mimosa and hold at room temperature.
Prepare Roasted Beet and Feta Salad up to step of tossing.

30 MINUTES BEFORE SERVING
Make 2 Zucchini-Basil Frittatas and hold at room temperature.

JUST BEFORE SERVING
Whip cream for Strawberry Shortcakes.
Toss Roasted Beet and Feta Salad.

Thanksgiving Dinner

MENU

Butternut Squash Soup • 77

Roast Turkey • 116

Holiday Stuffing • 185

Caramelized Brussels Sprouts • 164

Best Mashed Potatoes • 178

pumpkin pie *(purchased)*

SERVES 10

Wine pairing: choice of Chardonnay or Zinfandel

TIMELINE

UP TO 2 DAYS AHEAD OF SERVING
Make 2 recipes Butternut Squash Soup up to step of adding cream, and refrigerate.

1 DAY AHEAD
Season turkey and refrigerate.

4 HOURS AHEAD OF SERVING
Take turkey out of refrigerator.

3 HOURS BEFORE SERVING
Make 2 recipes Holiday Stuffing.

2½ HOURS BEFORE SERVING
Put turkey in oven.

1 HOUR BEFORE SERVING
Put 2–3 recipes' worth of potatoes on to boil.
Separate 5 recipes' worth of Brussels sprouts into leaves.

30 MINUTES BEFORE SERVING
Take turkey out of oven; make gravy and keep warm.

JUST BEFORE SERVING
Heat up Butternut Squash Soup and add cream.
Sauté Brussels sprouts.
Mash potatoes.

Christmas Dinner

MENU

French Onion Soup • 81

Roast Beef with Yorkshire Pudding • 98

Ginger Carrot Salad • 155

Celery Root Purée • 169

Ginger Cake with Hard Sauce • 202

SERVES 8

Wine pairing: Cabernet Sauvignon

TIMELINE

UP TO 2 DAYS AHEAD
Make French Onion Soup up to step of broiling (grilling), and refrigerate.
Make Ginger Cake and hold wrapped at room temperature.
Make Hard Sauce and refrigerate.

1 DAY AHEAD
Season beef roast and refrigerate.

4 HOURS BEFORE SERVING
Take beef out of refrigerator.

2 HOURS BEFORE SERVING
Put beef in oven.
Make 2 recipes Ginger Carrot Salad.

30 MINUTES BEFORE SERVING
Take Roast Beef out of oven.
Make Yorkshire Pudding.
Put 2 recipes' worth of celery root on to boil.

JUST BEFORE SERVING
Broil (grill) topping of French Onion Soup.
Purée celery root.

Glossary

Artichoke hearts: The heart is the most delicious part of an artichoke, and trimming artichokes is a labor of love. Keep jarred artichoke hearts, either marinated or packed in water, on hand in the pantry to use for impromtu appetizers or as part of a pasta or other dish.

Arugula: The leaves of this dark green plant, also called rocket, resemble deeply notched, elongated oak leaves. They have a nutty, tangy, and slightly peppery flavor. The larger leaves may have a coarser texture and more pungent flavor than small ones.

Asian skimmer: This mesh tool is useful for scooping food from hot oil when deep-frying or hot water when blanching.

Baking dish: Shallow, rectangular dishes made of tempered glass, porcelain, or earthenware are all-purpose vessels that work for roasting meat or vegetables and baking brownies or bread pudding. Items will cook more slowly in opaque ceramic than they will in clear glass.

Baking sheet: A baking sheet is a rectangular metal pan with shallow, slightly sloping rims. Choose sturdy stainless-steel ones that will last for years.

Blender: When shopping for a blender, features to look for are sturdiness and a tight-fitting lid that allows you to add ingredients as you blend. Blenders can sometimes substitute for food processors, but create a smoother purée and incorporate less air.

Boning knife: This knife features a thin, flexible blade whose shape is designed to follow along the curve of a bone as you cut away the meat.

Box grater: This useful tool offers four different sizes of rasps or holes, allowing you to grate hard cheeses into fine powder for quick melting or shred raw vegetables or semifirm cheeses such as Cheddar on the largest holes.

Brandy: This distinguished spirit is distilled from wine or fermented fruit juice. It's used in both sweet and savory dishes, often flambéed to burn off some of its alcohol content while leaving behind its delicious flavor. The finest type of brandy is Cognac, which is made in the regions around the town of Cognac in western France.

Broccoli rabe: Related to broccoli, cabbage, and mustard, this cruciferous vegetable has slender stalks with small, jagged leaves and florets that resemble tiny heads of broccoli. Broccoli rabe has a mild, pleasantly bitter taste with overtones of sweet mustard.

Brushes: When choosing brushes for the kitchen, look for natural bristles that are firmly attached to a handle. Keep one brush for savory uses and another for sweet, and if you like to grill, look for a long-handled brush for basting meat.

Bulgur: Nutty-tasting bulgur, also known as bulghur or burghul, is made by steaming wheat, partly removing the bran, and then drying and cracking the grains. It is commonly used in Middle Eastern and Balkan cooking as the basis for pilafs, salads, and stuffings. Sold in fine, medium, and coarse grinds, it has a mild flavor and firm texture that make it a good vehicle for the flavors of other ingredients.

Cake comb: Also called a decorating comb or icing comb, this triangular tool has jagged teeth of varying size on each edge to make decorative patterns in cake icing.

Cake pan: Round pans, generally 2 inches (5 cm) deep and 8 or 9 inches (20 or 23 cm) in diameter, used especially for baking cakes. You will want to have at least two on hand for making layer cakes.

Can opener: Because you will use this so often, buy a good one, whether manual or electric. Newer manual can openers are ergonomically designed to save your hand from cramping as you wrestle to open a can.

Chef's knife: This is the most useful all-purpose knife: a large, evenly proportioned, tapered blade, of which the most useful are generally 6 to 9 inches (15 to 23 cm) long. You will use this knife to make nearly every dish, for slicing, dicing, chopping, julienning, or mincing ingredients.

Chicory: This family of bitter greens includes Belgian endive (chicory/witloof), curly endive, escarole (Batavian endive), frisée, green endive, and radicchio. These sturdy and distinctively flavored greens make an interesting addition to or basis for salads and are at their best in autumn and winter, when cool weather brings out their sweetness.

Chili powder: Finely ground dried chilies, pure chili powder is not to be mistaken for the commercial spice blend known as chili powder, which usually combines ground dried chilies, cumin, corinader, garlic, oregano, and other seasonings and is used to flavor the well-known American Southwest stew of the same name. Pure chili powder, whether made from ancho or another chili variety, can be found in well-stocked markets and Mexican grocery stores.

Chimney starter: See page 228.

Chinese five-spice powder: This seasoning blend is common in the kitchens of southern China and of Vietnam, where it is often used to flavor poultry for roasting. It is readily available in well-stocked food stores.

Chocolate: The chocolate-making process begins with cacao beans. The beans are fermented, roasted, shelled, and crushed into bits that are then ground and compressed to become chocolate liquor. Unsweetened, or bitter, chocolate is pure chocolate liquor with no sugar added. Depending on the amount of sugar added, the chocolate liquor becomes the more familiar semisweet and sweet chocolate. The addition of milk solids results in milk chocolate. Always use the chocolate type specified in the recipe, since different varieties behave differently and should not be substituted one for another.

Citrus reamer: A tool designed to squeeze the juice from lemons, usually by means of a mound-shaped ridged surface pressed and twisted against and into a lemon half.

Coffeemaker: Modern electric versions of the classic French drip coffeepot can grind the coffee, brew it, keep it warm in a thermos rather than scorching it on a burner, and do this all on a timer so that hot coffee is ready for you when you get up in the morning.

Colander: A large and sturdy sieve, this tool is indispensable for draining boiled foods such as potatoes or pasta and for rinsing large quantities of fruits or vegetables. A colander lined with damp cheesecloth (muslin) can also be used for straining stock.

Cookie sheets: These flat metal pans are usually rimless on two or three sides to allow for sliding cookies onto a cooling rack. Avoid very dark sheets, which may cause your cookies to overbrown or burn. Nonstick cookie sheets work well and are easy to clean. You will want to have at least two cookie sheets on hand for baking large batches of cookies.

Cooling racks: Baked goods just out of the oven are usually cooled on wire racks, which permit air to circulate on all sides. The racks, which come in various shapes and stand on short legs, should be made of sturdy metal. Have on hand enough racks to handle two baking sheets of cookies.

Cream of tartar: This white powder is potassium tartrate, a by-product of wine making. It is used to stabilize egg whites so that they whip up more easily.

Crepe pan: The most common size for this shallow pan 9 inches (23 cm). Its flat base and long handle make it easy to spread batter in an even circle by rotating the pan, and its low slanting sides allow you to lift an edge of the crepe with ease for flipping.

Cutting boards: The best cutting boards are made of wood or polyethylene. Keep separate boards for raw meat and poultry and other foods, and wash them in hot, soapy water after use. An oniony board can be freshened by rubbing it with the cut side of a lemon.

Decorating turntable: Anyone who does a lot of cake decorating appreciates a turntable. Frosting and piping are much easier if the cake is raised above the work surface and if you can turn the cake with a slight push.

Double boiler: A double boiler is a set of two pans, one nested atop the other, with room for water to simmer in the bottom pan. Delicate foods such as chocolate and custards are placed in the top pan to heat them gently, or to melt them in the case of chocolate. The top pan should not touch the water beneath it, and the water should not be allowed to boil. A tight fit between the pans ensures that no water or steam can escape and mix with the ingredients in the top, which can cause melting chocolate to seize or stiffen. You can create your own double boiler by placing a heatproof mixing bowl or a slightly smaller saucepan over a larger one, although it may not be as steady or the fit as tight.

Dutch oven: These large, heavy round or oval pots with tight-fitting lids and two loop handles are used for slow cooking on the stove top or in the oven. Most are made of enameled cast iron, which will not react with acidic foods the way uncoated cast iron does. They are also called casseroles and stew pots.

Egg poacher: Eggs can be poached in a specially designed egg poacher, which is a shallow dish with three or six indentations, each one the right size to hold one egg.

Electric mixer: Handheld mixers are small, light, portable machines. Lacking the power and special attachments of stand mixers, these appliances are adequate for most batters and soft doughs but do not work well for stiff doughs. For long mixing tasks, such as making buttercream or beating volumes of egg whites, these mixers can become tedious to hold. They can be used with nearly any bowl or pan, however, even those set over a pan of simmering water on the stove top. See also stand mixer.

Epazote: Pungent epazote (also called wormseed) is looked on as a culinary treasure by Mexican cooks. Ideally, epazote is used fresh, but dried epazote, stocked in Mexican markets, can be used in beans and soups. Enclose about 1 teaspoon in a tea ball for easy removal of the woody stems.

Fennel: Also known as sweet fennel or finocchio, a fennel plant's leaves, seeds, and stems have a sweet, faint aniselike flavor. Similar in appearance and texture to celery, fennel has stems that overlap at the base to form a somewhat flat bulb with white to pale green ribbed layers. The leaves are light and feathery. It is available year-round but is at its peak from October to March. Select creamy-colored bulbs topped by fresh-looking stems and feathery green tops.

Fermented black beans: Also called salted or preserved black beans, fermented black beans are soybeans that have been dried, salted, and allowed to ferment until they turn black. They are distinctly pungent, have an almost smoky character, and are used mainly in Chinese cooking.

Food mill: Used to purée cooked or soft foods, this tool looks like a saucepan with a perforated bottom and an interior crank. A paddle-shaped blade at the base rotates against a disk perforated with small holes. As the handle is turned, the blade forces the food through the holes.

Food processor: The all-purpose, spiral-shaped metal blade chops, blends, mixes, and purées. Other attachments include disks for shredding or grating and slicing, a plastic blade for kneading dough, and a paddle for beating batters. A feed tube allows you to add ingredients while the food processor is running. Despite their popularity, food processors are not capable of performing every kitchen task. They are not recommended for mashing potatoes, nor can they normally be used for beating egg whites or whipping cream. If you plan to mix very dense dough, make sure your processor motor is powerful enough, or the motor may dangerously overheat.

Frying pan: This broad pan is similar to a sauté pan, but differs in that its flared sides make it useful for cooking foods that must be stirred or turned out of the pan. Stainless steel, anodized aluminum, and cast iron are good materials for frying pans.

Ginger: This knobby rhizome, or underground stem, enlivens many sauces, salads, and marinades; it is excellent to keep on hand year-round to mix with dried ginger in holiday cakes and cookies. Look for firm ginger with no discoloration. Peel ginger and slice, chop, mince, or grate it before using in a recipe. You can store an entire piece of ginger in the freezer and grate it, still frozen, as needed.

Grappa: This rustic Italian spirit is made from the remnants of grape pressings—stems, seeds, and skins—after the juice has been extracted to make wine.

Griddle: Flat rectangles or rounds of cast iron or cast aluminum, often with a nonstick finish, griddles sit flat on the stove top and are designed to be heated over 1 or 2 burners. Sometimes the second side is a grill pan. They are ideal for cooking pancakes, eggs, bacon, thin steaks, cheese sandwiches, and more. Most have depressed rims to catch grease.

Grill: Even set to high, a gas grill can never achieve the high temperatures of hardwood and charcoal, and purists claim that the food never acquires the flavor delivered by a good charcoal fire. Nonetheless, for most backyard cooks, the convenience of the gas grill more than makes up for any difference.

Haricots verts: Literally translated from the French, haricots verts are "green beans." These small, slender green beans are favored in France. Delicately flavored, they are more elegantly shaped than other green beans and are also referred to as French green beans or filet beans. Young, slender Blue Lake or other green beans may be substituted.

Ice cream maker: Most ice cream and sorbet recipes require the use of an ice cream maker that contains a canister and a churn. The old-fashioned kind requires the use of ice and rock salt, not to mention elbow grease, but most contemporary ice cream makers use a frozen or refrigerated canister and usually an electric motor.

Ice cream scoop: Two styles of scoop are popular: the dipper scoop and the half-sphere scoop. The dipper has a thick handle and a rounded, shallow bowl. The handle is hollow and transmits heat from your hand to the dipper. The half-sphere scoop has a full, deep bowl and a trigger-released metal wire that pushes the ice cream from the scoop.

Icing spatula: Also called a frosting spatula or pastry spatula. This long, flat metal utensil with its slender, flexible blade resembles a round-tipped knife without a sharp edge. When the handle angles off the blade, the spatula is called an offset spatula. Both types make frosting and decorating cakes easier.

Kitchen scale: Most American home bakers rely on volume rather than weight to measure ingredients, but weight is more accurate and is used in professional kitchens. Choose a kitchen scale capable of weighing up to 10 lb (5 kg) in no larger than ¼-oz (7-g) increments. The best scales allow you to weigh ingredients in any bowl or container. Make sure that the scale weighs light items as accurately as heavy ones.

Kitchen shears: Every kitchen should have a pair of shears in the drawer to cut parchment (baking) paper, kitchen string, cheesecloth (muslin), fresh herbs, fruits, and even pickles. Basic kitchen scissors have stainless-steel blades and one serrated edge. Heavier and longer poultry shears are useful for cutting chicken pieces and trimming fat and skin.

Kitchen string: Kitchen string, also called kitchen twine, is used for trussing chicken and tying roasts, as well as numerous other tasks. The linen string should be soft, pliable, and natural (no dye).

Kitchen timer: This invaluable little gadget is your best friend if you're cooking several dishes at once, cooking in the midst of company, or doing other tasks at the same time as cooking. Timers range in complexity from the simple spring-activated ones to digital timers that can time 3 dishes at once. Newer stoves have built-in oven timers. A clip-on timer that attaches to your apron is helpful when you need to leave the kitchen and move around the house.

Ladle: At least one ladle is essential in every kitchen. The bowl should be made of stainless steel or rigid, heat-resistant plastic and large enough to scoop up a good measure of soup or stew. The handle should be heat-resistant and long enough for easy use.

Loaf pan: Loaf pans give form to breads that are too moist to hold their own shape. They range in size and shape, but the standard size is 8½ by 4½ inches (21.5 by 11.5 cm). Be careful when trying to substitute a pan of a different size than the one called for in a recipe. The batter should fill the pan about two-thirds full. With less batter, you will have a flat loaf. With too much, you will have a top-heavy loaf that looks awkward and is difficult to slice.

Mâche: Also called corn salad or lamb's lettuce. This very delicate and mild salad green has oval leaves that grow in a small, loose bunches.

Mallet: Mallets are useful for pounding boneless meat and poultry pieces until thin for quick and even cooking. Also called meat pounders, although pounders tend to have one smooth side, while mallets often have two sides, like a double-headed hammer, both with blunt teeth that help break down fibers in the meat, tenderizing it.

Mandoline: This narrow, rectangular tool, usually made of stainless steel, is used for slicing and julienning. It sits at an angle on the work surface, and the food to be cut is moved over a mounted blade (with a strumming motion, which gives the tool its name). This handy tool simplifies the task of creating thin, uniform slices.

Mascarpone cheese: Thick enough to spread when chilled, but sufficiently fluid to pour at room temperature, this Italian cream cheese is noted for its rich flavor and acidic tang. Similar to crème fraîche, it is sold in tubs in well-stocked food stores and in the cheese cases of Italian delicatessens.

Melon baller: Also known as a vegetable scoop, potato baller, or melon-ball scoop, this hand tool has a small bowl at one end, about 1 inch (2.5 cm) in diameter, used for making decorative balls from melon or other semifirm foods. It is useful for seeding or coring some foods, such as cucumbers and pears, or preparing them for stuffing.

Molasses: A thick, robust-tasting syrup, molasses is a by-product of cane sugar refining. Each step in the molasses-making process produces a different type of molasses. Mixed with pure cane syrup, light molasses has the lightest flavor and color. Dark molasses is thicker, darker, stronger in flavor, and less sweet than light molasses. Both light and dark molasses may be bleached with sulfur dioxide. Processed without sulfur, unsulfured molasses has a milder flavor. Molasses gives a distinctive flavor to many sweet and savory baked foods.

Mortar and pestle: These ancient tools are effective for pulverizing spices and making pastes. Mortars are bowl shaped, made of stone, wood, or pottery, with a smooth or coarse-textured interior. The bat-shaped pestle is the grinding tool. To grind ingredients, place them in the mortar, then grasp the pestle and rotate and press down on the ingredients to crush them with the blunt tip.

Mozzarella: Originally from Italy, mozzarella cheese was traditionally made from the milk of water buffaloes, but now it is usually made from cow's milk. It is available in both the familiar supermarket version and in a fresh version—rolled by hand into small or medium balls, packed in water or whey, and offering a more distinctive milky flavor.

Muffin pan: Standard muffin and cupcake pans have 6 or 12 cups, each capable of holding 6 to 7 tablespoons of batter. Jumbo and miniature muffin tins are also available. Muffin cups can be lined with paper liners (although the crust is likely to come off with the paper) or greased before being filled. Although aluminum and steel are common materials, cast-iron pans with nonstick surfaces are ideal for making muffins.

Mushrooms: The common white, all-purpose mushrooms sold in most grocery stores are generally called button mushrooms, although this term refers specifically to young, tender white mushrooms with closed caps. Cremini mushrooms, also called common brown mushrooms or Italian mushrooms, are closely related to button or common white mushrooms. The two varieties are interchangeable. Large, fully mature cremini are known as portobello mushrooms. To clean mushrooms, wipe them with a clean, damp cloth or mushroom brush, or swish them very briefly in water. Mushrooms soak up water like sponges and should not be soaked.

Nonstick baking liner: Silicone pan liners are a boon to the cookie baker. They prevent cookies from sticking to a baking sheet and make cleanup very easy.

Nutmeg: The large, oval, brown seed of a soft fruit, nutmeg has a warm, sweet, spicy flavor. Whole nutmeg keeps its flavor much longer than ground nutmeg. Always grate nutmeg just before using. Use the finest rasps on a box grater, or a specialized nutmeg grater.

Oil, olive: A staple of Mediterranean cooking, olive oil is both delicious and healthful. Southern France, Spain, Italy, Greece, California, Tunisia, Israel, and Australia all produce high-quality olive oils. Extra-virgin oils are pressed without the use of heat or chemical solvents. Depending on the location and type of olive, the color of these oils can range from a rich gold to a murky deep green. Oils made from mature olives, like those from southern Italy, are more golden and buttery. Oils made from younger olives, characteristic of Tuscany, have a clear, greenish hue and a flavor that is fruity and sometimes peppery. Show off the rich flavor of extra-virgin olive oil by using it uncooked in vinaigrettes, as a seasoning, or as a condiment. "Pure" olive oil is extracted from a subsequent pressing, usually by means of heat or chemicals, and generally has a less distinctive olive flavor. It is often labeled simply "olive oil" and is good for general cooking, frying, or sautéing. Olive oil will solidify at cold temperatures; store it in a cool dark place rather than in the refrigerator.

Olives: Olives pass through stages of ripeness, producing many nuances of colors from green to pale beige to chocolate brown to deep purple and all the way to shiny black. Richly flavored, dark ripe olive varieties include the little French Niçoise, Greek Kalamatas, Italian Gaetas, and the very mild, very large black Cerignola olive from southern Italy. Picholines are a mild, green olive from France. Wrinkled herb-seasoned black olives are typically labeled Moroccan.

Oyster knife and glove: Oyster knives have thick handles for easy gripping and turning. Their wide, dull blades are strong enough to lever open the shell by inserting and twisting near the hinge. (Although similar, oyster knives are stubbier than clam knives.) Stainless-steel oyster knives will not transfer any metallic flavor to the oyster. An oyster glove is a metal mesh glove that protects the hand holding the oyster from a slip of the knife.

Pancetta: A flavorful, unsmoked Italian bacon, pancetta is made from the same cut, pork belly, as the more common bacon, but it is salt-cured instead of smoked and has a subtler taste and silky texture. Look for pancetta at delicatessens and Italian markets.

Parchment (baking) paper: Treated to withstand the high heat of an oven, parchment paper resists moisture and grease and has a smooth surface ideal for lining pans. Look for parchment paper in well-stocked markets and cookware shops.

Paring knife: A small, evenly proportioned blade usually 3 to 4 inches (7.5 to 10 cm) long. Used for paring, peeling, and slicing fruits and vegetables and for chopping small quantities.

Parmesan cheese: A firm, aged, salty cheese made from cow's milk. True Parmesan, produced in the Emilia-Romagna region of Italy, is known by the trademarked name Parmigiano-Reggiano. Look for the name stamped in a pattern on the rind. To ensure freshness, purchase the cheese in wedges and grate or shave it only as needed for use in a recipe. Store the cheese wrapped in waxed paper or plastic in the refrigerator for up to 3 weeks.

Parsley: Flat-leaf parsley, also called Italian parsley, has a more complex and refreshing flavor than curly-leaf parsley. For best results, always use fresh flat-leaf parsley for cooking.

Pastry bag: Different pastry tips can be inserted into the narrow end of this conical bag and frosting, whipped cream, or a similar mixture can be spooned into the wide end and piped out of the narrow end. Pastry bags should be washed in warm, soapy water and turned inside out for drying. If you don't have a pastry bag, spoon the filling into a heavy-duty zippered plastic bag and snip off one of the bottom corners.

Pastry board: Rolling out pastry calls for a smooth, hard, preferably cool surface. A pastry board may be made of hardwood or marble. Do not use it as a cutting board, or the surface will become rough (and marble will dull your knives). Marble boards stay cool, which is important for flaky pie dough. They can even be chilled in the refrigerator or on a back porch in cold weather.

Pecorino Romano: This sharp, firm Italian grating cheese is made from sheep's milk. American Romano cheeses are made from cow's milk, alone or combined with sheep's or goat's milk.

Pepper mill: Pepper mills are available in a wide range of materials and shapes. When choosing a pepper mill, keep in mind that you may want a coarseness of pepper for different uses. Look for a mill that can be adjusted for coarse or fine grind.

Pernod: This liqueur is an absinthe substitute made by Pernod et Fils in France, a company that produced true absinthe before it was banned in 1914. Although far sweeter than absinthe, Pernod shares its anise flavor. Pernod is yellowish in color but, like other anise-flavored liqueurs, turns cloudy when mixed with water.

Pie pan: Buy metal pie pans or glass pie plates in 9- and 10-inch (23- and 25-cm) sizes. Glass pie plates let you see how the bottom crust is browning, although they are sometimes overzealous heat conductors that lead to a brown crust and an undercooked middle. Look for a wide rim to hold up the fluted edge of the crust.

Pizza cutter: Although pizzas and open tarts can be cut with serrated knives, using a rotating pizza wheel, or pizza cutter, is more efficient. The sharp-edged wheels are 2 to 4 inches (5 to 10 cm) in diameter; the handles are short and sturdy and are fitted with a protective thumb guard. Buy the sturdiest pizza wheel you can find, making sure it has a strong handle and a large thumb guard.

Pizza peel: Using this wooden paddle, topped pizzas can be slid into the oven safely and with ease. Peels measure 24 inches (60 cm) or more in diameter and have a thin edge and long handle. A cookie sheet can be used for the same purpose.

Pizza stone: Also called a baking stone or baking tile, this square, rectangular, or round slab of unglazed stoneware creates the effect of a hot brick oven in a home oven. A stone should be preheated in the oven for at least 45 minutes or up to 1 hour before baking. The pizza or other bread is slid onto the hot stone from a pizza peel.

Polenta: Polenta is cornmeal that is cooked in either water or broth until it thickens and the grains of the cornmeal become tender. Polenta may be either yellow or white, made from either coarsely ground or finely ground cornmeal, but the classic version is made from coarsely ground yellow corn. Traditionally, it was poured right onto the middle of a wooden table or onto a wooden board, cooled, and then cut with a string for serving.

Potatoes: Starchy potatoes—the familiar brown russet, baking, or Idaho potatoes—are perfect for baking and mashing. They are different from waxy potatoes, thin-skinned white or red potatoes with a low starch content. These potatoes hold their shape after cooking and are ideal for potato salads. All-purpose potatoes, such as Yukon golds, contain a medium amount of starch can be used for either purpose.

Potato masher: A handheld masher yields mashed potatoes with a coarse texture. Unlike a food processor, it will not overwork the potatoes, which can result in a gluey texture. Look for a masher with a sturdy handle and a mashing grid with some flat portions to help mash the lumps more efficiently.

Potato ricer: Ideal for preparing fluffy mashed potatoes and other purées, this utensil has a perforated container to hold cooked vegetables and fruits. When the ricer's handles are pressed together, the food is forced through the perforations, and any fibers or peels are left behind in the container.

Pot holders: Essential for taking pots from the stove and pans from the oven, pot holders and oven mitts should be thickly padded and large enough to perform their designated tasks with safety. Do not skimp on these. Square pot holders should be generous in size and protection. Glovelike oven mitts should reach above the wrist and be well insulated. Those designed to reach nearly to the elbow are especially useful for taking large pans from the oven and for working over a hot grill.

Puff pastry: One of the glories of French cuisine, puff pastry is made by adding layers of butter to pastry dough through repeated rollings and foldings, producing a rich, flaky dough used in savory and sweet dishes. Frozen puff pastry dough is a fine substitute for labor-intensive homemade.

Quince paste: Quince paste—made by cooking the pulp of this fruit with a high proportion of sugar, puréeing, and molding into a sliceable loaf—is served with soft cheese is a favorite Spanish and Latin dessert. It is also known by its Spanish name, *membrillo*.

Ramekins: A ramekin is a small, usually round ceramic baking dish with straight sides. They come in many sizes, but 4-, 6-, and 8-fl oz (125-, 180-, and 250-ml) are the most common. Ramekins are frequently used when making custards, puddings, and mousses.

Rice: Long-grain rice has elongated, slender grains that are much longer than they are wide. When cooked, the grains remain fluffy and separate, making them popular for pilafs and soups. Short-grain rice varieties tend to clump up and stick together when cooked, and are preferred for Asian and Caribbean cooking. Arborio and Carnaroli are Italian rices whose high starch content make them perfect for risotto. Jasmine rice is a perfumed rice popular in Thailand, and basmati rice, an aromatic, nutty rice, is used in Indian cooking.

Rice cooker: Also called a rice steamer, this electric appliance takes the guesswork and worry out of cooking rice. The cooker sits on the countertop and is fitted with an insert for steaming rice. Some models have additional inserts for steaming other foods.

Ricotta salata: This aged ricotta cheese has a soft but crumbly texture and a salty tang. Usually, the older the cheese, the saltier. In the spring, look for young ricotta salata in your cheese shop (it is sometimes labeled "spring ricotta salata"); this tends to be less salty and a bit softer.

Roasting pan: A roasting pan has low sides in order to allow the oven heat to reach as much of the surface of the food as possible, while catching any juices from the roasting food. For roasts and poultry, choose a heavy roasting pan to keep the bottom of the food and the pan juices from burning. Although a pan with a nonstick surface makes cleanup easy, a regular surface allows more browned bits to stick to the pan during roasting, which means better gravy.

Rolling pin: Chief among the essential tools for pie and tart bakers, rolling pins come in

various styles. A heavy, smooth hardwood or marble pin at least 15 inches (38 cm) long is best. Some bakers prefer a French-style pin without handles, either a straight dowel or a dowel with tapered ends, while others prefer pins with handles. If you choose the latter, look for one with handles that move on ball bearings for the smoothest roll.

Roux: A mixture of flour and a fat such as butter or oil, roux is a common thickening agent in sauces and in gravies. Roux is made by stirring flour into hot oil or butter and stirring the mixture over the heat for a minute or two, or sometimes longer.

Saffron: The stigmas of a type of crocus, saffron is used in many regions of Italy to add a subtle flavor and appealing yellow color to many dishes, including risottos, soups, and stews. For the best flavor, buy saffron in whole "threads," or stigmas, and check the date on the package to make sure the saffron has not been on the shelf too long.

Salad spinner: Consisting of a lidded container with an inner colanderlike basket, a salad spinner makes short work of drying lettuce and other greens, preventing the salad dressing from becoming too watery.

Santoku knife: A multipurpose knife, the Santoku ("three benefits" in Japanese) is used for mincing, dicing, and slicing.

Saucepan: A simple round pan usually with either straight or sloping sides. In general, saucepans range in size from 1 to 5 qt (1 to 5 l). Most useful is the 2-qt (2-l) size. Straight- and high-sided saucepans are ideal for cooking sauces, since the liquid will not boil away so quickly. The best materials for saucepans are anodized aluminum or aluminized steel.

Sauté pan: A straight-sided pan with a high, angled handles, designed to flip foods easily without fear of spilling, and usually a lid. Sauté pans are also useful for braised dishes or any stove-top recipe that calls for a lot of liquid.

Savory: Winter savory, a shrublike Mediter-ranean evergreen herb, has a strong, spicy

flavor. It goes well with dried beans and lentils, meats, poultry, tomatoes, and other vegetables. More delicate than its cousin winter savory, summer savory has a scent reminiscent of thyme and a faintly bitter, almost minty flavor.

Serrated bread knife: A straight, serrated blade at least 8 inches (20 cm) long. The serrated edge cuts easily through the tough crusts of breads.

Serrated utility knife: Like a miniature bread knife, with a blade 6 to 8 inches (15 to 20 cm) long. Used for peeling and slicing or for carving small cuts of meat, or cutting through the delicate skins of tomatoes that might otherwise be crushed by an ordinary knife.

Sesame oil: A dark amber-colored oil pressed from toasted white sesame seeds, Asian sesame oil has a rich, distinctive nutty aroma and taste. Like a good extra-virgin oil, sesame oil does not heat well. It's best used in small amounts as a flavoring agent for marinades and dressings or for soups and braised or stir-fried dishes during the final minutes of cooking. Don't confuse Asian sesame oil with the clear-pressed sesame seed oil sold in natural-foods stores, which is made from raw white sesame seeds.

Sharpening steel: Before you put a knife away after use, it's a good idea to hone it. The best—and most classic—home tool to use is a sharpening steel, available wherever good-quality knives are sold. Swipe each side of the blade's cutting edge a few times across and along the length of the steel, alternating sides and holding the blade at about a 15-degree angle to the long metal rod.

Sieve, fine-mesh: A sieve, also called a strainer, is used to separate lumps or larger particles of food from smaller ones. It also is used to drain pieces of food of their liquid, and to purée soft foods, which are pushed through the strainer with the back of a large spoon. Wire-mesh strainers come in a variety of sizes, from very small to large, with either fine or coarse mesh. Some strainers have a long handle plus a metal hook that allows them to fit onto a bowl. Strainers are used in blanching to move food quickly from boiling water into an ice bath. Use fine-mesh strainers to strain delicate foods such as custards; to make the strainer even more efficient, line it with a double thickness of cheesecloth (muslin).

Sifter: Shaped like a canister, and activated by a handle that is turned or squeezed, a flour sifter forces flour, powdered (icing) sugar, or other ingredients through a layer (or two or three) of wire mesh. A fine-mesh sieve may be used instead by simply tapping its rim to pass the flour through.

Skimmer, perforated metal: With a long handle and a large flat strainer or shallow bowl of wire mesh or perforated metal, a skimmer is designed to remove the scum or foam from the top of simmering stocks. It is also perfect for scooping small pieces of food from boiling water or hot oil.

Soufflé dish: Soufflé dishes, made of ceramic to help hold in the heat, have tall, straight sides that are usually greased and then dusted with sugar (or, for savory soufflés, bread crumbs) to help the batter climb the sides of the dish.

Spatulas: Cooks regularly use both metal and rubber spatulas. The offset spatula has a thin, flexible blade, usually of stainless steel, that rises in an angle off of the handle. These spatulas are ideal for removing cookies from baking sheets. Wide, flat, thin metal spatulas, also known as turners, are great for fried eggs or fish. Flexible rubber spatulas, available in varying sizes, are excellent for stirring or folding in ingredients and for scraping down bowl or food processor sides. The most versatile ones have blades made of silicone rubber, which won't melt or stick when used in a hot pan. Have a few different sizes on hand for different tasks.

Spoons: Stirring and spooning up food are simple tasks, but having a selection of different kinds of spoons to choose from makes them even easier. Wooden spoons

are indispensable in the kitchen, as they are sturdy, do not scratch bowls or pans or add a metallic taste to foods, and their handles do not get hot. Metal spoons with big bowls are nice for stirring large quantities of thick foods, such as stews, although their primary use is the spooning of food from one container to another. The slotted spoon is not used for stirring, but rather for transferring solid foods such as braised meat out of a liquid.

Springform pan: A deep, round cake pan with sides secured by a clamp, this pan is useful for cheesecakes and other solid cakes. The sides release when the clamp is released, making the cake easy to remove. A 9-inch (23-cm) diameter is the size most commonly used. Generally, springform pans should be used atop baking sheets to prevent batter from leaking onto the bottom of the oven.

Stand mixer: Stand mixers are heavy, stationary machines with large, removable bowls, a range of speeds, and a variety of attachments. The basic set usually includes a wire whisk for beating egg whites or whipping cream, a paddle for creaming together butter and sugar and mixing batters, and a dough hook for kneading bread. Some are equipped with meat grinders or other specialty attachments. Stand mixers work better for large amounts and heavy batters and free up your hands, which can be especially welcome when adding ingredients.

Steamer insert: Also known as vegetable steamer and folding steamer. Steamer baskets are collapsible contraptions made of perforated metal with fanned sides that allow them to fit into a number of different-sized pans. They sit on small feet so that they hold food above the boiling water, ensuring the steam will circulate around the food.

Stick blender: Also called hand or handheld blenders, immersion blenders have an extended blade that is immersed in a food or mixture to blend or purée it. Immersion blenders are great for puréeing food in the container in which it is mixed or cooked (bowls, saucepans). This means that they can blend larger amounts

of food than will fit in the jar of a standing blender. Immersion blenders also tend to incorporate more air into a liquid and as such can be used to make frothy foam on creamed soups. These blenders usually have only two speeds, and the blade must be completely immersed in the food to prevent spattering. Many are designed to hang in a wall mount for easy storage. Some have whisk attachments or small containers for blending small amounts.

Stock: A flavorful liquid created by slowly simmering chicken, meat, fish, or vegetables in water, along with herbs and aromatic or flavorful ingredients such as onions, carrots, and celery. Stock can be made easily at home and frozen for future use (pages 216–17). Canned broths are also available, but they tend to be saltier than homemade stock, so seek out those labeled "low-sodium" to most effectively control the flavoring in your dish. For best quality, seek out cartons of broth or good frozen broths. Some delis sell stock.

Stockpot or soup pot: Also known as a soup pot, a stockpot is a high, narrow pot designed for minimal evaporation during long cooking. It is essential for making stock or cooking large quantities of soup. Stockpots are fitted with two looped handles for easy lifting and with tight-fitting lids. They should be made of heavy-gauge metal with good heft. Anodized aluminum or enameled steel are good choices because they absorb and transfer heat efficiently, clean up easily, and do not react with the acidity of wine or citrus juice. The smallest stockpots have an 8-qt (8-l) capacity, but most cooks find stockpots with 10- to 12-qt (10- to 12-l) capacities to be the most useful.

Tart pan: Tarts are baked in pans with shallow, usually fluted vertical sides. Look for ones with removable bottoms, which allow you to free a tart easily from its pan by placing the baked tart on a large can or small canister and letting the sides drop away. The tart and pan bottom may be placed on a serving plate.

Thermometer, instant-read: Inserted near the end of cooking, instant-read thermometers are more accurate and make smaller holes in the meat (and release fewer juices) than other types of thermometers. The temperature reading appears within seconds. When testing for doneness, be sure the thermometer is not touching a bone, and do not leave the thermometer in the meat or poultry while it is still roasting in the oven.

Thermometer, oil and candy: The best candy thermometers are fitted with a clip that attaches to the side of a pan. For an accurate reading, submerge the tip of the thermometer in the liquid, but for an accurate reading do not let it touch the bottom of the pan.

Thermometer, oven: Use an oven thermometer—available at kitchen shops, hardware stores, and food markets—to determine an oven's accuracy. Hang the thermometer from the rack in the middle of the oven, and then turn on the oven. Check the temperature after at least 20 minutes have passed. If it is off by just a few degrees, adjust for it when you set the dial. Or, depending on the type of oven you have, call your local electric and/or gas company; most will send a technician to your house to calibrate the oven, thus eliminating the need to make an adjustment each time you bake. Nevertheless, it is a good idea to leave the thermometer in the oven all the time to track its accuracy.

Toaster: When selecting a toaster, consider whether you'd like to be able to toast more than 2 slices at a time, or if you'd like a wide slot for toasting bagels and other thick slices.

Tongs: No cook should be without a pair of tongs for cooking meat and poultry. Tongs allow you to turn and transfer these foods without piercing them and losing juices. A long pair of tongs is especially useful grilling.

Tube pan: Any pan with a central tube, a feature that helps the center of a cake to rise and bake evenly, is called a tube pan, but several different styles exist. Angel food cake pans have removable bottoms and small "feet" (or an extra-tall central tube) extending above the rim, which permit the inverted pan to stand clear of the counter during cooling

so no moisture is trapped. Fluted tube pans (called Bundt pans) and fluted and flared kugelhopf (also called kugelhupf or gugelhopf) pans have fixed bottoms and no feet. Tube pans hold from 1½ to 4 qt (1.5 to 4 l) of batter. A 10-inch (25-cm) inch tube pan is the most common size.

Vanilla: Vanilla extract, also known as vanilla essence, is made by chopping vanilla beans and soaking them in a mixture of alcohol and water, then aging the solution. Look for pure extracts made from beans from Tahiti (more subtle flavor) or Madagascar (stronger flavor). Imitation vanilla has a thin, chemical flavor that dissipates quickly, and should be avoided. Always let hot foods cool off for a few minutes before adding vanilla extract; otherwise, the heat will evaporate the alcohol, and along with it some of the vanilla flavor.

Vegetable peeler: Sharp-edged blades and easy-to-hold handles define good vegetable peelers. Swivel-bladed peelers are more maneuverable, hugging the curves of vegetables and lessening your work. They will dull after several years of use and usually are replaced, not sharpened.

Vinegar: *Vinaigre,* the French word for vinegar, means "sour wine." After an initial fermentation turns the grape juice into wine, a second bacterial fermentation turns the wine's alcohol into acid, creating wine vinegar. The best vinegars are slowly fermented from good wine; lower-quality vinegars are made from poor wines that have been inoculated with yeasts for quick fermentation. Because of its high acidity, vinegar has a long shelf life and does not need to be refrigerated. Red wine vinegars is the most commonly used one, although balsamic vinegar (see page 27) is gaining in popularity. For all-purpose use, look for a good aged red wine vinegar. White wine vinegar made with Champagne grapes is lighter and milder than most white wine vinegars. Sherry vinegar, another wine vinegar, is a mildly acidic vinegar with a trace of sweetness. Vinegar may also be made from other bases, such as cider. Do not substitute distilled

white vinegar, made from grain alcohol, for white wine vinegar, as it is tart but flavorless.

Waffle iron: A Belgian waffle and a standard American waffle are substantially different. Belgian waffles are also much thicker than American waffles, which is why they must be made in a deep Belgian waffle iron. The resulting texture accommodates luscious toppings such as berries and whipped cream.

Watercress: A member of the mustard family, watercress grows wild in cold, shallow streams and along the edges of cold springs. Commercially, it is cultivated both in moist soil and hydroponically; in the latter case, it is sold with the roots intact and wrapped in cloth. It has a refreshing peppery flavor and brilliant green leaves, which add a bright note to salads.

Whisk: With a head of looped thin metal wires, a whisk is used to rapidly beat or whip ingredients. Also known as whips, whisks are made in various sizes and shapes for various uses. Elongated flat sauce whisks, or roux whisks, are the basic model and are used to mix ingredients thoroughly without adding excess air. Balloon whisks, which are more rounded, are used to incorporate the maximum amount of air when whipping egg whites and cream.

Wok: This ingenious Chinese pan is a multi-purpose cooking device ideal for stir-frying, deep-frying, and steaming. The rounded bottom heats quickly when set over a gas burner and allows small pieces of food to be rapidly tossed and stirred, while the gradually sloping sides help to keep the food in the pan.

Zester, citrus: A handheld tool with a row of circular holes at the end of its metal blade, specially designed to remove the zest from citrus efficiently.

Index

FREE PRESS

A Division of Simon & Schuster, Inc.
1230 Avenue of the Americas
New York, NY 10020

WILLIAMS-SONOMA

Founder & Vice-Chairman Chuck Williams

WELDON OWEN INC.

Chief Executive Officer John Owen
President and Chief Operating Officer Terry Newell
Chief Financial Officer Christine E. Munson
Vice President International Sales Stuart Laurence
Creative Director Gaye Allen
Publisher Hannah Rahill
Associate Publisher Sarah Putman Clegg
Editorial Assistant Juli Vendzules
Art Director Colin Wheatland
Senior Designer Lisa Milestone
Production Director Chris Hemesath
Color Manager Teri Bell
Production and Reprint Coordinator Todd Rechner
Photo Coordinator Meghan Hildebrand

THE WILLIAMS-SONOMA BRIDE & GROOM COOKBOOK

Conceived and produced by Weldon Owen Inc.
814 Montgomery Street, San Francisco, CA 94133
Telephone: 415 291 0100 Fax: 415 291 8841

In collaboration with Williams-Sonoma, Inc.
3250 Van Ness Avenue, San Francisco, CA 94109

A WELDON OWEN PRODUCTION
Copyright © 2006 by Weldon Owen Inc. and Williams-Sonoma Inc.

For information regarding special discounts for bulk purchases,
please contact Simon & Schuster Special Sales at 1 800 456 6798 or
business@simonandschuster.com

Set in Myriad MM, Perpetua, Marydale

Color separations by Bright Art Graphics, Hong Kong
Printed and bound in China by Midas Printing Limited

First printed in 2005.

10 9 8 7 6 5

Library of Congress Cataloging-in-Publication data is available.

ISBN-13: 978-0-7432-7855-3
ISBN-10: 0-7432-7855-0

ACKNOWLEDGMENTS

Weldon Owen wishes to thank the following people for their generous support in producing this book:

Photographer David Matheson
Photo Assistants Antony Nobilo, Tom Hood
Food and Prop Stylist Ben Masters
Assistant Food Stylist Ann Kidd
Copy Editor Sharron Wood
Consulting Editor Sharon Silva
Proofreaders Carrie Bradley, Desne Ahlers
Indexer Ken DellaPenta
Designer Marianne Mitten
Production Editor Joan Olson

Heather Wheatland
Sean Clegg
Agostino Fortunati
Nima Oberoi
Alec Nicolajevich
Leigh Noe
Joy Coakley

Additional photography:
pages 21, 22 center, 23 center, 66, 80, 96, 113,
and 146 by Food Stylist George Dolese and
Associate Food Stylist Elizabet der Nederlanden;
pages 220, 232, and 234 top by Photographer
Jeff Kauck; pages 226 and 227 by Photographers
Jeff Tucker and Kevin Hossler; pages 233 top,
233 bottom, 234 bottom, 235 top, and
235 bottom by Photographer Bill Bettencourt

Ben Masters would like to thank Accoutrement in
Mosman, Essential Ingredient in Paramatta Road,
Murdoch Produce, and Broadway Butchery.

A NOTE ON WEIGHTS AND MEASURES
All recipes include customary U.S. and metric
measurements. Metric conversions are based on
a standard developed for these books and have
been rounded off. Actual weights may vary.